A Modern Elementary Logic

L. Susan Stebbing

Revised By
C.W.K. Mundle

Routledge
Taylor & Francis Group

First published in 1943 by Methuen & Co.
Revised edition published in 1952

This edition first published in 2017 by Routledge
2 Park Square, Milton Park, Abingdon, Oxon, OX14 4RN
and by Routledge
711 Third Avenue, New York, NY 10017

Routledge is an imprint of the Taylor & Francis Group, an informa business

Publisher's Note
The publisher has gone to great lengths to ensure the quality of this reprint but points out that some imperfections in the original copies may be apparent.

Disclaimer
The publisher has made every effort to trace copyright holders and welcomes correspondence from those they have been unable to contact.

A Library of Congress record exists under LC control number: 53034340

ISBN 13: 978-1-138-23185-6 (hbk)
ISBN 13: 978-1-315-27001-2 (ebk)
ISBN 13: 978-1-138-28379-4 (pbk)

Routledge Revivals

A Modern Elementary Logic

First published in 1943, and revised for this 1952 edition, this book, which was intended for use by students of philosophy, combines traditional and modern developments in logic. The author envisaged this volume as filling a gap for a simple, introductory text on formal logic, written from a modern point of view and unencumbered by traditional doctrine. It provides a thorough introduction and grounding in the philosophy of logic, and was later revised after the author's death to correct a number of logical errors, making this edition the most complete version of the work.

A Modern Elementary Logic

BY

L. SUSAN STEBBING

REVISED BY

C. W. K. MUNDLE

First published August 12, 1943
Reprinted five times
Fifth edition, revised, 1952
Reprinted three times
First published in this series 1961
Second Printing 1963
for Barnes & Noble Inc.
Reprinted 1966
1.3
by Butler & Tanner Ltd, Frome and London
Catalogue no. (Methuen) 02/6766/49
Printed in Great Britain

University Paperbacks are published
by METHUEN & CO LTD
11 New Fetter Lane, London E.C.4
and BARNES & NOBLE INC
105 Fifth Avenue, New York 3

Reviser's Note to Fifth Edition

In the course of using this book for teaching purposes, I discovered a number of logical errors, most of them in the first five chapters. Although I have now made a systematic search for such errors I cannot guarantee that none have been overlooked, for several which I had not noticed have since been pointed out to me by Mr R. N. W. Smith of St Andrews University. I have limited myself to such alterations to the text as could be effected by the deletion, amendment or insertion of not more than a single sentence or group of logical symbols except in the following cases: the second paragraph on p. 87 has been rewritten, and the set of diagrams given on p. 96 has been altered. Regarding this last change, Miss Stebbing followed J. N. Keynes in acknowledging only seven of the ten possible cases. Keynes gave only seven diagrams because he was restricting his attention to the cases where $\bar{S}$ and $\bar{P}$, as well as S and P, have members, but Miss Stebbing does not seem to have intended to adopt this restriction. In the course of looking for logical errors I have noticed and corrected a few grammatical slips.

C. W. K. MUNDLE

University College
Dundee, 1952

Publisher's Note

Readers should bear in mind that this book was written during the Second World War. For this reason a number of examples have a military flavour.

Preface

The aim of this book is extremely limited. It is definitely a textbook primarily intended for the use of first-year students reading Logic for a University examination. The present conditions of examinations in this country make it necessary to include some trivial technicalities with which, in time, teachers of elementary logic will be able to dispense. Already the situation is much more hopeful than it was a few years ago. Teachers and examiners have made some progress in the task of carting away some dead wood. Accordingly, it has been possible to reduce the discussion of technical trivialities in this book to a small space, thus leaving the student time to consider the wider implications of logic as a formal discipline instead of a depository of antiquities.

Within the limited number of pages available it has not been possible to treat of methodology, or scientific method, as fully as is necessary for covering all the topics dealt with in examinations in elementary logic. Only the last chapter touches upon these topics and hardly does more than indicate to the student what the problems are about which he must seek fuller information elsewhere. This omission is the less to be regretted in that there are several books on scientific method well suited to the purpose and obtainable in most university and public libraries. The case of formal logic is, however, very different. So far as I know, there is no simple, introductory textbook on formal logic, written from a modern point of view, that is both unencumbered with much dead traditional doctrine and yet meeting the needs of students preparing for an examination. I have tried to repair this omission. I have kept especially in mind the student who is reading by himself, without any guidance from a teacher. There are, I understand, not a few such students today, many of them in H.M. Forces. To aid this class of reader I have included some typical questions, together with a key indicating the way in which the questions should be answered.

These are given in an Appendix, which can be neglected by those who are fortunate enough to have someone at hand to deal with their perplexities. In the answers I have given I have had in mind the sort of difficulties which years of teaching have shown me to be very commonly felt by young students who are not 'born logicians' and yet can gain something (besides the advantage of passing an examination) from a course in elementary logic. I am convinced that the careful consideration of logical principles, even in the simple form in which they are presented in this book, is well worth while for any student. This belief, I am aware, may be the result of my own interest in, and liking for, logical studies; in other words, I am perhaps allowing myself to be too partial to my main preoccupation. It remains possible that a statement that is not impartial may nevertheless happen on the truth.

I regret very much that I have given no references to *Formal Logic*, by Prof. A. A. Bennett and Prof. C. A. Baylis (Prentice-Hall, New York). Although I possessed a copy war conditions deprived me of it, and it is only recently that I have been able to read it. It can be unreservedly recommended.

I am much indebted to Mr A. F. Dawn for reading the Appendix and making many valuable suggestions, and to Professor D. Tarrant and Miss M. E. F. Thomson for help in the reading of the proofs. To Professor Tarrant I owe more than help in proof-reading; her critical mind and sound sense have saved me from many blunders.

War-time economy forbids a dedicatory page; it is, however, permitted to express the wish to dedicate this textbook to my students, present and past, in appreciation of the help they have often given me, unsuspected by themselves.

L. SUSAN STEBBING

Bedford College
London, May 18th, 1943

Contents

CHAPTER I

The Study of Logic

§ 1. REFLECTIVE THINKING

When we are told something that is startling or unpleasant we may be moved to ask our informant: 'How do you know that?' Usually such a question is a demand for reasons: we want to know the grounds for the statement rather than to inquire what were the processes of thought through which our informant was led to make the statement in question; we are asking for some assurance; we are not willing to accept the statement without evidence. The sort of answer that would satisfy such a questioner would take the form: 'Because it (i.e. what was originally stated) follows from so-and-so.'

The reader, it is assumed, will have no difficulty in understanding the above paragraph; he is already familiar with a notion of great importance in the study of logic, namely, the notion of evidence in support of a statement. In this book it is taken for granted that our interest in logic is, for the most part, confined to the domain of evidence. Our purpose is to examine the principles in accordance with which it is reasonable to accept, or to reject, statements made by ourselves or by other people. During the greater part of our daily life we unhesitatingly accept what we hear or read and the answers given to our questions. It seldom occurs to us to question what generally passes as true; for example, that our cat will produce kittens and not puppies, that if we sow seeds from a poppy we shall get poppies and not sweet-peas, that a stone thrown into a pond will sink and ripples will spread outwards from the spot where the stone struck the water, that – in the northern hemisphere – we shall never see the sun due north, that we shall eventually all of us die. Examples could be added indefinitely. Most of us could give reasons for these beliefs but usually it does not seem necessary to ask for them.

Our common daily activities are for the most part carried on without reflection: the paper knife will slit the envelope if we make the usual movements, the upset cup of coffee will stain the tablecloth, the electric light will come on if we turn the switch. Unless we could take such things for granted our more or less orderly lives could not go on as they do.

This unreflective state of mind cannot always be maintained: our statements are challenged or some unexpected change occurs in our environment. We may even have enough leisure and alertness of mind to be curious and thus to begin to ask questions simply to satisfy our curiosity, as intelligent children do. To be in a questioning frame of mind is to be thinking; reflective thinking essentially consists in attempting to solve a problem and thus in asking questions and seeking answers to these questions so as to solve the problem. We distinguish reflective thinking from idle reverie or day dreaming. In reflective thinking our thoughts are directed towards an end – the solution of the problem that set us thinking. Thinking is a mental process in which we pass from one thought to another. A thought is an element in this process which requires for its full expression a complete sentence. When one thought is more or less consciously connected with another in order to elicit the conclusion towards which our thinking is directed we are *reasoning*.

Reasoning is a familiar activity; we all reason more or less, badly or well. We connect various items of information and draw conclusions; we judge that, if certain statements are known to be true, then certain other statements are also true and must be accepted. In saying that the latter *must* be accepted we are saying that, *provided we are thinking logically*, we shall accept them; that is to say, we should not be rational beings if we accepted the former statements and rejected the latter.

§ 2. ARGUMENT

Consider the following passage taken from Boswell's *Life of Johnson*.

I introduced the subject of toleration. JOHNSON: 'Every society has the right to preserve public peace and order, and therefore has a good right to prohibit the propagation of opinions which have a dangerous tendency. To say the *magistrate* has this right, is using an inadequate word; it is the *society* for which the magistrate is agent. He may be morally or theologically wrong in restraining the propagation of opinions which he thinks dangerous, but he is politically right.' MAYO: 'I am of opinion, Sir, that every man is entitled to liberty of conscience in religion; and that the magistrate cannot restrain that right.' JOHNSON: 'Sir, I agree with you. Every man has a right to liberty of conscience, and with that the magistrate cannot interfere. People confound liberty of thinking with liberty of talking; nay, with liberty of preaching. Every man has a physical right to think as he pleases; for it cannot be discovered how he thinks. He has not a moral right, for he ought to inform himself and think justly. But, Sir, no member of a society has a right to *teach* any doctrine contrary to what the society holds to be true. The magistrate, I say, may be wrong in what he thinks: but while he thinks himself right, he may and ought to enforce what he thinks.' MAYO: 'Then, Sir, we are to remain always in error, and truth never can prevail; and the magistrate was right in persecuting the first Christians.' JOHNSON: 'Sir, the only method by which truth can be established is by martyrdom. The magistrate has a right to enforce what he thinks; and he who is conscious of the truth has a right to suffer. I am afraid there is no other way of ascertaining the truth, but by persecution on the one hand and enduring it on the other.'*

This conversation is an example of argumentative discourse. It is argumentative because the thoughts of the speakers are connected in such a way as to lead to a conclusion, that is to say, there is direction towards a statement which logically concludes the argument. Certain statements were taken for granted *from which* the conclusion was obtained; these statements are called *premisses*. A *premiss* is a statement from which another statement, called the *conclusion*,

* Boswell's *Life of Johnson* (Globe edition, 1922), p. 265.

is drawn. Thus *premiss* and *conclusion* are correlatives. Not every statement is put forward as a premiss, any more than every man is a husband. But just as men become husbands by entering into the relation of marriage so a statement becomes a premiss when it is put into the relation of providing *evidence for* a conclusion. Usually more than one premiss is required to establish a conclusion, and more than one conclusion can be drawn from the same statement or set of statements.

Whenever we use such words as 'therefore', 'it follows', 'hence', 'consequently', we profess to have offered premisses from which our conclusion may be drawn; when we use such words as 'because', 'for', 'since', 'for the reason that', we profess to offer premisses for a conclusion already stated, that is to say, we are offering evidence in support of our conclusion. The premisses are evidence for the conclusion only in virtue of certain relations in which they stand to the conclusion. The relation between premiss and conclusion which justifies the assertion that the conclusion follows from the premiss is a relation of *implication*. When this relation holds, the premisses *imply* the conclusion, and the conclusion *follows from* the premisses. For example, the conjoint assertion of the two statements, *Every society has the right to prohibit the propagation of opinions having a dangerous tendency* and *These opinions have a dangerous tendency*, implies *Society has the right to prohibit the propagation of these opinions*. Provided that the premisses are true, the conclusion is true. We might refuse to admit that one of the premisses is true, or we might deny both; in that case we are not rationally bound to accept the conclusion, but we must, in our turn, give reasons for denying the premiss or premisses. To do this is to argue.

If the reader looks back to the conversation reported by Boswell, he will see that Johnson was engaged in putting forward premisses to justify his conclusions.* The reader may

* The student should re-read Johnson's argument and attempt to determine its structure. It should be noticed that Johnson (i) asserts his belief [on the topic for discussion] and gives a reason for it; (ii) points out (in response to a comment made by another participant in the discussion) the need to make certain distinctions; (iii) makes further statements on the basis of these distinctions; (iv) answers an objection to his original contention by accepting the objection as an unavoidable consequence.

very well dissent from Johnson's conclusions; if so, he will in his turn be engaged in reflective thinking – arguing from premisses to conclusion or seeking premisses to establish *as a conclusion* a statement which, perhaps, had been previously accepted without question. Johnson's argument was on a controversial topic and carried on in a somewhat controversial manner. This is not the essential characteristic of argument. Even though we often dispute heatedly with one another we do sometimes enter into an argument solely in order to arrive at correct conclusions. It is this sense of "argument" which concerns the logician, and from this point of view an argument is simply a set of statements in which one statement (the conclusion) is accepted on the evidence of the remaining statements (the premisses). Frequently the conclusions we seek to establish do not stand to the premisses in so strict a logical relation as that of *being implied by* the premisses; the premisses may provide evidence in support of the conclusion without providing logically *conclusive evidence*; in this case the relation may be said to be a *probability relation*. When the conclusion is implied by the premisses the argument is *deductive*; when the premisses do not suffice to imply the conclusion but nevertheless have some weight as evidence in favour of it the argument is said to be *inductive*. In an inductive argument the premisses may be true and yet the conclusion may be false; the evidence, however strong, is thus inconclusive. With arguments of this kind we shall be concerned later. In a deductive argument the conclusion could not be false and yet the premiss be true; hence, in this case, the evidence is rightly called conclusive.

In ordinary discussions we seldom state fully all the premisses which we should on reflection unhesitatingly admit to be required for establishing our conclusion; still less do we recognize exactly how it is that the premisses do suffice (when they do) to establish the conclusion. In practice our arguments are often very much abbreviated; we omit premisses because they are self-evident or are regarded as accepted by everyone. This procedure is good enough for most of our purposes and is further necessary in order to avoid intolerably long and prolix statements. It is not, however, free from danger, for it may be that the validity of the argument depends upon an unstated, or implicit, premiss which would not be accepted had it been made explicit what the required premiss is. The omission of premisses is, as we shall see later, a common cause of fallacious arguments.

§ 3. VALIDITY AND TRUTH

We have just used the phrase, 'the validity of the argument'. An argument is valid if the truth of the premisses necessitates the truth of the conclusion; this is equivalent to saying that the premisses cannot be true and the conclusion false, or, in other words, that the premisses logically imply the conclusion. We have just used three alternative expressions to state the relation holding between premisses and conclusion in a valid argument. It should be noted that we do not define these expressions but assume that the reader understands at least one of them – for example, 'the premisses cannot be true and the conclusion false'; he has then to see that the other two expressions are alternative ways of saying the same thing. It is, moreover, taken for granted that we know what is meant by "true" and "false". The logical relation of implication holding between a premiss and a conclusion does not determine whether the premiss is true; hence, the validity of an argument is in no way a guarantee that the conclusion is true. For example, *Boccaccio died before Dante* and *Dante died before Voltaire* together imply *Boccaccio died before Voltaire.* Logical considerations alone suffice to assure us that the conclusion is true *provided that* the premisses are, for the premisses certainly imply the conclusion. In fact, the first premiss is false, the second is true, and the conclusion is true. We know this (if we do know it) not from logic but from historical records. Again, it may be true that Bothwell loved Mary, Queen of Scots, and also that she loved Bothwell; but, from *Bothwell loved Mary* it does not follow that *Mary loved Bothwell*; there are, unfortunately, many unrequited lovers. Both these statements may be true or one may be true with the other false; hence neither implies the other. But *Darnley married Mary* does follow logically from *Mary married Darnley*, and indeed, conversely; if one statement be true, the other is; if one is false, the other is. It is impossible for *A* to be married to *B* without its being true that *B* is married to *A*; this logical impossibility is involved in the meaning of "*married to*". But logic does not determine who marries whom, who loves whom, nor when men are born or die.

Consider the following examples of arguments:

(1) All Athenians are Greeks and no Greeks are barbarians; therefore, no Athenians are barbarians.
(2) All Austrians are Germans and all Germans are Europeans; therefore, all Austrians are Europeans.
(3) No insects have six legs and all spiders are insects; therefore, no spiders have six legs.
(4) All members of Parliament have great responsibilities, and Winston Churchill has great responsibilities; therefore, Winston Churchill is a member of Parliament.
(5) Some poets are not Roman Catholics and all who acknowledge the authority of the Pope are Roman Catholics; therefore, none who acknowledge the authority of the Pope are poets.

We shall examine each of these five examples in order to answer two questions: (i) Are the premisses true? (ii) Is the argument valid? [The student should carry out this examination for himself before he reads further.]

We summarize the result of the examination as follows:

(i) *Are the premisses true?*	(*Is the conclusion true?*)	*Is the argument valid?*
1. Both premisses true.	Conclusion true.	Valid.
2. First premiss false.	Conclusion true.	Valid.
3. Both premisses false.	Conclusion true.	Valid.
4. Both premisses true.	Conclusion true.	Invalid.
5. Both premisses true.	Conclusion false.	Invalid.

In addition to answering the two questions posed to us we have noted whether the conclusion is true or false. From these examples we can see that there can be (*a*) a true conclusion from a valid argument although the premisses are false; (*b*) an invalid argument with both premisses true and the conclusion true; (*c*) a false conclusion in an invalid argument with true premisses. Validity, then, is not dependent upon truth. On reflection we see that this must be so. Every statement has implications, or, as we sometimes say, *consequences*. For instance, a scientist may wish to determine whether a possible hypothesis, which would account for the phenomena he is investigating, is true or false. An hypothesis is a statement of the form *If so and so, then such and such* (e.g. *If light has a finite velocity, then the light from different stars reaches us after a longer or shorter time depending upon the distances of the stars from the earth*). The consequences are deduced, and, when possible, tested. If the implied consequence is false, there is no reason to accept the hypothesis; if the implied consequence is true, then the hypothesis may be true. When the premisses of a *valid* argument are true, then the conclusion must also be true. When the argument is valid and the premisses are false, we do not know whether the conclusion is true or not; consequently, we should have no reason for accepting the conclusion as true. When the argument is invalid and the premisses are true, we again have no reason for accepting the conclusion; in such a case we might say that the 'conclusion' is not properly a *conclusion* since it does not follow logically from the premisses; hence, the argument is *inconclusive*.*

We had no difficulty in determining whether the statements (premisses and conclusions) in our five examples were true or false, since these statements were about familiar subject-matter. Anyone who reads this book (it is assumed) knows that Austrians are not Germans but that both Austrians and Germans are Europeans; and so on, in each of the other examples. The question whether these statements are true is a question concerning matters of fact, or, as we shall say, it is a *factual* question. The question whether the premisses suffice to prove the conclusion is a question about the logical form of the argument. As logicians we do not care whether Austrians are Germans, or whether Athenians are not barbarians; our concern is wholly with the conclusiveness of the arguments, for unless our arguments are conclusive we

* As the logician, Augustus de Morgan, has said: 'It is not therefore the object of logic to determine whether conclusions be true or false; but whether what are asserted to be conclusions *are* conclusions.'

have no logical reasons for accepting the conclusions. If the conclusion does follow from the premisses, the argument is valid; if the conclusion does not follow from the premisses the argument is invalid. The validity of an argument depends entirely upon the logical form of the argument. What, then, do we mean by *logical form*?

§ 4. FORM AND LOGICAL FORMS

We are all familiar with the notion of change of form: butter left standing in the sun becomes a runny mess; water heated to boiling-point becomes steam, frozen it becomes ice; an orderly procession of civilians suddenly charged by mounted police becomes a disorderly crowd, and so on. What is meant by 'and so on', in the last sentence? It is used to invite the reader to supply other examples, in the confident expectation that he will be able to do so, for the examples have all been of the same form: something that in one sense remains the same and in another sense is different. The crowd and the orderly processions are composed of the same people but they have entered into new combinations; the shape made by them as they march in procession is quite different from the varying shapes made as they huddle together or push one another in various directions. Probably we should say that the crowd was a 'shapeless mass', for we tend to use the word 'shape' only when the elements that are shaped stand in relatively constant relations to one another. But shape is a matter of degree; when we press a piece of rubber we change its shape; when we blow into a toy balloon we transform it from a relatively shapeless bit of stuff into shapes of various sorts, perhaps ending with a round ball-shape. *Shape* is the most common meaning of the word "form", but we frequently use it in greatly extended senses. How widely we understand this notion of form is shown by its numerous synonyms or partial synonyms, e.g. arrangement, orderliness, type, norm, standard, design, pattern. The paper pattern for a dress has the same form, or shape and size, as the material of the dress when the material has been cut to pattern. This is what we mean by saying that the paper pattern is a *pattern*.

The design of the English penny and twopenny stamps (current issue) is the same but they differ in colour; the design as well as the colour of the shilling stamp differs from that of either of the other stamps. A meat-mould, a jelly, and a blancmange may all have the same shape or form but they differ in the materials of which they are made. Everyone understands this distinction between *material* and *form*, or, as we sometimes say, between *matter* and *form*. When a child builds a house out of his toy bricks he is arranging the bricks (i.e. the matter) in a certain way, viz. in the form of a house; this is a *construct*. Not all that is constructed, or has form, is material. Consider, for instance, musical form. A scale is a musical form consisting of notes, but these notes cannot be taken in any order; they must be put together in a certain definite way. We might use the same notes put in a different order and thus get a singable melody, quite different from the scale. We distinguish between hymn form, fugue form, sonata form; we might say that a symphony is a sonata for the orchestra.

Why do we call the musical scale a *scale*? Obviously because the *order* of the successive notes is felt to resemble the order of rungs as one goes up and down a "scale" or "ladder". A *ladder* means originally a certain material thing, but we have come to recognize a ladder-like arrangement in many other things, e.g. a ladder in a stocking, and even more abstractly, as when we speak of the educational ladder. Our manner of speaking shows that we implicitly recognize a common form in diverse material; we see a relation that is analogous between the notes of a scale from lower to higher and the colour-scale from dark to light colours. Analogy is the recognition of a common form or structure in very unlike things.

Our thoughts have form. When we are successfully engaged in reflective thinking our thoughts occur in an orderly way; what does not fit in is, as far as possible, kept out of mind. Our languages are adapted, somewhat imperfectly, to express our thoughts; hence, we have grammatical form. Words cannot be put into any order to make a sentence. The student who knows a little Latin but not much finds in translating 'unseens' that he sometimes knows all the words but 'can't get the hang of the sentence', but sometimes he can get the hang of the sentence but does not know what some of the words *mean*. In the first case his knowledge of syntax is inadequate; in the second case it is his vocabulary that is at fault. Syntax is the *formal structure* of a language; vocabulary is its *material*.

In learning Latin syntax *Balbus murum aedificavit* does just as well as but no better than *Caius puellam a mavit* to illustrate the use of the accusative case. Analogously, the logician can use any material to illustrate logical forms. As soon as we are able to frame sentences correctly we have gained an implicit knowledge of grammatical form; as soon as we are able to reason, and to demand reasons, we have an implicit knowledge of logical form. Our apprehension is at first implicit; if it were explicit we should not merely apprehend but comprehend: we should thus understand just *why* this combination of words, in grammatical form, was right for our purpose, and just *why* that special combination of statements was logically right for sound reasoning. In studying logic we extract this implicit knowledge from the particular instances in which it is present, and are thus able to state the logical principles to which our reasoning must conform if it is valid. Our interest is wholly in the formal combinations of statements.

Consider the statement *If Jones is a painter, and all painters are irascible, then Jones is irascible.* This is a compound statement consisting of three statements each of which could be separately asserted. This compound statement is true in virtue of its form; if the first two statements are true, the third must also be true, but, as we have seen, the implication holds even if the first two statements (joined by *and*) are false. Thus the whole compound proposition is true in virtue of its form. The implication does not depend upon any characteristics *Jones* may possess other than his *being a painter*; we could then say, *If Robinson is a painter, and all painters are irascible, then Robinson is irascible.* It is not difficult to see that we could likewise replace *painters* by *musicians*, by *schoolmasters*, or by anything else that would make sense, provided we made the substitution in both statements; likewise with *irascible*. Let us then replace *Jones* by *X*, *painters* by *C's*, and *irascible people* by *D's*; we thus obtain, *If X is a C, and all C's are D's, then X is a D*. We have now no longer a definite statement about certain persons or classes of things but a logical form or structure. If we substitute for *X*, *C*, *D* anything yielding a statement which makes sense, we shall have an *instance* of a valid implication instead of an *implicational form*. What makes the implication valid (and thus the statement that it holds true) is the form of the separate statements and the mode in which they are combined, i.e. the way in which the three statements are inter-related.

Logic is a formal science. What exactly is involved in saying that logic is formal will be clear only after we have studied in detail various logical forms. For this purpose we need to make explicit the forms we implicitly apprehend. Consequently, at times we shall need to use special symbols, since we want to consider forms of reasoning without paying attention to the subject-matter, or material, of specific arguments.

§ 5. LOGICAL SYMBOLISM AND FORM

We are all familiar with such symbols as the national flag, a flag at half-mast, the wearing of a crown. Language is a symbolism. We use language not only to express our feelings but to communicate what we feel and know to others. So long as men were confined to a spoken language they could not communicate more than those living were able to remember. With a written language it is possible to communicate what we know to those who live centuries after we and all our contemporaries are dead. We communicate by using signs to convey our meanings. A word is a special sort of sign. A sign indicates something other than itself. For example, a rapid upward movement of the arm until the tips of the fingers touch the cap is a visible sign conventionally expressive of courteous recognition of a superior in rank. But to whom is this sign significant? Only to those who are aware of this special convention of a salute. Signifying is a relation requiring three terms: a sign, that of which the sign is significant, and an interpreter for whom the former indicates the latter. The appearance of the sunset-sky is a sign to a weather-wise countryman of what tomorrow's weather will be; it is significant for him because he has had experience of connecting a certain sunset-appearance with a certain kind of weather next day; to the ignorant townsman there may be no significance. A symptom, in the medical sense, is a sign characteristic of a certain sort of disease. These are natural signs; they are to be contrasted with conventional signs which owe significance to the actions of men who seek to fulfil their needs and desires.

The words in our languages are conventional signs. Aristotle (thinking of the spoken language) called them 'sounds significant by convention'. They are not merely sounds but *significant sounds*; in the written language words are *significant marks*; but a word must not be identified with any particular sound uttered by someone on a particular occasion, nor with any particular mark written by someone in a particular place. For example, in this paragraph the mark *sounds* occurs more than once, but these separate, numerically different, but recognizably the same, marks are each an instance of the one word *sounds*. In sending a telegram we count the number of words in the sense of marks; if the mark *five* occurs twice we count it twice in estimating the cost of the telegram at so much *per word*; in the sense of the mark's *meaning* there is only the one word *five*. Sometimes a mark may exemplify more than one word, e.g. 'patient', 'bull'. *Bull* is a mark that may be used to signify a certain kind of *animal* or it may be used to signify a certain sort of *ludicrous jest*.

A conventional sign is called a *symbol*. The kind of symbols we are most familiar with are ordinary words; these are called *verbal symbols*. Anyone who knows our language knows what it is we are referring to when we use words in the language. For many scientific purposes we find it more convenient to use *non-verbal* symbols. There are various kinds of non-verbal symbols, of which we shall here distinguish only two kinds. A third will be dealt with later.*

* See Ch. VII.

(i) *Shorthand symbols.* These are either abbreviations for words or concise marks substituted for words, directly representing what they symbolize. For instance *this* is used as a road-sign symbolizing that there is a double bend ahead. This shorthand symbol can be more easily apprehended by a rapid driver than the words 'double bend ahead'.

In mathematics shorthand symbols make it possible to express a complicated idea so briefly that it can be apprehended at a glance. For example, $\sqrt{\ }$ is easier to grasp in a formula than 'the square root of'; similarly, $+$ instead of 'plus', $\times$ instead of 'multiply', and so on. The student will recognize that shorthand symbols are indispensable in practice if we wish readily to grasp even comparatively simple algebraical expressions. For example,

$$ax^2 + bx + c = a\left(x + \frac{b + \sqrt{b^2 - 4ac}}{2a}\right)\left(x + \frac{b - \sqrt{b^2 - 4ac}}{2a}\right)$$

will be easily read by anyone with the most elementary knowledge of algebra; if the student attempts to write out this equation using only English words he will soon find that it is difficult to keep his head. The choice of appropriate marks, i.e. shorthand symbols, is often very important. Compare, for example, the difficulty of working out a long sum in multiplication using Roman numerals with the ease of working it out when expressed by means of the Arabic notation.* In logic we find such shorthand symbols as $\equiv$ to stand for 'is equivalent to'; $=$ for 'equals', $\supset$ for a special sense of *implication*, extremely convenient both for brevity and ease of apprehension. We shall see later that it is a help to use different shorthand symbols for distinguishing between different meanings of the word "is".

(ii) *Illustrative symbols.* Suppose someone contends that all who

* A simple example of a shorthand symbol of great utility is provided by $10^{7^{10}}$; this is short and easily apprehended (once the notational rules have been learnt), but written out in full, in the usual manner, it would require so many zeros after the unit 1 that it would be difficult to grasp what number it is. Sir Arthur Eddington believes that the number of electrons in the universe is 136×2^{256}, a number which requires 1 followed by 79 other digits to write out in full (see *The Philosophy of Physical Science*, p. 171).

have been at Public Schools are fair-minded. Someone may reply, 'I don't agree. A, who was at a Public School, is grossly unfair.' Granted the truth of the second statement, the generalization that all Public School men are fair-minded is disproved. The symbol 'A' was used to stand for a definite person who was not specified. In the trial of blackmailers it is sometimes necessary to conceal the name of the victim from the public press; accordingly, he may be referred to as 'Mr A'. This device is convenient for it permits an individual to be uniquely referred to throughout the trial without disclosing his identity to the general public. The 'A' and the 'Mr A' used in the above examples are instances of the use of illustrative symbols. Our purpose in using illustrative symbols in logic is analogous to the purposes in the examples; we want to refer to some one definite object but not to an identifiable object; hence we use capital letters of the alphabet to serve as an arbitrary, undescriptive name. An illustrative symbol signifies a definite object, or characteristic, but not a *specified* one. The use of x for the 'unknown' in solving algebraic equations is an example of the use of an illustrative symbol.

The combination of shorthand and illustrative symbols enables us to exhibit explicitly the forms of our arguments. To understand why it is that a given argument is valid and another invalid, we must be able to discern clearly their respective forms since it is upon their form that their validity depends.

CHAPTER II

Propositions and Their Relations

§ 1. PROPOSITIONS AND SENTENCES

In discussing examples of argument we have hitherto used the word 'statement' to refer to *what is stated* by someone or other. This word is ambiguous for it may mean either *what is stated* or the verbal expression used by a speaker in stating something. The ambiguous word was deliberately used because we did not then wish to raise the question of distinguishing these two meanings. The word 'proposition' is frequently used for the former. A proposition is anything that can significantly be said to be true or false. A proposition stated in thought, in speech, or in writing, must be expressed in words or other symbols arranged in the sort of order which we recognize as constituting a sentence. A proposition must not be confused with a sentence; not all sentences express propositions. When King Lear exclaims,

Why should a dog, a horse, a rat, have life,
And thou no breath at all?

he is asking a question, not stating anything true or false although he was certainly presupposing the truth of a proposition concerning the comparative value of 'his fool's' life. Again, when he cries, 'Pray you, undo this button', he is making a request, not stating anything. In the context of a conversation an interrogative sentence may be apprehended as having the force of a proposition, but, if so, the sentence-form is simply disregarded. A rhetorical question is intended to be understood as a statement:

What's Hecuba to him or he to Hecuba
That he should weep for her?

In thus passionately asking himself this question Hamlet uses the question-form to emphasize the inevitable answer – an answer which his further argument assumes. It is not a genuine question for the questioning-attitude was not present, but it is present when, in the same soliloquy, he asks himself, 'Am I a coward?' This time he is not sure what the answer is.

The same proposition may be stated by using different sentences, e.g. "I have a dog", "I possess a dog", "Ich habe einen Hund", "J'ai un chien". These four different sentences all express the same proposition. We shall see later that sometimes the same sentence may be used to express different propositions, for sentences no less than single words may be ambiguous.

§ 2. PROPOSITIONS, MENTAL ATTITUDES, AND FACTS

The four sentences given above which express the same proposition have the same meaning; indeed, the proposition just is what these sentences mean. What the sentence *means* can be believed, disbelieved, doubted, or merely entertained at a supposition. A thinker may have any one of these attitudes, at different times, to the *same* proposition. The preceding sentence expresses a proposition which I, the author of this book, believe; you, the reader, may be willing to suppose the proposition to be true in order that you may further inquire what follows if it *is* true; you may doubt it and subsequently resolve your doubt and come to have the attitude of believing the proposition in question; or you may disbelieve it.

"Belief" as ordinarily used may be ambiguous, for it may mean the mental act of *believing* or *that which is believed.* For the purpose of this book "belief" will always be used to mean *that which is believed.* In this sense a belief means a proposition that is believed; all beliefs are then propositions, but many propositions are not believed. Many beliefs are not true but every belief (being a proposition) either is true or is false and not both true and false. A proposition, whether believed or not, is true or false. Whether a proposition is true is determined by what is in fact the case, or, more shortly, by facts. Facts simply *are*; they are neither true nor false. If anyone were to judge that Sir Walter Scott wrote *Marmion*, he would be judging truly; it is in fact the case that Sir Walter Scott wrote *Marmion*, and it would still be a fact if no one except Sir Walter Scott knew that it was so. Obviously no example can be given of what no one has ever thought of, but there are many facts that have not been thought of and never will be thought of.

Philosophers are by no means agreed as to the nature of truth and falsity or with regard to the relation of facts to propositions in virtue of which relation we can say that a given proposition is true or that it is false. The discussion of this topic belongs to the branch of philosophy called epistemology or theory of knowledge and lies outside the scope of this book. We must be content with the dogmatic assertion that facts determine whether propositions are true or false.

To disbelieve that *Sirius is the nearest star to the earth* is to believe that *Sirius is not the nearest star to the earth*. Propositions can always be paired in this way so that one contradicts the other; that is, one must be true and one must be false. To disbelieve a proposition is thus logically equivalent to believing its contradictions. We are not at all concerned with the differences there may be between the mental attitudes of believing and disbelieving but only with the logical relations between what is believed and what is disbelieved. Connected with believing and disbelieving are affirming and denying. These are mental acts familiar to everyone. If I* am asked: 'Is equality of incomes desirable?' and I answer 'Yes', then I am in effect *affirming* that equality of incomes is desirable; if I answer 'No', then I am in effect denying that equality of incomes is desirable. Suppose my belief is that the *No*-answer is correct: then I might say 'Equality of incomes is not desirable' but I might equally well have said 'Equality of incomes is undesirable'. In one case I use an affirmative, in the other a negative sentence to express my belief, but either sentence expresses equally well that I am *denying* that equality

* 'I' stands – here and elsewhere in this book – for *any* thinker, unless it is explicitly qualified to show that 'I', in the given context, stands for the author of this book, viz. Susan Stebbing.

of incomes is desirable. The distinction between affirming and denying is fundamental: whether I affirm or deny that such and such things are related may be of the utmost importance, and should I pass from denying to affirming I have changed my mind; the difference, however, between using an affirmative or a negative sentence to express either my denial or my affirmation is not a logical difference; the verbal statements will be different but both are used to state the same belief or proposition. Every affirmative sentence can be translated into an equivalent negative sentence, and conversely, just as I can translate 'J'ai un chien' by 'I have a dog'.

§ 3. ASSERTION, INFERENCE, AND IMPLICATION

It is characteristic of the study of logic that at the beginning we *use* certain words in the confident expectation that they will be understood, but, later, we *talk about* these words, perhaps raising difficulties that do not ordinarily occur to us as we go about our daily business, making inferences and seeing the implications of other people's statements. "State", "affirm", "deny" are instances of this procedure. The reader has had no difficulty in our *using* these words. Now, however, we must inquire what precisely is meant by "*stating a proposition*": how does a stated proposition differ from that proposition *unstated*?

In ordinary conversation when we use a sentence in the indicative we intend our hearers to understand that we believe the proposition. If I say 'The Russians' resistance at Stalingrad is magnificent', I should be understood to be stating that I believe this proposition, and am not merely putting it forward for contemplation, provided that I say the sentence in the course of a discussion or in silent meditation about the war situation in September 1942. In teaching logic we often take examples of propositions merely in order to investigate the logical relations between propositions of various forms; it by no means follows from the fact that we use a given example of a proposition that we wish to assert it. Our attitude to the example is purely contemplative. We do wish to make assertions to the effect that a given proposition (contemplated as an example) does stand in a certain relation to another proposition (also contemplated). Nearly the whole of this book consists of assertions which the author believes and hopes the reader will also believe.

Without *assertion* there is no argument; this is equivalent to saying that without assertion there is no *inference*. Since our usual attitude is one of making declarations, putting forward our point of view, informing one another of our beliefs, we do not ordinarily need to call attention to the distinction between *asserting a proposition* and *contemplating it*. The distinction is nonetheless of vital importance. Even in ordinary conversation we do not always intend to assert the propositions we state; sometimes we take to a proposition an attitude of *hypothetically entertaining* the proposition in order to see what follows from it. But we do intend, somewhere or other, to break the chain of hypothetically entertained propositions and *make an assertion*: 'So *this* is *true*'. For example, 'If the Russians' continued resistance implied that the German army could be defeated by the Russians alone, and the Russians could continue to resist, then the German army could be defeated by the Russians alone' *asserts nothing more than* 'if a given implication were true and a given proposition were true, then a given conclusion would follow'. This is not the sort of statement we should wish to make if we were anxiously (however amateurishly) considering the possible outcome of the war. Contrast this with, 'Since the Russians can continue to resist, and since their continued resistance implies that the German army can be defeated by the Russians alone; *therefore*, the German army can be defeated by the Russians alone.' Here two assertions are made: *If so-and-so, then such-and-such* is replaced by *since so-and-so*; *therefore such-and-such*. The conclusion has been detached from the *if . . . then . . .* statement and has been put forward *as true*, and thus as capable of standing by itself. To assert a proposition is to put forward the claim that the proposition is *true*; from the point of view of the speaker the assertion of a proposition is the putting forward of a *belief*. *That* the proposition is asserted forms no part of the proposition itself. Affirming and denying are assertive acts. The difference between the assertive and the contemplative attitudes is fundamental; inference is assertive. Propositions have implications whether anyone thinks of them or not; inference involves a thinker.

Inference is a process of thought in which the thinker passes from a certain proposition (the premiss) to another proposition (the conclusion) because he apprehends, or believes himself to apprehend, certain evidential relations holding between the premiss and the conclusion, in virtue of which relations he asserts the conclusion. It should be noticed: (i) that evidential relations are not necessarily *conclusive*; they may be probability relations; (ii) a thinker may falsely believe that he is apprehending an evidential relation, when, in fact, no such relation is present. He is nonetheless *inferring*, but he is not justified in inferring the conclusion unless his belief that the evidential relations are present is not mistaken. Unfortunately, we often do make mistakes of this kind. It is a mistake to define "inference" so narrowly that it covers only *deducing*. This mistake is frequently made. It is even worse to define inference in such a way that "inferring invalidly" is excluded from the definition. Whether an inference is deductive or inductive depends upon the relations holding between the premiss and the conclusion.

§ 4. THE TRADITIONAL ANALYSIS OF PROPOSITIONS

Aristotle is commonly and justly regarded as the founder of the science of logic. As Professor A. N. Whitehead says: 'Aristotle founded the science by conceiving the idea of the form of a proposition, and by conceiving deduction as taking place in virtue of the forms.'* Unfortunately his successors, for nearly two thousand years, studied in detail only a very few forms of propositions; they tried to express anything that anyone might want to say in one or other of four propositional forms together with a few other forms that were not carefully studied at all. No clear distinction was made between a proposition and a sentence so that some important distinctions were relatively neglected whilst differences in verbal statements were treated as differences in propositional forms.

* *Proceedings of the Aristotelian Society*, N.S. XVII, p. 72.

In this section we shall be concerned with the traditional scheme.

Consider the following propositions:

(1) *All Cornishwomen are good cooks.*
(2) *No British Ambassadors are women.*
(3) *Some poets are pacifists.*
(4) *Some voters are not householders.*

Each of these propositions contains three elements – *subject, copula, predicate* – and in addition a sign of quantity. The *subject* and *predicate* are called the 'terms' of the proposition; the *copula* (some part of the verb *to be*) connects the predicate with the subject; the sign of quantity shows whether reference is made to *all* or to *some* of the members of the class constituting the subject-term. (1) and (2) differ in *quantity* from (3) and (4), the former being called *universal*, the latter *particular* propositions. (1) and (3) are affirmative, (2) and (4) are negative; this is said to be a difference in *quality*. This classification of propositions rests upon the assumption that any proposition is a statement to the effect that one class is – either wholly or partially – included in, or excluded from, another class. Certainly many propositions are quite naturally expressed in one or other of the four forms exemplified above; our examples are not at all odd in expression. On the other hand, many statements do not resemble any of these four in form and cannot, without distortion of meaning, be put into one of them. For example, 'To know all is to pardon all.'

At present we neglect these difficulties, but they must not be entirely forgotten. We shall now use the illustrative symbols, *S*, *P*, to stand respectively for the subject and predicate of the propositions; the four traditional forms can then be symbolized as follows:

All S is P	*SaP*	*A*	Universal affirmative.
No S is P	*SeP*	*E*	Universal negative.
Some S is P	*SiP*	*I*	Particular affirmative.
Some S is not P	*SoP*	*O*	Particular negative.

The third column gives the letters customarily used to name

these forms; the vowels are derived from the first two vowels in *affirmo* (I affirm) and from the vowels of *nego* (I deny). They provide a convenient shorthand symbolism. The second column shows the quantity and quality of the proposition by putting the appropriate vowel between the illustrative symbols, *S* and *P*. If the terms of the proposition were symbolized by *M* and *N*, then the four propositions would be written as follows: *MaN*, *MeN*, *MiN*, *MoN*. The student should familiarize himself with this shorthand symbolism. It has long been used for convenience only but it has one special merit – it serves to remind us that we are concerned not with specified classes, e.g. *Cornishwomen* and *good cooks*, but with *any* class. The four propositions listed on page 22 are true or are false, i.e. they really are propositions. The second list is a list of *propositional forms*: *All S is P* does not assert anything that is true or that is false; it may be regarded as an empty schema into which may be fitted a proposition such as no. 1 on page 22.

It should be noticed that universal propositions are distinguished from particular propositions in that the former are unrestricted generalizations and the latter are restricted. In stating *All Archbishops are males*, reference is made to every member of the class *archbishops*; in stating *Some architects are women* reference is not made to every member of the class *architects*. This difference is technically named a difference in distribution. The decision whether a term is distributed or not is of primary importance in determining the validity of certain of our inferences. Hence, it is desirable for the student to familiarize himself with this notion; the following definitions should be learnt:

A term is *distributed*, in any proposition, if reference is made to every member of the class for which the term stands.

A term is *undistributed*, in any proposition, if reference is not made to every member of the class for which the term stands. It is easy to see that the subject-terms of universal propositions are distributed, whilst the subject-terms of particular propositions are undistributed. With regard to the predicate-terms the determination is not so simple. *No Eskimos are sculptors* does clearly exclude the whole class of *sculptors* from the class of *Eskimos* no less than it excludes the *Eskimos* from the *sculptors*. Hence, the predicate-term is also distributed. In the particular proposition, *Some socialists are not Marxists*, it is stated that the whole class of *Marxists* is excluded from *some socialists*. Thus the predicate-term is distributed. In the proposition *All Cabinet Ministers are Members of Parliament* the reference is not to the whole class of *Members of Parliament*; consequently the predicate-term is not distributed. Likewise in the proposition *Some policemen are detectives* the predicate-term is not distributed. The following table sums up these conclusions which we have obtained by considering specific examples of the four forms:

	Proposition	*Subject*	*Predicate*
A	*All S is P*	distributed	undistributed.
E	*No S is P*	distributed	distributed.
I	*Some S is P*	undistributed	undistributed.
O	*Some S is not P*	undistributed	distributed.

It should be noted that in these forms "some" must be taken to mean "some at least", which is equivalent to "some and perhaps all". In ordinary English we most commonly use "some" to mean "some only"; thus *Some A.R.P. workers are paid* would probably be understood to mean that some were paid and some were not paid. But it might be used to mean that *some at least* were paid, leaving it still open to question whether all were. Now, if we were to interpret "some" in *Some S is P* to mean "some only", then this proposition would be in fact, though not in linguistic form, the conjoint assertion of both the *I* and the *O* propositions, for it would assert *Some A.R.P. workers are paid and some A.R.P. workers are not paid.* It is, therefore, desirable to give the minimum interpretation to "some"; we thus interpret "some" so that it is consistent with "all" but excludes the meaning of "none". Accordingly propositions *A* and *I* are consistent, and *E* and *O* are consistent as thus interpreted.

If we take *S* and *P* to stand for two different unspecified classes, there are five different relations possible between them, ranging from complete coincidence to complete mutual exclusion:

1. The two classes may completely coincide.
2. The first may be wholly included in the second without coinciding with it.
3. The first may wholly include the second but not coincide with it.
4. The two classes may partially overlap, i.e. each partially includes and partially excludes the other.
5. The two classes may wholly exclude each other.

The mathematician Euler (1707–83) represented these class relations diagrammatically, using circles whose spatial relations have some analogy with the logical relations of the two classes. These diagrams, known as Euler's Circles, are:

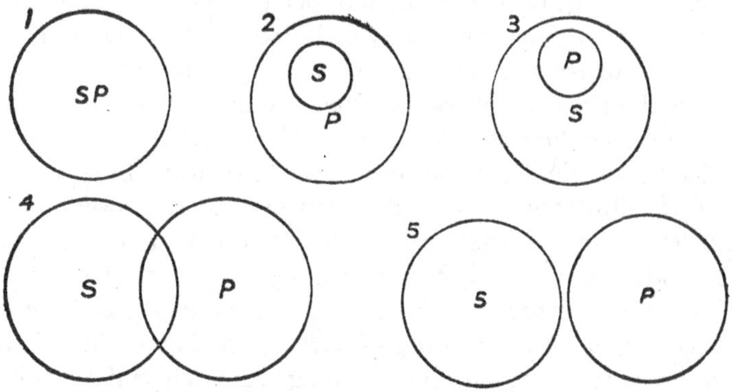

It is important to notice that there are four propositional forms and five diagrams; hence there is not a simple correspondence between the propositional forms and the circles. This is due to the fact that propositions are used to state what we know or believe; and what we know is usually not determinate. If we knew, with regard to some class *S* and some other class *P*, that they were related precisely in the way in which the two circles in diagram 4 are related, we should know more than any one of the *A*, *E*, *I*, *O* propositions can state. Since an undistributed term is indeterminate in its reference, a proposition containing an undistributed term cannot be represented by any *one* of Euler's diagrams. Only diagram 5 corresponds to a single proposition of the four-fold scheme, viz. *E*, which is the only proposition in which both terms are distributed, thus giving information with regard to the whole extent of each term. To state the information provided by each of the first four diagrams it is necessary to affirm conjointly two or more of the propositions. The following table expresses in terms of Euler's diagrams the information provided by each of the four propositions:

A	allows 1, 2;	excludes 3, 4, 5.
E	allows 5;	excludes 1, 2, 3, 4.
I	allows 1, 2, 3, 4;	excludes 5.
O	allows 3, 4, 5;	excludes 1, 2.

Unless at least one possibility represented by the five diagrams is excluded no information has been given; to know that *trepangs* are wholly or partially included in, or excluded from, the class of *echinoderms* is to know nothing more about trepangs than can be known by logic alone. We might just as well replace *trepangs* by *T*, and *echinoderms* by *E*. This is indeed equivalent to what we have done by using the symbols *S*, *P*, to illustrate any two different classes. If, however, we are told that trepangs are wholly included in the class of echinoderms, we know that diagrams 3, 4, and 5 are excluded. If, now, we further know that *trepangs are wholly included in echinoderms without exhausting that class*, we know that their relation corresponds uniquely to diagram 2. This information can be given by the conjoint assertion of an *A* and an *O* proposition: *All trepangs are echinoderms and some echinoderms are not trepangs.*

At this point an intelligent student might well ask such questions as the following:

1. What about those things which are neither trepangs (whatever these may be) nor echinoderms? Are they supposed to lie outside the circles? If so, where in the diagram are they represented?

2. If I say, 'Ghosts are not always draped in sheets', am I to draw a circle representing ghosts even if there aren't any ghosts in the world?

To answer these questions it will be necessary to raise other questions which go beyond the traditional treatment of propositions. Accordingly these questions will be answered in a later chapter.

§ 5. SIMPLE, COMPOUND, AND GENERAL PROPOSITIONS

Among the simplest statements we can make are those which attribute a characteristic or property to an individual thing, e.g. *That leaf is green*, *That table is round*, *Roosevelt is wise*. We shall adopt the convention that such propositions as these are *simple* and that they are *subject-predicate* propositions. The subject is that to which some characteristic is attributed; the predicate is that which is attributed to the subject. *Simple* propositions are to be contrasted with *compound* propositions and with *general* propositions. Consider the following:

A. (1) The line *AE* is equal to the line *BC*.
(2) Aristotle was tutor to Alexander the Great.

B. (3) If the angle *BAC* is not equal to, or less than, the angle *EDF*, then it is greater than the angle *EDF*.
(4) If Winston Churchill has visited Moscow, then Stalin will be pleased.
(5) If Tom has matriculated, then he cannot be less than sixteen.
(6) Either Sirius is not larger than the sun or it is much farther from the earth than the sun is.
(7) It is not the case both that fuel economy is unnecessary and that also the production of coal is decreasing.
(8) Paul is in the R.A.F. and Marion has joined the A.T.S.

According to the convention we have adopted, the propositions of set A, as well as those in the first paragraph above, are simple. Those of set B are compound. A compound proposition contains two or more component propositions. Thus in (4) there are the two components: *Winston Churchill has visited Moscow* and *Stalin will be pleased*. Each of these could significantly be separately asserted but they are not so asserted; what is asserted is that the second is consequent upon the first, hence, the second is called the *consequent* and the first is called the *antecedent.* (3) and (5) are other examples of this form; they are called *hypothetical* propositions. What is common to these three propositions is that each as a whole asserts that the antecedent implies the consequent, in the sense that the antecedent cannot be true without the consequent's also being true. The antecedent is the *implying* proposition, the consequent the *implied* proposition. The relation between these in virtue of which the implication holds is different in different cases, e.g. in (3) it is due to certain definitions in geometry, in (4) to certain political and military conditions in Europe in 1942, in (5) to certain university regulations. It should be noted that the truth of the hypothetical depends not at all on the truth of the antecedent or the consequent separately considered but only on the relation asserted to hold between them. It has sometimes been held that a hypothetical proposition expresses doubt. This is a mistake. The intention of anyone who asserts (4), for instance, is not to express doubt whether Churchill has visited Moscow but to assert a consequence of the visit were it in fact made.*

(6) is an example of an *alternative* proposition; it asserts that *at least one* of the two component propositions is true, not excluding the possibility that both are. The component propositions are called *alternants*; there may be any number of alternants. The interpretation of *either . . . or . . .* as non-exclusive has the same logical justification as the interpretation of *some*, in *I* and *O* propositions, to mean *some at least and perhaps all*; namely, that ambiguous expressions should be given minimum significance. Common usage of *either . . . or . . .* varies. To say 'Tom is either stupid or idle' does not necessarily exclude the possibility that he is both. On the other hand, to say 'either immediate aid must be given to U.S.S.R. or national unity will be split from top to bottom' would probably be intended to be taken as asserting exclusive alternatives.

(7) is an example of a *disjunctive* proposition; it asserts that

* The student who knows some Latin should consider, from this point of view, the logical basis of the rules for conditional sentences in Latin.

not both of two component propositions are true, and is consistent with neither's being true. The component propositions are called *disjuncts*; there may be any number of *disjuncts*.

Compound propositions fall into two distinct kinds: (i) *composite*, including hypothetical, alternative, and disjunctive propositions; (ii) *conjunctive* propositions. (8) is an example of a conjunctive proposition. The three forms of composite propositions are related to one another in such a way that anything stated in one of these forms can be equivalently stated in either of the other two forms. How this can be done will be explained in § 6.

At the beginning of this section we said that certain propositions, of which examples were given, would be regarded by us as simple subject-predicate propositions. Set A provides other examples of simple propositions but they are not subject-predicate propositions; they are relational propositions: *The line AE is equal to the line BC* states that the relation of *equality* holds between the two lines named respectively *AE*, *BC*. There are various kinds of relations which must later be distinguished. At present it is enough to notice that a relation requires at least two entities standing in the relation; the entities between which a relation holds are called the *terms* of the relation. In the proposition *Andrew is twin of Mary*, the terms are obviously *Andrew*, *Mary*.

The notion of a simple proposition is itself not at all simple. Some logicians consider that, for instance, *This is white* is an absolutely simple proposition. We reject this view but must here be content to say only that we regard a proposition as simple provided that (i) it does not contain other propositions as components (ii) and includes in its verbal expression a word, or set of words, which uniquely indicates an identifiable object.* The traditional Logicians did not approach the analysis of propositions from this point of view. They seem to have assumed that a grammatically simple sentence expressed always a simple proposition, and that a grammatically complex sentence expressed always a compound proposition.

* We shall see later that this is equivalent to saying that a simple proposition is one that does not involve any reference to *variables* in its analysis.

Thus the sentence "All schoolmasters are fallible" and the sentence "Thomas Arnold is fallible" were regarded as alike expressing simple propositions; whereas the sentence "If a man is a schoolmaster, he is fallible" was taken to express a compound proposition. This is a mistake – "All schoolmasters are fallible" and "If a man is a schoolmaster, he is fallible" are verbally different statements of the same proposition, and it is not simple. The proposition expressed by "All schoolmasters are fallible" is clearly an A proposition. Propositions stating that one class is, wholly or partially, included in, or excluded from, another are *general* propositions. These, it will be remembered, are the *A*, *E*, *I*, *O* propositions of the traditional schema. It is a complete muddle to regard such propositions as simple although it is true that they cannot be analysed into the combination of two, or more, simple propositions. We must, then, distinguish these *general* propositions both from simple propositions and from the compound propositions with which we have so far been concerned. We shall see later exactly why it is that particular propositions (*I*, *O*) are correctly said to be general.

§ 6. THE SEVEN RELATIONS BETWEEN PROPOSITIONS AND THE FIGURE OF OPPOSITION

We have already seen how the possible truth or falsity of one or more propositions limits the truth or falsity of others, and we have had no difficulty in recognizing, in earlier sections, pairs of contradictory propositions and pairs of equivalent propositions. Unless we were able to recognize some cases of contradiction and to discern equivalence in spite of verbal difference we could hardly begin the study of logic, since logic arises from reflection upon our attempts to think problems out. But to be able to recognize logical relations in some instances is not the same as knowing clearly exactly what these relations are. In this section we shall be concerned with seven relations between propositions which are of fundamental importance. Every discussion concerning valid inferences in the book may be regarded as illustrating one or other of these seven relations; it is thus important that they should be thoroughly understood. Consider the following eight propositions:

(*a*) Human nature never changes.
(*b*) If human nature never changes, wars will not cease.
(*c*) If human nature does change, wars will cease.
(*d*) Wars will not always go on.
(*e*) Wars will not cease.
(*f*) Human nature always remains the same.
(*g*) Human nature can rise to sublime heights.
(*h*) Human nature does change.

These propositions are either about human nature or about wars or about the connexion between human nature and war. But propositions may be about the same subject-matter and yet not be logically connected, e.g. (*a*) and (*g*). These could both be true or both be false or one true with one false; thus, the truth or falsity of one is *logically independent* of the truth or falsity of the other. Other pairs of independent propositions are contained in the list, e.g. (*g*), (*h*). The student should select for himself other pairs. Some propositions in the list are not independent of others in the list; (*a*) denies what (*h*) asserts; these are contradictories of each other. At first sight it may seem that (*b*) and (*c*) are contradictories; a little reflection, however, will show that this is not the case: there is no contradiction in saying that wars will go on under certain conditions (e.g. provided that human nature does not change) but not under other conditions (e.g. provided that human nature does change); hence (*b*) and (*c*) are also independent of one another.

Let us now assert (*b*) *together with* (*a*), thus obtaining the conjunctive proposition: *If human nature never changes, wars will not cease and human nature never changes.* What is the relation between this conjunctive proposition and (*e*) given above? If (*b*) and (*a*) are both true, then (*e*) must also be true; but (*e*) may be true even though the *conjunction of* (*b*) *with* (*a*) is false. Thus the truth of (*e*) leaves the truth of the conjunction of (*b*) *with* (*a*) undetermined. Other propositions thus related will be found in the list; propositions so related that if the first is true the second is true, but if the second is true the truth or falsity of the first is not thereby determined, are said to be in the relation of *superimplicant to subimplicant.*

(*a*) and (*f*) are verbally different but both assert the same matter of fact; hence, either they are both true or both false. These propositions are said to be *equivalent.*

We have now recognized, by means of significant examples, four of the seven distinct logical relations that may hold between one proposition, or set of propositions, and another proposition, or set of propositions. We shall now define these and the remaining three relations. Using p, q as illustrative symbols for different propositions, the definitions are as follows:

(1) *Equivalence or Co-implication:* p and q are equivalent, or co-implicant, when they are so related that if p is true, q is true, and if q is true, p is true; and if p is false, q is false, and if q is false, p is false. Thus, $p \equiv q$, if they are true together or false together. This is the relation that holds when p implies q and q implies p. The name co-implicant brings out this relation.

(2) *Superimplication or Superalternation:* p is *superimplicant to* q provided that if p is true, q is true, but q may be true although p is false. Thus the truth of q leaves the truth of p undetermined.

(3) *Subimplication or Subalternation:* p is subimplicant to q provided that if q is true, p is true, but p may be true although q is false. The relation of subimplication is the converse of the relation of superimplication; hence, when p is *superimplicant to* q, then q is *subimplicant to* p.

(4) *Independence:* p is independent of q when neither the truth nor falsity of p determines the truth or falsity of q; and conversely.

(5) *Subcontrariety:* p is *subcontrary to* q provided that, if p is false, q is true, and if q is false, p is true, whilst p and q can be true together. The excluded case is the conjoint falsity of p and q.

(6) *Contrariety:* p is *contrary to* q provided that, if p is true, q is false, and if q is true, p is false, whilst p and q can be false together. The excluded case is the conjoint truth of p and q.

(7) *Contradiction:* p and q are *contradictories* of one another provided that, if p is true, q is false, and if p is false, q is true;

hence, p and q cannot be true together or false together, i.e. one must be true and one false.

These relations are relations of consistency or inconsistency; if any of the first five hold between propositions they are consistent, if either of the last two, they are inconsistent. The relation of independence combines consistency with complete lack of any conditions necessary for inference. This lack of any possible inferential connexion is clearly shown by propositions (*g*) and (*d*), for instance, on page 31; it is present equally in the case of (*b*) and (*c*) although not so easily apprehended. Contraries are not less mutually inconsistent, or incompatible, than contradictories; the former differ from the latter in that there are non-equivalent alternatives to both of two contrary propositions.

These seven relations are summed up in the following table, in which *p is true* is represented by p, *p is false* by $\bar{p}$, and likewise with q, and $\bar{q}$.

Relation	Given	then q or $\bar{q}$	Given	then q or $\bar{q}$
p equivalent to q	p	q	$\bar{p}$	$\bar{q}$
p superimplicant to q	p	q	$\bar{p}$	undetermined
p subimplicant to q	p	undetermined	$\bar{p}$	$\bar{q}$
p independent of q	p	undetermined	$\bar{p}$	undetermined
p subcontrary to q	p	undetermined	$\bar{p}$	q
p contrary to q	p	$\bar{q}$	$\bar{p}$	undetermined
p contradictory to q	p	$\bar{q}$	$\bar{p}$	q

In considering these relations between propositions we have not confined our attention to the traditional schema, the *A*, *E*, *I*, *O* propositions. Since every proposition stands to every other proposition in one or other of these seven relations, they must be so defined as recognizably to hold between propositions of any form whatever. The traditional Logicians, thinking of propositions as differing only in quantity and quality or both, constructed 'the Square of Opposition'. The word "opposition" is here used in a technical sense which permits compatible propositions to be opposed. Thus "opposition" must be defined as follows: Two propositions are *opposed* if they differ in quantity or in quality or in both quantity and quality. Those differing in quality but not in quantity are *contraries* (if quantity *universal*), *subcontraries* (if quantity *particular*). Those differing in quantity and quality are *contradictories*. Those differing in quantity but not in quality are *subaltern*. It is easy to construct the Square of Opposition by taking the diagonals of the Square as joining respectively the two pairs of contradictories, viz. *A* and *O*, *E* and *I*. The student may be left to work this out for himself. Here the traditional oppositions will be represented by an incompletely symmetrical figure, since the perfect symmetry of a square is not fitted to represent unsymmetrical relations.

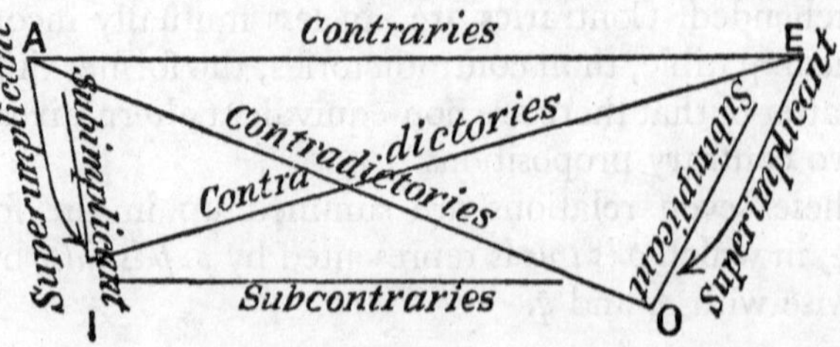

This Figure of Opposition illustrates the following facts:

(i) No two of the traditional *A*, *E*, *I*, *O* propositions are equivalent and no two are independent.
(ii) The two universal forms are contraries.
(iii) The two particular forms are subcontraries.
(iv) Universals and particulars differing in quality are contradictories.
(v) The universal form is superimplicant to the particular of the same quality, the latter being subimplicant to the former.

The traditional *Square* does not illustrate clearly the important distinction between superimplication and its converse.

The following table presents in summary form what may be validly inferred, given the truth or the falsity of these propositions:

Given	It can be inferred		
A true	*E* false	*I* true	*O* false
E true	*A* false	*I* false	*O* true
I true	*A* undetermined	*E* false	*O* undetermined
O true	*A* false	*E* undetermined	*I* undetermined
A false	*E* undetermined	*I* undetermined	*O* true
E false	*A* undetermined	*I* true	*O* undetermined
I false	*A* false	*E* true	*O* true
O false	*A* true	*E* false	*I* true

It will be seen that the *truth* of either of the universal propositions determines the truth or falsity of the other three; the *falsity* of either of the particular propositions determines the truth or falsity of the other three. But the *truth* of the particulars leaves two undetermined cases, and the *falsity* of the universals leaves two undetermined cases.

§ 7. IMMEDIATE INFERENCES

We have already seen that propositions whose verbal statement is different may be equivalent. Consider the following two pairs of propositions: (i) *All canned meats are rationed goods*; *No canned meats are unrationed goods*; (ii) *Some Cabinet Ministers are intelligent*; *Some Cabinet Ministers are not unintelligent.* In each pair the propositions are equivalent, their subject-terms are the same but their predicate-term are contradictories. Terms are contradictory when they stand respectively for two classes which are mutually exclusive and together exhaust the wider class within which both fall. Thus, for example, if the wider class is *goods*, then every member of this class falls either under the subclass *rationed goods* or under the subclass *unrationed goods.* Hence to assert that all canned meats are included in the class of *rationed goods* is equivalent to asserting that no canned meats fall in the class of *unrationed goods.* It may be objected that this is not the case with pair (ii) since *being intelligent* is not exactly the same as *being not unintelligent.* This may be admitted since we ordinarily so use "not unintelligent" as to suggest a considerable degree of intelligence. This illustrates the figure of speech *meiosis,* in which what is said intentionally gives an impression that something is less than is really the case; hence the terms may be regarded as contrary rather than contradictory. To avoid misunderstanding we can always affix *non* to the affirmative term, e.g. *non-intelligent.* It must always be remembered that in ordinary discourse what we convey is in part dependent not only upon the context but also upon intonation, emphasis, and even subtle changes in facial expression. For the purpose of discussing logical relations we ignore these characteristics of speech.*

It is a distinguishing characteristic of equivalent propositions that one can be substituted for the other, in any

* To ignore them is justifiable in an elementary textbook, but this does not mean that they do not need investigation.

argument in which either occurs, without affecting the validity of the argument. Equivalent propositions can be inferred one from the other.

It has been customary to distinguish inferences as being either *mediate* or *immediate*. Usually a conclusion is inferred from one premiss together with one or more other premisses; in such cases the inference is said to be a *mediate inference*. An inference is said to be *immediate* if the conclusion is inferred from a single proposition. This distinction is not of fundamental logical importance but it is convenient to retain it. Certain forms of immediate inference are traditionally recognized; we shall deal with them briefly.

In inferring one proposition from another care must be taken to see that the inferred proposition (or conclusion) does not assert anything not implied in the original proposition constituting the single premiss; it is, however, legitimate to assert less. This restriction is a special application of an important principle of deduction: *Do not go beyond the evidence*. Hence, if in the given proposition a term is undistributed, that term must not be distributed in the inferred proposition. It has been customary to allow a conclusion having an undistributed term to be inferred from a premiss in which that term is distributed. In such cases the given proposition will be superimplicant to the conclusion.*

Before we state the immediate inferences customarily accepted we must consider an assumption upon which their validity, in some cases, rests. Suppose we wish to consider a set of students as possessing or not possessing the characteristics of being able and hard-working. We should expect to find the following cases: those who are both able and hard-working; those who are able but not hard-working; those who are not able but are hard-working; those who are neither hard-working nor able. We have, then, four mutually exclusive and collectively exhaustive classes of students. Using *H* to stand for *hard-working*, *non-H* for its contradictory, *A* for *able*, *non-A* for its contradictory, the four classes can be symbolized by *AH*, *A non-H*, *non-AH*, *non-A non-H*. We have assumed that students are contained in each of these four

* We shall see later that such inferences are not strictly valid.

classes. It might be the case that there were no students who are both *non-H* and *non-A*; the fourth class will then be said to be empty. If any class contains members, we say that the class (which will be determined by one of the characteristics) is existent. Representing any subject-term and any predicate-term and their contradictories respectively by *S*, *non-S*, *P*, *non-P*, the assumption upon which the validity of the traditional immediate inferences is based can be stated as follows: *S*, *non-S*, *P*, *non-P* all exist, i.e. no one of the classes is empty.

Traditional immediate inference depends upon two fundamental operations, namely, *obversion* and *conversion.*

(1) *Obversion.* To assert *S is P* is equivalent to denying *S is non-P*. Thus it is always possible to obtain a proposition equivalent to a given proposition by substituting for the original predicate its contradictory and by changing the quality of the proposition. Its technical definition is: *Obversion is a process of immediate inference in which from a given proposition another is inferred having for its predicate the contradictory of the original predicate.*

SCHEMA OF OBVERSION

	Original proposition		Obverse	
A	*All S is P*	≡	*No S is non-P*	*E*
E	*No S is P*	≡	*All S is non-P*	*A*
I	*Some S is P*	≡	*Some S is not non-P*	*O*
O	*Some S is not P*	≡	*Some S is non-P*	*I*

The symbol '≡' between the original proposition (called the *obvertend*) and the obverse shows that they are equivalent: the quality is changed but the quantity remains unchanged.

Examples of significant obversion:

Obvertend		*Obvert*
No snobs are welcome guests	≡	All snobs are unwelcome guests.
All Quislings are contemptible	≡	No Quislings are other than contemptible.

(2) *Conversion.* By the converse of a proposition is ordinarily

meant another proposition in which the terms are interchanged. For example, *All equilateral triangles are equiangular* and *All equiangular triangles are equilateral* would be regarded as converses. But neither can be said to be immediately inferred from the other since such an inference would violate the rule that no term may be distributed in the inferred proposition unless it was distributed in the original proposition. These are both *A* propositions, in which the subject-term is distributed but the predicate-term is undistributed. The technical definition is: *Conversion is a process of immediate inference in which from a given proposition another is inferred having for its subject the original predicate.*

From *No snobs are welcome guests* we can infer *No welcome guests are snobs*. In each of these propositions both terms are distributed: the propositions are equivalent. From *Some Irishmen are air-gunners* we can infer *Some air-gunners are Irishmen*. These propositions are also equivalent since, in each of the propositions, both terms are undistributed.

From *All landowners are capitalists* we cannot infer that *All capitalists are landowners*, since the subject of the converse is distributed but was given undistributed in the original affirmative proposition of which it is predicate. Hence, such a converse is illegitimate; we must infer the weaker proposition, *Some capitalists are landowners*. The proposition thus inferred is said to be 'weaker' than the original since it is not possible to pass back from it to the original; the converse in the case of an *A* proposition is subimplicant to the original. Accordingly, it is said that an *A* proposition admits only of *conversion by limitation*; this is commonly called by the Latin term *conversion per accidens.*

From the proposition, *Some brachiopods are not bivalves* we cannot infer *Some bivalves are not brachiopods*, since, in the inferred proposition the predicate (*brachiopods*) is distributed, whereas it was given undistributed as the subject of a particular proposition. It is in fact true that some bivalves are not brachiopods, and in fact, *no* brachiopods are bivalves. But we assert this from information not provided by the original statement, which was in the form of an *O*, not an *E*, proposition.

SCHEMA OF CONVERSION

	Original proposition		Converse	
A	*All S is P*	→	*Some P is S*	I
E	*No S is P*	≡	*No P is S*	E
I	*Some S is P*	≡	*Some P is S*	I
O	*Some S is not P*		*None*	

It should be noted that the converse is the same in quality as the original. The symbol → shows that the converse of *A* is not equivalent to *A* but subimplicant to it.

(3) *Contraposition.* The converse of a proposition can, of course, be obverted, and an obverse be converted. Hence, other forms of immediate inference may be obtained by successively converting and obverting, in either order. There are two forms which have received special names, namely, contraposition and inversion.

Contraposition is a process of immediate inference in which from a given proposition another is inferred having for its subject the contradictory of the original predicate. From *No mammals are fish* we obtain by obversion *All mammals are non-fish*; from this, by conversion, *Some non-fish are mammals*; and by obverting this we obtain, *Some non-fish are not non-mammals.* The two latter satisfy the definition of contraposition, and are obverts of one another.

SCHEMA OF CONTRAPOSITION

Original proposition		Contrapositive		Obverted contrapositive
(*A*) *All S is P*	≡	*No non-P is S* (*E*)	≡	*All non-P is non-S* (*A*)
(*E*) *No S is P*	→	*Some non-P is S* (*I*)	→	*Some non-P is not non-S* (*O*)
(*I*) *Some S is P*		*None*		*None*
(*O*) *Some S is not P*	≡	*Some non-P is S* (*I*)	≡	*Some non-P is not non-S* (*O*)

It should be noted that *I* has no contrapositives, since *I* obverts to *O*, and *O* has no converse. *E* has not an equivalent contrapositive, since *E* obverts to *A*, and *A* has a non-equivalent converse.

(4) *Inversion* is a process of immediate inference in which from a given proposition another is inferred having for its subject the contradictory of the original subject. Thus it is

required to obtain from a proposition of the form *S-P* (where quantity and quality are not specified) a proposition of the form *non-S – non-P*, or *non-S – P*. By obversion we obtain the contradictory of the predicate-term. Hence, if we can infer a proposition having *S* as predicate, its obvert would have *non-S* as predicate; if this proposition admits of being converted we should have a proposition of the required form. If the last proposition is an *O* proposition it cannot be converted. On trial it will be found that by alternately obverting and converting (in that order) we can obtain from *A* a proposition of the required form; by alternately converting and obverting (in that order) we can obtain from *E* a proposition of the required form. An inverse cannot be obtained either from the *I* or the *O* proposition, since, in each case, in attempting to obtain a proposition with *non-S* as subject we succeed only in obtaining one with *non-S* as predicate in an *O* proposition, which cannot be converted. The process required to obtain inverses from *A* and from *E* are set out below:

A	*All S is P.*	E	*No S is P.*
obv.	*No S is non-P.*	conv.	*No P is S.*
conv.	*No non-P is S.*	obv.	*All P is non-S.*
obv.	*All non-P is non-S.*	conv.	<u>*Some non-S is P.*</u>
conv.	<u>*Some non-S is non-P.*</u>	obv.	<u>*Some non-S is not non-P.*</u>
obv.	<u>*Some non-S is not P.*</u>		

The required inverses are the underlined propositions. It will be seen that the obverted inverse of *A* is *Some non-S is not P*. This inference, therefore, breaks the rule of distribution, since *P* was not distributed in *All S is P*. Yet this inference has been obtained by using only the processes of obversion and conversion which are taken to be valid. This result ought to puzzle us. If we take a significant example the result may well be absurd, e.g. *All honest politicians are mortals* has, as its obverted inverse, *Some dishonest politicians are not mortals*, and for the other inverse, *Some dishonest politicians are immortals*. The result is absurd because, relying on information about the world not derived from logic, we claim that the original proposition is true and the inverses are false. But any proposition implied by a true proposition is true; if, therefore, using only the processes of obversion and conversion we obtain a false proposition from a proposition admittedly true, we must begin to doubt whether these processes are valid. We find it necessary, then, to examine the assumptions upon which the validity of conversion and obversion rest. Our reason for thinking that *Some dishonest politicians are immortal* is false is that we do not believe that there are any *immortal men*; accordingly, we assented to the statement that all honest politicians are mortals. If, however, there are immortal men and honest politicians are wholly included in the contradictory class, viz. *mortal men*, then immortal men must include *dishonest politicians*. But it is by no means logically necessary that every class represented by *S*, *non-S*, *P*, *non-P*, should have members; hence, the assumption that none of these classes is empty must be made explicit. If we assume *Something is not P*, then we have an additional premiss in which *P* is distributed, but if inversion requires this additional premiss it can hardly be regarded as a process of *immediate* inference in the sense in which "immediate inference" has been defined. The difficulty we find in the illicit process of the predicate-term in passing from *All S is P* to *Some non-S is not P* suggests that immediate inferences may not be valid apart from implicit assumptions, which must be made explicit. The relevant assumption is that *S*, *non-S*, *P*, *non-P* are none of them empty. If this be admitted, then, if *All S is P*, it follows that

SUMMARY OF IMMEDIATE INFERENCES

Form	*A*	*E*	*I*	*O*
Original proposition . .	SaP	SeP	SiP	SoP
Converse	PiS	PeS	PiS	
Obverse	$Se\bar{P}$	$Sa\bar{P}$	$So\bar{P}$	$Si\bar{P}$
Obverted converse . .	$Po\bar{S}$	$Pa\bar{S}$	$Po\bar{S}$	
Contrapositive . . .	$\bar{P}eS$	$\bar{P}iS$		$\bar{P}iS$
Obverted contrapositive .	$\bar{P}a\bar{S}$	$\bar{P}o\bar{S}$		$\bar{P}o\bar{S}$
Inverse	$\bar{S}i\bar{P}$	$\bar{S}iP$		
Obverted inverse . .	$\bar{S}oP$	$\bar{S}o\bar{P}$		

non-P cannot be *S*, so that *non-P* must be *non-S*, i.e. some *non-S* is *non-P*. We shall see later that an assumption of existence is always required to render valid the inference of a particular proposition from a universal proposition.

The traditional immediate inferences we have been considering may be conveniently summed up in the table given on page 41. We shall henceforth write *non-S* as $\bar{S}$, and *non-P* as $\bar{P}$.

CHAPTER III

Compound Propositions and Arguments

§ 1. EQUIVALENTS AND CONTRADICTORIES

In § 5 of the last chapter we distinguished two kinds of compound propositions, namely, *conjunctive* and *composite* propositions. In this chapter we shall be concerned to see what exactly is asserted by stating any one of these propositions. We shall begin by considering two propositions, illustratively symbolized by p and by q respectively, and their contradictories, symbolized by $\bar{p}$, $\bar{q}$. These may be combined conjunctively as follows: (1) p *and* q, (2) $\bar{p}$ *and* q, (3) $\bar{p}$ *and* $\bar{q}$, (4) p *and* $\bar{q}$. The *order* in which the conjuncts are asserted is indifferent; for instance, there is no logical difference between *Dickens is a great novelist and Anthony Trollope is a good storyteller* and *Anthony Trollope is a good storyteller and Dickens is a great novelist.* Which of the two components in each proposition we assert first will be determined by the context of the discussion in which one or other of them happened to be asserted. If one compound were asserted no one would feel any need to assert the other.

It may seem easy to state the denial of any proposition; we all know how to contradict our neighbour. But it is not always easy to distinguish at once between *denial by affirming the contrary* and *denial by affirming the contradictory.* We sometimes fly to extremes and thus assert more than we need. In some cases, in everyday discussion, we even at times mistake two independent propositions for contradictories.* How should we contradict *Every prospect pleases and only man is vile?* This asserts both conjuncts to be true; to deny it must mean to assert either that both conjuncts are false or that at least one is false. The former is the assertion of the contrary of the

* For example, propositions (*b*) and (*c*) on page 31. The student should formulate the contradictories of these propositions.

original conjunctive proposition, the latter of the contradictory. These are often confused. The contrary is: *Neither does every prospect please nor is man only vile*; the contradictory is: *Either not every prospect pleases or not only man is vile.* This contradictory can be also stated in the form, *It is not the case that every prospect pleases and also that only man is vile.* The student should convince himself that both these contradict the original proposition. The conjoint assertion of p with q is equivalent to the denial that p and q can be disjoined; hence the disjunctive *Not both p and q* contradicts *Both p and q*; it is also clear that if *not both* of two propositions can be asserted, then *at least one* must be denied; hence a conjunctive can be equally well denied by an alternative proposition.

Ordinary statements in different composite forms can easily be seen to be equivalent. Consider the following:

(i) Either Martin is stupid or Jones is a bad teacher.
(ii) If Martin is not stupid, Jones is a bad teacher.
(iii) If Jones is not a bad teacher, Martin is stupid.
(iv) Not both Martin is not stupid and Jones is not a bad teacher.

If we write p for *Martin is stupid*, q for *Jones is a bad teacher*, and $\bar{p}$, $\bar{q}$ for their respective contradictories, we can exhibit the form of these four propositions as follows: (i) *Either p or q*; (ii) *If $\bar{p}$, q*; (iii) *If $\bar{q}$, p*; (iv) *Not both $\bar{p}$ and $\bar{q}$*. These are all equivalent to one another and are consequently alike contradicted by the conjunctive *Both $\bar{p}$ and $\bar{q}$*.

It will be noticed that we have two hypothetical propositions in the list above and that they are equivalent. The one is constructed from the other by separately contradicting the original antecedent and consequent and then reversing them, so that the contradictory of the original consequent is the new antecedent and conversely. We saw that the order of the components of a conjunctive proposition is logically indifferent; the same holds of the order of the disjuncts in a disjunctive, and of the alternants in an alternative proposition. In the case of hypothetical propositions this is not so. *If he is a hard worker, he will be successful* is not equivalent to *If he will be successful, he is a hard worker*; there are other conditions of success – he may be lucky or unusually clever. Using X to stand for any one statement, and Y for any other, we must notice that *If X, then Y* is logically independent of *If Y, then X*: the former asserts that *X* is sufficient to the truth of *Y*; the latter that *Y* is sufficient to the truth of *X*. These may both be true, but either may be true without the other being true. We must also notice that *unless* ordinarily means *if not* . . ., and is not equivalent to *only if not* . . .; the former states a condition that is *sufficient*, the latter a condition that is *necessary*; but a condition may be sufficient without being necessary; for example, *Unless it is wet, I shall go for a walk* asserts that I shall go for a walk if it is not wet, but this is not equivalent to saying *Only if it is not wet, I shall go for a walk*, for I might go for a walk *even if it were wet* because I am tired of staying indoors or I want to please a friend. In an ordinary conversation the context should suffice to show in which sense "unless" is being used.

The lack of symmetry in the relation of *p* to *q* in *If p, then q*, which makes the simple conversion *If q, then p* invalid, is again due to our accepting the *minimum* interpretation of statements, as in the case of *Either p or q*. To interpret *either . . . or . . .* exclusively is equivalent to asserting *Either p or q and not both p and q*, i.e. to the conjunction of an alternative and a disjunctive proposition. To interpret *If p, then q* as asserting that *p* is *sufficient* to the truth of *q* without at the same time asserting it to be necessary to the truth of *q* is to avoid committing ourselves to the *maximum* assertion that *p* is *both sufficient and necessary* to the truth of *q*. If we wish to make this latter assertion we can do so by the conjunctive *If p, then q, and if q, then p*. In science we frequently wish to assert that *p* implies *q* and also *q* implies *p*; i.e. we seek a pair of propositions in which the implying component of one is the implied component of the other. Frequently, however, this is not possible: we know that loss of appetite is consequent upon a certain bodily disease, but it may also be consequent upon a deep sorrow. Medical scientists seek to find whether there are common factors, which could be medically treated, in these two cases, and, if so, what they are; but medical scientists are not always successful. Hence, we must avoid the mistake of invalidly inferring *If q, then p* from *If p, then q*. The conjoint assertion of these two propositions is of special importance for the advance of knowledge; they have been called *complementary* propositions. Likewise *Either p or q* and *Not both p and q* are called complementary propositions.

> The term complementary [says W. E. Johnson] is especially applicable where propositions are conjoined in either of these ways, because separately the propositions represent the fact partially, and taken together they represent the same fact with relative completeness.*

This point may be further illustrated by the pair of general propositions represented by *SaP*, *PaS*. These are complementary; they are consistent but neither can be validly inferred from the other. Together they assert that the class *S* is wholly included in the class *P* and the class *P* is wholly included in the class *S*, i.e. the classes *S* and *P* are co-extensive; e.g. *Every triangle whose base angles are equal is isosceles and every isosceles triangle has its base angles equal.* The contradictory of the conjunctive proposition *SaP and PaS* is *Either SoP or PoS.* Thus *All Germans are Nazis and only Germans are Nazis* is contradicted by *Either some Germans are not Nazis or some Nazis are not Germans.* It must be remembered that *either . . . or* is interpreted as non-exclusive.

The table below sums up the equivalences between the composite forms, together with the contradictory in each case. It should be observed that *If p, then q* and *If q, then p* are

EQUIVALENCES AND CONTRADICTORIES OF COMPOSITE PROPORTIONS

Equivalent hypotheticals			Disjunctive		Alternative	Contradictory
1. *If* p, *then* q	$\equiv$ *If* $\bar{q}$, *then* $\bar{p}$	$\equiv$	*Not both* p *and* $\bar{q}$	$\equiv$	*Either* $\bar{p}$ *or* q	p *and* $\bar{q}$
2. *If* $\bar{p}$, *then* $\bar{q}$	$\equiv$ *If* q, *then* p	$\equiv$	*Not both* $\bar{p}$ *and* q	$\equiv$	*Either* p *or* $\bar{q}$	$\bar{p}$ *and* q
3. *If* p, *then* $\bar{q}$	$\equiv$ *If* q, *then* $\bar{p}$	$\equiv$	*Not both* p *and* q	$\equiv$	*Either* $\bar{p}$ *or* $\bar{q}$	p *and* q
4. *If* $\bar{p}$, *then* q	$\equiv$ *If* $\bar{q}$, *then* p	$\equiv$	*Not both* $\bar{p}$ *and* $\bar{q}$	$\equiv$	*Either* p *or* q	$\bar{p}$ *and* $\bar{q}$

the same in form, for it is logically indifferent what *letters* we use as illustrative symbols; we used *X*, *Y* above to illustrate antecedent and consequent respectively. But, on the assump-

* W. E. Johnson, *Logic*, Part I, p. 37. Mr Johnson points out that complementary propositions 'are frequently confused in thought and frequently conjoined in fact'. It should, however, be noted that they are sometimes not conjoined in fact; hence, their tendency to be confused in thought may lead us astray.

tion that p stands for *some one definite* proposition and q for *some other definite* proposition, then *If p, then q* is distinguished from *If q, then p* as its complementary. Both will, therefore, be included in the list.

Certain observations on this table are important and should be carefully noted. (i) Propositions on different lines are independent; (ii) as any proposition contradicting a given proposition also contradicts any equivalent propositions, the proposition on the right of the black line contradicts all four propositions left of it on the same line; (iii) the propositions, on different lines, along the principal diagonal are stated in terms of p, q, and are clearly independent; (iv) propositions in the same column are the same in form but – on the assumption we have been making, viz. that p stands for *p is true*, $\bar{p}$ stands for *p is false* (likewise with q, $\bar{q}$) – these are conveniently distinguished, and have, therefore, been separately considered.

The significance of the composite forms can be brought out by formulating specific rules for inferring the various equivalent propositions when one is given. It will suffice to give these for the case of the hypothetical *If p, then q*. It must be remembered that *If . . . then . . .* can be interpreted as *implies*, in the sense that, when *p implies q*, q is true provided p is true. Given *If p, then q*:

(1) The denial of the antecedent is implied by the denial of the consequent; hence, *If $\bar{q}$, then $\bar{p}$*.
(2) Either the antecedent must be denied or the consequent asserted; hence, *Either $\bar{p}$ or q*.
(3) The assertion of the antecedent is not consistent with the denial of the consequent; hence, *Not both p and $\bar{q}$*.

It is not difficult to formulate corresponding rules for obtaining equivalents from one of the other two composite forms. The student should construct significant examples and transform them in the equivalent propositions; he may then intuitively apprehend the validity of these inferences. We shall consider one example.

Example. The British Government in the summer of 1942 desired to impress the people with the need for economizing in fuel in order that the war industries should not be hampered for lack of fuel. The Government's exhortations might be summed up in the short statement, *If we waste fuel, we lose the war*. To this proposition the three following are equivalent: (1) *If we do not lose the war, we have not wasted fuel*; (2) *Either we do not waste fuel or we lose the war*; (3) *It is not the case both that we waste fuel and do not lose the war*. In the next section we shall see that once we have fully grasped these rules, and have thus understood the precise significance of the various composite forms, we shall be in a good position for understanding certain forms of arguments of common occurrence in everyday reasoning. If we understand these forms we may be on our guard against mistakes in reasoning which occur all too frequently from an imperfect apprehension of what precisely has been asserted in the premisses.

§ 2. COMPOUND ARGUMENTS WITH ONE OR MORE COMPOSITE PREMISSES

Let us consider the following examples of arguments, taken from everyday conversation; some are valid, some are invalid.

(1) Two boys are watching the approach of an aeroplane. One says, 'That's a bomber; I think it is a Stirling.' The other replies, 'It has four engines and I think it must be a Stirling or a Liberator, but I don't think it is a Stirling.' As the aeroplane approaches nearer, the first boy says, 'You are right; it has twin-fins and rudders, so it is a Liberator.'

(2) 'You cannot maintain that after the war there should continue to be unrestricted competition among the nations for the world's natural resources and yet, at the same time, hold that we ought to aim at giving to all nations economic security. But you do admit the latter; hence, you must reject unrestricted competition. Moreover, if there is unrestricted competition, there will be more world wars, and you have agreed that there must be no more world wars.'

(3) 'If Prock's book deepens our sense of humanitarian values, it is worth writing even in time of war; but it is certainly worth writing in time of war, so I conclude that his book deepens our sense of humanitarian values.'

(4) 'If a man is a coward, he will seek to evade military duties, but Tobias is not a coward; so he won't attempt to get out of military duties.'

(5) 'For a novelist to be sure of getting his books properly reviewed, he must be either already famous or have written a really first-rate book; but Jensen is already famous, so his novel is not first-rate.'

It is not difficult to determine the structure of these arguments.* It will suffice to examine in detail only the first. It presents a common form of reasoning – something is recognized as being *this* or *that*; then, some characteristic is looked for that would suffice *to distinguish this from that.* The argument can be formally analysed as follows:

(i) *Either the aeroplane is a Stirling or a Liberator;*
(ii) *If it has twin-fins and rudders, it is not a Stirling, but it has twin-fins and rudders; hence, it is not a Stirling.*
(iii) Combining (i) and the conclusion of (ii) yields the conclusion: *It is a Liberator.*

The logical structure can be exhibited as follows:

Either A or B	(i)
If F, then not-A *F ∴ not-A*	(ii)
∴ B	(iii)

In the following table we set out formally the four modes of argument corresponding to the four varieties of composite premisses, adding the Latin name traditionally used in each case:

COMPOUND MODES

Modus†		*Form of Composite Premiss*
1. *Ponendo ponens:*	*If p, then q; but p; ∴ q*	*Hypothetical*
2. *Tollendo tollens:*	*If p, then q; but $\bar{q}$; ∴ $\bar{p}$*	*Hypothetical*
3. *Ponendo tollens:*	*Not both p and q; but p; ∴ $\bar{q}$*	*Disjunctive*
4. *Tollendo ponens:*	*Either p or q; but $\bar{p}$; ∴ q*	*Alternative*

* The student should before reading further determine for himself whether the conclusion, in each case, does in fact follow from the premisses.

† These barbarous names are derived from the Latin verbs: *ponere* = to affirm; *tollere* = to deny; hence, they can be interpreted as follows: (1) by affirming, affirms; (2) by denying, denies; (3) by affirming, denies; (4) by denying, affirms.

The rules for these modes are:

(1) *Ponendo ponens*: From the affirmation of the antecedent, the affirmation of the consequent follows. (2) *Tollendo tollens*: From the denial of the consequent, the denial of the antecedent follows. (3) *Ponendo tollens*: From the affirmation of one disjunct, the denial of the other disjunct follows. (4) *Tollendo ponens*: From the denial of one alternant, the affirmation of the other alternant follows.

From these rules it is easy to see that, in the examples given above, (3) is invalid because the antecedent is affirmed on the ground of an affirmation of the consequent; (4) is invalid because the consequent is denied on the ground of a denial of the antecedent; (5) is invalid because one of the alternants is affirmed and the other is denied *in consequence*. These three fallacies are all due to the failure to appreciate what exactly the relevant composite premiss asserts. To affirm the antecedent *because* the consequent has been affirmed is to confuse an hypothetical with its complementary; similarly, in denying the consequent *because* the antecedent has been denied. To deny an alternant *because* the other alternant has been affirmed is to confuse an alternative proposition with the complementary disjunctive, or to treat it as though it were the *conjunction* of the alternative with the complementary disjunctive. That this is a confusion should be clear from our previous discussion of the composite propositions. These invalid modes of inference can be summarized as follows:

1. *Hypothetical:* If p, then q; but q; $\therefore p$ (consequent affirmed).
2. *Hypothetical:* If p, then q; but $\bar{p}$; $\therefore \bar{q}$ (antecedent denied).
3. *Alternative:* Either p or q; but p; $\therefore \bar{q}$ (alternant affirmed).
4. *Disjunctive:* Not both p and q; but $\bar{q}$; $\therefore p$ (disjunct denied).

Since the same statement can be made in any one of the four composite forms of propositions, the compound modes can be reduced to one another.

Equivalent arguments

Ponendo ponens		*Tollendo ponens*
If you paid £2, he overcharged you;	≡	Either you did not pay £2 or he overcharged you;
You paid £2;		You paid £2;
∴ he overcharged you.		∴ he overcharged you.

In the same manner the *ponendo tollens* and *tollendo tollens* can be obtained, the conclusion in each case being the same.

The Dilemma. As the popular use of the phrase, 'I am in a dilemma' shows, the dilemma is a form of *argument*, the purpose of which is to prove that from either of two alternatives an unwelcome conclusion follows. If skilfully employed, it can be made effective by an orator and amusing to an audience; it can also be used seriously. For these reasons, no doubt, a disproportionate amount of space has been given to it in books on logic – 'disproportionate' because no new logical principles are involved. We shall deal with it shortly.

A dilemma is a compound argument consisting of a premiss in which two hypotheticals are conjunctively affirmed and a premiss in which the antecedents are alternatively affirmed or the consequents alternatively denied. If there are three hypotheticals conjunctively affirmed the argument is called a *trilemma*, if four, a *quadrilemma*, if more than four a *polylemma*. These are of rare occurrence; sometimes 'dilemma' is used to cover all these forms.

Four distinct kinds of dilemma are recognized:

1. *Complex Constructive:*

If *p*, then *q*, and if *r*, then *t*,
But either *p* or *r*,
∴ either *q* or *t*.

2. *Simple Constructive:*

If *p*, then *q*, and if *r*, then *q*,
But either *p* or *r*,
∴ *q*.

3. *Complex Destructive:*

If *p*, then *q*, and if *r*, then *t*,
But either not-*q* or not-*t*,
∴ not-*p* or not-*r*.

4. *Simple Destructive:*

If *p*, then *q*, and if *p*, then *r*,
But either not-*q* or not-*r*,
∴ not-*p*.

It is obvious that the rules for the hypothetical and alternative modes of argument directly apply to the dilemmatic forms, so that they need not be re-stated here.

The dilemma is often regarded as a peculiarly fallacious mode of argument. This is, however, a mistake; any form of argument can be, and most are, fallaciously used either through stupidity or cunning. In so far as there are any difficulties in using valid dilemmas these arise from the difficulty of finding premisses both significant and pertinent which are true and also fulfil the conditions imposed by the form. The force of the dilemmatic situation presented in the alternative premiss depends upon the condition that the alternants must be exhaustive. If there is a third alternative, we can 'escape between the horns of the dilemma'.* Thus, a too-anxious parent might argue: 'If my son is idle, he will fail in his examination; and if he overworks, he will be ill; but either he will be idle or he will overwork; therefore, my son will either fail in his examination or be ill.' The third alternative is too obvious to require stating; it is, however, just possible that some people may be as silly as this argument suggests. An example of a valid dilemma is the following: 'If you reflected carefully you would have seen your mistake; and if you were honest you would have admitted it; but either you do not see your mistake or you do not admit it; therefore, either you have not reflected carefully or you are not honest.' This is a complex destructive dilemma; the conclusion can be avoided only by objecting correctly to the factual truth of the hypothetical premiss. But this way of rejecting a conclusion is not confined to dilemmatic arguments.

A dilemma is said to be *rebutted* if another dilemma be constructed leading to a conclusion which seems to contradict the original conclusion. Thus an Athenian mother is reported to have presented her son with the dilemma:

'If you say what is just, men will hate you; and if you say

* This phrase emphasizes the fact that the dilemma has been regarded as essentially a *disputatious* argument; the speaker seeks 'to impale his adversary upon the horns', i.e. the unwelcome alternatives; but we do not always argue to refute *adversaries*; we may seek to *convince* those who oppose our view, even, sometimes, to convince ourselves.

what is unjust, the gods will hate you; but you must say what is just or what is unjust; hence either men will hate you or the gods will hate you.'

To this the son replied:

'If I say what is just, the gods will love me; and if I say what is unjust, men will love me; but I must say one or the other; therefore, either the gods will love me or men will love me.'

The rebuttal consists in transposing the two consequents and contradicting* them. Thus the form of the mother's dilemma is: If *p*, then *q*; and if *not-p*, then *r*; but *p* or *not-p*; therefore, *q* or *r*.

The son's rebuttal is of the form: If *p*, then *not-r*; and if *not-p*, then *not-q*; but either *p* or *not-p*; therefore, either *not-r* or *not-q*.

It is clear that *q or r* is not contradicted by *not-r or not-q*; these propositions are independent. What the son needed to prove in order to allay his mother's fears was *Both men and gods will love me.*

A dilemma is said to be 'taken by the horns' when the alternatives are accepted but the consequences drawn from them are denied. These picturesque modes of argument have no special logical significance. As tests of our ability to use logical principles and to discern violations of principles they have some utility, but not much.

* Miss Stebbing here treats "loving" and "hating" as contradictory terms, though they would usually be regarded as contrary terms. [C. W. K. M.]

CHAPTER IV

The Traditional Syllogism

§ 1. DEFINING CHARACTERISTICS OF A SYLLOGISM

Formal immediate inference is trivial. When we seem to have inferred a non-trivial conclusion from a single premiss it is because we have tacitly made assumptions or have presupposed a premiss without noticing that we have done so. At least two premisses are required for a properly formal inference which is not trivial. Such inference is *mediate* inference. It is seldom that we state both premisses explicitly, but it is possible to find examples. Sir Henry Campbell-Bannerman was making an informal speech to his neighbours at Montrose. In the course of it he said: 'An old friend of mine, Wilfrid Lawson, was accustomed to say: "The man who walks on a straight road never loses his way." Well, I flatter myself that I have walked on a pretty straight road, probably because it was easier, and accordingly I have not gone astray.'* The conclusion *I have not gone astray* is implied by the conjoint assertion of two premisses, *The man who walks on a straight road never loses his way* (i.e. does not go astray) and *I have walked on a (pretty) straight road.* No one should have any difficulty in seeing that the conclusion does indeed follow from the premisses. Arguments of this kind, in which a conclusion is inferred from two premisses, can often be stated in a traditional form called the syllogism. For example:

(1) All human beings are liable to make mistakes.
All philosophers are human beings.

∴ All philosophers are liable to make mistakes.

* Quoted by Lord Oxford and Asquith in *Fifty Years of Parliament*, Vol. II, p. 51.

(2) No vain people are trustworthy.
All great leaders are trustworthy.

∴ No great leaders are vain.

(3) All policemen are tall.
Some policemen are Cockneys.

∴ Some Cockneys are tall.

In each of these examples there are three propositions and three different terms, each of which occurs twice. The term which occurs in both premisses but not in the conclusion is called the *middle* term; it is connected in one premiss with the predicate of the conclusion, and in the other with the subject of the conclusion. The subject and predicate of the conclusion were called by Aristotle 'the extreme terms', because they are connected by a middle term. The predicate of the conclusion is called the *major* term; the subject of the conclusion is called the *minor* term. The premiss containing the major term is called the *major premiss*; the premiss containing the minor term is called the *minor premiss*. The major premiss is traditionally stated first, then the minor, and then the conclusion. This is the order followed in the three examples above, but the order of the premisses is logically irrelevant. The line drawn between the premisses and the conclusion is intended to mark the difference between them – the premisses are taken for granted or asserted to be true, the conclusion is drawn from the premisses.

Aristotle defined the syllogism widely. He said, 'a syllogism is discourse (*λόγος*) in which, certain things being stated, something other than what is stated follows of necessity from their being so', and he adds, 'I mean by the last phrase that they produce the consequence, and by this, that no further term is required from without to make the consequence necessary'.* But the syllogism has traditionally been more narrowly interpreted so that an argument, even when valid and in accordance with this definition, can in various ways fail to fall into syllogistic form. This narrower specification of

* *Analytica Priora*, 24*b* 18.

traditional syllogistic arguments can be stated in three defining rules:

1. *Every syllogism comprises three propositions.*
2. *Each proposition in a syllogism must be in one of the A, E, I, O forms.*
3. *Every syllogism contains three and only three terms.*

Comments on these rules: (1) Syllogistic arguments are usually abbreviated so that one premiss is tacitly supplied by the context or is, perhaps, presupposed only in the sense that without it the argument is not valid. A syllogism thus incompletely stated is called an *enthymeme.* Sometimes the conclusion is omitted, mainly as the rhetorical device of innuendo. The following are illustrations of enthymemes as they might very well occur in ordinary conversation although not, as a rule, so tersely expressed:

(i) 'Dictators are ruthless for all ambitious men are ruthless.'
(ii) 'No honest men are advertisers because all advertisers are liars by profession.'
(iii) 'Sailors are handy folk, so they are always welcome guests.'

In (i) and (ii) the minor premiss is omitted; in (iii) the major premiss is omitted.*

(2) The singular proposition, e.g. *De Valera is not wholly Irish, She is reckless*, is not excluded by this rule since, for the purposes of syllogistic inference, singular propositions are regarded as *A* or *E* propositions.

(3) This rule is most commonly violated by equivocation, i.e. by using the same word or phrase with different meanings in its two occurrences. When this happens the syllogism has more than three terms or – as it would be more correct to say – the argument is not syllogistic although it appears to be so because one word, or phrase, is being used ambiguously.†

These rules suffice to determine what is to be understood as a categorical syllogism, but they do not suffice to deter-

* Polysyllogisms are also enthymematic. See below, p. 71.

† On this topic see further, p. 101.

mine the conditions under which an argument conforming to them is valid. That the arguments given on page 55 are valid will be easily seen, but such 'seeing' is not *proof*. We need to see further how it is that the conclusion of a valid syllogism is valid and to understand exactly why some of the conclusions we are tempted to draw in arguing are in fact invalid. For this purpose we must state certain rules or axioms:

I. *Axioms of Distribution.*

1. The middle term must be distributed in at least one of the premisses.
2. A term that is distributed in the conclusion must be distributed in the corresponding premiss.

II. *Axioms of Quality.*

3. At least one premiss must be affirmative.
4. With one premiss negative, the conclusion must be negative.
5. With both premisses affirmative, the conclusion must be affirmative.

From these axioms we can deduce three corollaries, which we shall find useful in determining which combinations of *A*, *E*, *I*, *O* propositions yield valid syllogisms. Some writers of elementary textbooks in Logic include these corollaries among the rules, or axioms, but it is desirable to prove them. A corollary is a theorem, and a theorem is a general proposition which is proved entirely by reference to the axioms and definitions. For the three following theorems we shall use the traditional name *corollary*.

Corollaries. (i) *At least one premiss must be universal.* This can be established by indirect proof; i.e. by supposing that both premisses could be particular, which is the contradictory of the theorem asserted.

Proof: There are three cases to be considered. (*a*) *Both premisses are negative.* This violates axiom 3; hence the original supposition is impossible; therefore, its contradictory, the theorem, is proved.

(*b*) *Both premisses are affirmative.* Then, since both are particular (assumed), no term in either premiss is distributed;

hence, the middle term is undistributed; accordingly axiom 1 is violated.

(*c*) *One premiss is affirmative, the other negative.* Since only one term is distributed, it must, by axiom 1, be the middle term; but, by axiom 4, the conclusion must be negative [and would thus have a distributed term, viz. its predicate]; therefore, axiom 2 is violated.

(ii) *Given that one premiss is particular, the conclusion must be particular.*

Proof: There are again three cases: (*a*) *Both premisses are negative.* This is excluded by axiom 3.

(*b*) *Both premisses are affirmative.* Since one premiss is particular (*given*) and both are affirmative, only one term is distributed in the two premisses; this, by axiom 1, must be the middle term; therefore, by axiom 2, the minor term cannot be distributed in the conclusion, i.e. the conclusion must be particular.

(*c*) *One premiss is affirmative, the other negative.* Since one premiss is affirmative and one negative only two terms can be distributed in the premisses; of these one term, by axiom 1, must be the middle term, and the other, by axioms 4 and 2, must be the major term; therefore the minor term cannot be distributed, i.e. the conclusion must be particular.

(iii) *Given that the major premiss is particular, the minor premiss cannot be negative.* Since, *ex hypothesi*, the minor premiss is negative, then, by axiom 4, the conclusion must be negative, so that the major term will be distributed in the conclusion. But the major premiss is particular (*given*) and affirmative, by axiom 3; hence, neither term in the major premiss is distributed; therefore, by axiom 2, the minor premiss cannot be negative if the major premiss is particular.

§ 2. FIGURES AND MOODS OF THE SYLLOGISM

Not all combinations of *A*, *E*, *I*, *O* propositions will yield valid syllogisms; we must, therefore, determine which combinations are valid. Let us first, however, consider the four following arguments:

I. All ruminants are horned.
All cows are ruminants.

∴ All cows are horned.

II. No soldiers are pacifists.
All Quakers are pacifists.

∴ No Quakers are soldiers.

III. All film stars are famous.
Some film stars are frivolous.

∴ Some who are frivolous are famous.

IV. All snobs are obsequious.
No obsequious people are financiers.

∴ No financiers are snobs.

The student will have no difficulty in seeing that these arguments are valid. They differ in form in two ways: (i) in the position of the middle term; (ii) in the quantity and quality of the propositions involved.

(i) In I the middle term is subject of the major premiss and predicate of the minor; in II the middle term is predicate in both premisses; in III the middle term is subject in both premisses; in IV the middle term is predicate in the major premiss and subject in the minor premiss. Using *S*, *M*, *P*, to stand for minor, middle, and predicate term respectively, we can symbolize these forms as follows:

I	II	III	IV*
$M-P$	$P-M$	$M-P$	$P-M$
$S-M$	$S-M$	$M-S$	$M-S$
$\therefore S-P$	$\therefore S-P$	$\therefore S-P$	$\therefore S-P$

These differences are said to be differences in the *figure* of the syllogism. Accordingly, the figure of a syllogism is determined by the position of the middle term.

(ii) The propositions involved in example I are *AAA*, in II *EAE*, in III *AII*, in IV *AEE*. This difference is called a difference in *mood*. Accordingly, the mood of a syllogism is determined by the quantity and quality of the propositions involved. Thus I is in the mood *AAA*, II in the mood *EAE*, and so on.

Consider the argument: *All polite people are kind*; *Some customs officers are not polite*; therefore *Some customs officers are not kind*. Does this conclusion follow from the premisses? A little reflection should enable us to see that it does not – a man

* The position of the middle term in the four figures can be easily remembered by noticing that a line drawn through *M* in the above schemas gives roughly a W, viz. ╲ | | ╱.

may be impolite and yet in other respects kind. If the argument is examined it will be seen that the major term *kind* is distributed in the conclusion (being the predicate of a negative proposition) but not in the major premiss; hence axiom 2 is violated. The argument is in figure I and is in the mood *AOO*. The invalidity is due to its form; it has nothing to do with the characteristics of *polite people*, *kind people*, and *customs officers*. Accordingly, we can assert that the mood *AOO* is invalid in figure I, no matter what the propositions involved may be about. It is invalid because the major term is illegitimately distributed in the conclusion. This fallacy is called the fallacy of illicit process of the major term, or, more shortly, *illicit major*. Now consider the argument: *Some R.A.F. pilots are artistic*; *all R.A.F. pilots are intelligent*; therefore *All intelligent people are artistic*. This is again invalid; the minor term is illegitimately distributed; i.e. the syllogism is guilty of the *fallacy of illicit minor*. Finally, consider the argument: *All operatic singers are temperamental*; *all disillusioned poets are temperamental*; therefore, *all disillusioned poets are operatic singers*. The conclusion does not follow; axiom 1 has been violated, for, since both premisses are affirmative and the middle term is predicate in both, the middle term has not been distributed. This fallacy is known as the fallacy of *undistributed middle*. It is of common occurrence in our arguments, but it is not always easily detected when the argument is less tersely expressed.

The conventional restriction of the syllogism to the four traditional categorical forms limits the conclusions to one of the following, *SaP*, *SeP*, *SiP*, *SoP*. Negative terms are excluded so that, for example, we cannot have a conclusion involving $\bar{S}$ or $\bar{P}$. The major premiss may be any one of the *A*, *E*, *I*, *O* forms; so may the minor premiss. There are, then, sixteen possible combinations. These are written below; the first letter indicates the major, the second the minor premiss:

AA	*AE*	*AI*	*AO*
EA	*EE*	*EI*	*EO*
IA	*IE*	*II*	*IO*
OA	*OE*	*OI*	*OO*

Some of these combinations can be eliminated at once, by reference to the axioms. The axioms of quality exclude *EE*, *EO*, *OE*, *OO**; corollary (i) excludes *II*, *IO*, *OI*; corollary (iii) excludes *IE*. There are left eight combinations each of which will yield a valid syllogism in one or more of the figures. These are *AA*, *AE*, *AI*, *AO*, *EA*, *EI*, *IA*, *OA*.

Since the distribution of any term in these propositions depends upon its position as subject or as predicate, combinations not excluded generally by the axioms of distribution will nevertheless not yield a valid conclusion in every figure. We have already studied examples of such invalid combinations. We have now to deduce from the axioms special rules for each figure.†

Special Rules of Figure I. Schema

$$\frac{\begin{matrix} M - P \\ S - M \end{matrix}}{S - P}$$

(i) *The minor premiss must be affirmative. Proof:* Suppose the minor premiss is negative: then the conclusion must be negative (ax. 4) and the major premiss affirmative (ax. 3). Then the major term will be distributed in the conclusion but not in its own premiss, thus violating axiom 2. Therefore, the minor premiss cannot be negative, i.e. it must be affirmative.

(ii) *The major premiss must be universal. Proof:* Since the minor premiss must be affirmative, the middle term, its predicate, will be undistributed in the minor premiss; hence, the middle term must be distributed in the major premiss (ax. 1), of which it is subject; accordingly, the major premiss must be universal.

From these rules we can directly determine the valid moods in figure I. Granted the assumption that the classes denoted by *S* and *P* respectively contain members, then, any combination of premisses that justifies a universal conclusion also justifies a particular conclusion, since, in this case, the

* It should be noted that *OO* is also excluded by corollary (i), and *OE* by corollary (iii).

† This procedure is elegant and affords a useful exercise. Any student who has difficulty in following the deduction should turn again to the axioms. It is important to remember that a term is distributed if it is the *subject* of a *universal* proposition or the *predicate* of a *negative* proposition; it will be undistributed if it is the *subject* of a *particular* proposition or the *predicate* of an *affirmative* proposition.

particular conclusion would be subimplicant to the universal conclusion.

Valid Moods of Figure I. The combinations excluded by the special rules are: *AE*, *AO* excluded by rule (i); *IA*, *OA* excluded by rule (ii); accordingly, the valid moods are *AAA*, [*AAI*], *AII*, *EAE*, [*EAO*], *EIO*. The two moods given in brackets are the weakened moods, and may be disregarded. The unweakened moods have been given proper names which, since the thirteenth century, have been familiar to students of logic. They are now mainly of antiquarian interest but are of some use for purposes of reference. Keeping the same order in which the valid moods have just been listed and omitting the weakened moods, these names are, *Barbara*, *Darii*, *Celarent*, *Ferio*.*

Special Rules of Figure II. Schema

$$\frac{\begin{array}{c} P - M \\ S - M \end{array}}{S - P}$$

(i) *One premiss must be negative.*† This is necessary in order to secure the distribution of the middle term, which is predicate in both premisses.

(ii) *The major premiss must be universal.* This is to prevent illicit major, since the conclusion is always negative as a consequence of rule (i).

Valid Moods of Figure II. The combinations excluded by the special rules are: *AA*, *AI*, *IA* (by rule i), *OA* (by rule ii); accordingly, the valid moods are *AEE*[*AEO*], *EAE*[*EAO*], *EIO*, *AOO*, and their names are *Cesare*, *Camestres*, *Festino*, *Baroco*.

Special Rules of Figure III. Schema

$$\frac{\begin{array}{c} M - P \\ M - S \end{array}}{S - P}$$

* These names were invented for a special mnemonic purpose, viz. to reduce to a mechanical procedure the reduction of syllogisms in figures II, III, IV to figure I. It should be noted that the quantity and quality of the propositions involved in a given syllogism are shown by the vowels contained in the name, the canonical order of major, minor, conclusion, being preserved, e.g. C*e*l*a*r*e*nt. All other letters can be disregarded. Those interested in the purpose for which the other letters were used should consult *F.L.* § 258.

† The proofs of these special rules are very easy; in the case of figure I the proofs have been given in full; for the remaining figures the proofs are merely indicated.

(i) *The minor premiss must be affirmative.* This is for the same reason as in figure I, for the rule is required owing to the position of the major term, *P*, which is the same in both figures, and has no reference to the minor term, *S*, the position of which differs in the two figures.

(ii) *The conclusion must be particular.* This follows from special rule (i) together with axiom 2.

Valid Moods of Figure III. The combinations excluded by the special rules are *AE*, *AO* (by rule (i)); all other combinations are permitted but the conclusion must not be universal. For this reason there are six unweakened moods: *AAI*, *AII*, *IAI*, *EAO*, *EIO*, *OAO*, and their names are *Darapti*, *Datisi*, *Disamis*, *Felapton*, *Ferison*, *Bocardo*.

Special Rules of Figure IV. Schema

$$\frac{\begin{array}{c} P - M \\ M - S \end{array}}{S - P}$$

(i) *The major premiss cannot be particular if either premiss is negative.* Violation of this rule involves illicit major, since the major term is subject in its premiss.

(ii) *The minor premiss cannot be particular if the major premiss is affirmative.* Violation of this rule involves undistributed middle since the middle term is subject in the minor, and predicate in the major premiss.

(iii) *The conclusion cannot be universal if the minor premiss is affirmative.* Violation of this rule involves illicit minor.

It should be noted that rule (i) combines the two rules of figure II, rule (iii) the two rules of figure III. Rule (ii) is analogous to the two rules of figure I but, owing to the reversed position of the minor and major terms, it is required that an affirmative major premiss necessitates a universal *minor* premiss in order that the *middle* term should be distributed.

Valid Moods of Figure IV. The special rules exclude the combinations *AO*, *OA*, *AI*, and require that *AA* should have *I* as conclusion. Accordingly, the valid moods are: *AAI*, *AEE*, [*AEO*], *EAO*, *EIO*, *IAI*, and their names are, *Bramantip*, *Camenes*, *Fesapo*, *Fresison*, *Dimaris*.

It will be noticed that in the first three figures there are, including the weakened moods, six moods in each figure. In figure III there are no weakened moods, but *Darapti* and *Felapton* have two universal premisses with a particular conclusion. The middle term is unnecessarily distributed in both premisses. In figure IV one of the six moods is weakened and one (*Bramantip*) contains a premiss (the major) which could be weakened without affecting the validity of the conclusion; in this case the mood would be *IAI* (*Dimaris*) instead of *AAI*. In *Bramantip* we have an example of an over-distributed term, i.e. a term distributed in its premiss but not in the conclusion. We shall see later that there are difficulties about this mood, and, indeed, about all weakened moods.* If the same conclusion can, in any syllogism, be obtained although one of the premisses is weakened, the syllogism is said to be a *strengthened syllogism.*†

Figure IV is usually called the *Galenian figure*, because it is supposed to have been introduced by Galen; it is seldom given in books on logic before the eighteenth century. The following are examples in figure IV:

E No aeroplanes are balloons.
A All balloons are aircraft.
O ∴ Some aircraft are not balloons.

A All big men are jovial.
E No jovial men are non-smokers.
E ∴ No non-smokers are big men.

The student should notice that it would be possible to obtain the same conclusion, in each of these cases, by a syllogism in figure I. How this is possible will be explained in the next section.

§ 3. REDUCTION AND THE ANTILOGISM

By using the syllogistic axioms to deduce special rules for the figures, thus showing that certain moods must be excluded, we have not shown demonstratively that the remaining moods are valid. Aristotle, who may be said to have invented the theory of the syllogism, did not adopt this method of justification. He formulated an axiom which directly guarantees the valid moods of figure I. This axiom is called

* See p. 95, below.

† We shall see later that every syllogism in which there are two universal premisses with a particular conclusion is a strengthened syllogism, *with one* exception, viz. *AEO* in figure IV.

the *Dictum de omni et nullo* because it is an axiom concerning *all or none* of a class. It has been variously formulated; we shall formulate it as follows: *Whatever is predicated affirmatively or negatively of every member of a class can in like manner be predicated of everything contained in that class.* Thus, for instance, if *All scholars are inefficient in business affairs and all academic professors are scholars,* then it follows that *All academic professors are inefficient in business affairs.* Everyone will admit that, granted that the premisses (stated in the compound proposition) are true, then the conclusion is necessarily true. What Aristotle did was to generalize the grounds of this admission. At the moment we shall follow Aristotle and admit that the *Dictum* is not only true but necessarily true and, further, that it can be accepted as an axiom. It applies directly only to figure I. The *Dictum* permits us equally well to assert that *No scholars are inefficient,* or to assert that *Some academic professors are scholars* although, in that case, our conclusion must be an assertion about some academic professors not about all of them. Hence, the dictum gives us a schema for figure I:

If *Every M is P* (*or not*)
and *All* (*or some*) *S is M,*
then *All* (*or some*) *S is P* (*or not*).

From this schema we can directly obtain the two special rules of the figure and can see clearly why the middle term must be distributed in the major premiss and why the minor premiss must be affirmative.

There were reasons, bound up with his metaphysical views, which made Aristotle content to formulate an axiom for the first figure alone. Now, if it be granted that the *Dictum de omni* is properly axiomatic and, further, that it is the sole axiom guaranteeing the validity of syllogistic moods, then it must be admitted that the validity of moods in other figures than the first can be guaranteed only by showing that these moods are logically equivalent to first figure moods. This can be done by showing that a conclusion is obtainable in the first figure equivalent to or implying the original conclusion and from premisses equivalent to or implied by the premisses originally given. The process of thus testing the validity of moods is known as *reduction*, of which Aristotle recognized two methods: (1) direct reduction, performed by converting propositions or transposing premisses; (2) indirect reduction, which consists in proof by *reductio per impossibile*. These methods must now be illustrated.

(1) *Direct reduction.* Consider the pair of syllogisms below:

(α)		(β)
All Quakers are pacifists	⤭	No pacifists are soldiers.
No soldiers are pacifists		All Quakers are pacifists.
∴ No soldiers are Quakers	≡	∴ No Quakers are soldiers.

(α) is a syllogism in *AEE* in figure II (*Camestres*); (β) is *EAE* in figure I (*Celarent*); the two syllogisms are equivalent. In (β) the major premiss is the converse of the minor premiss of (α). Thus the premisses have been transposed and the original minor premiss, which has become the new major premiss, has been converted. Accordingly, since the minor premiss contains the subject of the conclusion, the new conclusion must be converted in order that the original conclusion may be obtained. It must be remembered that we are assuming that the validity of *Celarent* is established by the *Dictum de omni*, and we have thus shown that the mood *Camestres* in figure II is valid; we are not contending that the moods of figure I are superior in self-evidence to the moods of figure II. We are adopting an attitude of doubting something that seems to be self-evident, and we resolve the doubt by showing that the same conclusion can be obtained by means of a mood guaranteed by the *Dictum*; in doing so, we have used only simple conversion – which we have admitted to be valid – and transposition of the premisses. We shall now give one more example of direct reduction:

Figure III. AAI		*AII. Figure I*
All pedants are bores.		All pedants are bores.
All pedants are scholars.	→	Some scholars are pedants.
∴ Some scholars are bores.		∴ Some scholars are bores.

We do not need so much information as is provided in figure III, *AAI* (*Darapti*), in order to draw the same conclusion, since the middle term is unnecessarily distributed twice; hence we can convert the minor premiss (*A*) by limitation (*I*).

When both the premisses of a valid syllogism admit of simple conversion it is clear that the order of the terms is logically indifferent. This is the case when the major premiss is *E* and the minor *I*; hence, the mood *EIO* is valid in every figure. This is shown below:

I. Ferio		*II. Festino*		*III. Ferison*		*IV. Fresison*
MeP	≡	*PeM*	≡	*MeP*	≡	*PeM*
SiM	≡	*SiM*	≡	*MiS*	≡	*MiS*
∴ *SoP*	≡	∴ *SoP*	≡	∴ *SoP*	≡	∴ *SoP*

These four syllogisms are all equivalent no matter in what figure they may happen to be. They present indeed four ways of making the same set of statements. Syllogisms of which the premisses are *A* and *I* (in either order) or *A* and *E* (in either order) are also equivalent, in the sense that the same conclusion can be obtained from the given premisses, in several figures providing that transposition of the premisses is allowed.* These equivalences are exhibited below:

I. Celarent		*II. Cesare*		† *II. Camestres*		*IV. Camenes*
MeX	≡	*XeM*	≡	*XeM*	≡	*MeX*
YaM	≡	*YaM*	≡	*YaM*	≡	*YaM*
∴ *YeX*	≡	∴ *YeX*	≡	∴ *XeY*	≡	∴ *XeY*
I. Darii		*III. Datisi*		*III. Disamis*		*IV. Dimaris*
MaX	≡	*MaX*	≡	*MaX*	≡	*MaX*
YiM	≡	*MiY*	≡	*MiY*	≡	*YiM*
∴ *YiX*	≡	∴ *YiX*	≡	∴ *XiY*	≡	∴ *XiY*
				III. Felapton		*IV. Fesapo*
				MeX	≡	*XeM*
				MaY	≡	*MaY*
				∴ *YoX*	≡	*YoX*

(2) *Indirect reduction.* The moods *Baroco* (*AOO* in figure II) and *Bocardo* (*OAO* in figure III) lie outside this scheme of

* To bring out the equivalences in a brief form the regular order of the premisses is not always maintained; the minor premiss is that which contains the *subject* of the conclusion, the major premiss that which contains the *predicate* of the conclusion. Accordingly, the minor and major terms are to be identified by *looking at the conclusion.* The order of the premisses is always logically irrelevant.

† Notice that there is no equivalent argument in figure III in which the conclusion must always be particular.

equivalences; they cannot be reduced to the first figure, so that indirect reduction must be used. It must be remembered that we suppose ourselves to be *proving* that the conclusion is validly inferred and that we have accepted the validity of the moods of the first figure. It will suffice to exhibit this method in the case of *Bocardo*, i.e.

MoP
MaS
∴ *SoP*.

We reason as follows: If *SoP* is not true, then its contradictory, *SaP*, must be true; combining *SaP* with the minor premiss *MaS*, we obtain

SaP
MaS
∴ *MaP*,

which is in *Barbara*. But *MaP*, the new conclusion, contradicts *MoP*, which was *given true* as a premiss of the original syllogism; hence, its contradictory, *MaP*, must be false; but *MaP* is the conclusion of a valid syllogism in figure I; hence it is true if its premisses are true; since it is not true at least one premiss must be false; this cannot be *MaS*, since that was given as true; therefore *SaP*, its other premiss, must be false; therefore, *SoP* is true, and that is the original conclusion.

The reasoning upon which indirect reduction is based rests upon the principle that, if the conclusion of a valid syllogism is false, then *at least one* of the premisses must be false. This principle can be stated generally, in the form of an hypothetical proposition with a compound antecedent. Let *p*, *q*, *r*, be illustrative symbols for the major and minor premisses and the conclusion of a valid syllogism. Then we have: *If p and q, then r*. This is equivalent to *If not r, then either not-p or not-q*; i.e. if the conclusion, *r*, is false, then at least one of the premisses, *p*, *q*, is false. Again, *If p and q, then r* is equivalent to *Not (p and q) and not-r*. This disjunction was called, by Mrs Ladd-Franklin, an *inconsistent triad*; she invented the name *antilogism* for the triad of propositions constituted by the two premisses of a syllogism and the contradictory of its conclusion. The following is an example of an antilogism:

p No pets are ugly.
q All cats are pets.
$\bar{r}$* Some cats are ugly.

Any two of these propositions imply the falsity of the third; hence, we obtained three valid syllogisms.

Celarent	*Festino*	*Disamis*
p *No pets are ugly.*	p *No pets are ugly.*	$\bar{r}$ *Some cats are ugly.*
q *All cats are pets.*	$\bar{r}$ *Some cats are ugly.*	q *All cats are pets.*
r ∴ *No cats are ugly.*	$\bar{q}$ *Some cats are not pets.*	$\bar{p}$ ∴ *Some pets are ugly.*

These three syllogisms are respectively in figures I, II, and III. It will be found that, starting with a valid syllogism in *any one* of these three figures two other syllogisms will be obtained, one in each of the other figures, if the contradictory of the first conclusion is combined first with one premiss and then with the other premiss; the new conclusion thus obtained will contradict the omitted premiss. It follows that there must be an equal number of valid syllogisms in each of the first three figures, and that they can be arranged in sets of equivalent triads.†

Figure I can be regarded as asserting that a general rule applies to a particular case; thus, in the example of *Celarent* given above, a rule is negatively asserted, viz. *No pets are ugly*, the case of *cats* is subsumed under it, and the conclusion that none of them is *ugly* is deduced. We shall see that, from this point of view, we can again bring out the interdependence of the first three figures. For example:

If All great statesmen sometimes lie
and George Washington is a great statesman,
then George Washington sometimes lies.

* $\bar{r}$, $\bar{p}$, $\bar{q}$ stand respectively for *not-r*, *not-p*, *not-q*.

† These triads are: *Barbara*, *Baroco*, *Bocardo*; [*AAI*, *AEO*, *Felapton*]; *Celarent*, *Festino*, *Disamis*; [*EAO*, *EAO*, *Darapti*]; *Darii*, *Camestres*, *Ferison*; *Ferio*, *Cesare*, *Datisi*. Triads containing weakened conclusions or strengthened premisses are included in brackets. Figure IV is self-contained; the equivalent sets are all in the same figure, and are: [*Bramantip*, *AEO*, *Fesapo*]; *Camenes*, *Fresison*, *Dimaris*.

Now, if we deny that George Washington sometimes lies but admit the rule, we must deny that he is a great statesman; then we get, *Denial of Result* combined with *Rule* yields *Denial of Case*. This will be a syllogism in figure II. If, however, we deny that George Washington sometimes lies but contend that he is a great statesman, we are forced to deny the rule. Then we get, *Denial of Result* combined with reassertion of *Case*, yields *Denial of Rule*. This will be a syllogism in figure III.

This interrelation of the three figures suggests that we can easily formulate *dicta* for figures II and III analogous to the *Dictum de omni* for figure I. *Dictum for figure II:* If every member of a class has (or does not have) a certain property, then any individual (or individuals) which do not have (or have) that property must be excluded from that class. *Dictum for figure III:* If certain individuals have (or do not have) a certain property, and these individuals are included in a certain class, then not every member of that class lacks (or has) that property.

These *dicta* are self-evident in the same sense as the *Dictum de omni* is self-evident; probably they would be most easily apprehended in the first instance by means of a significant example, explicitly stated; once the dictum has been clearly seen to be exemplified in a particular case, it can be generalized to cover other cases.*

Each of the four figures has certain distinctive characteristics. In the first figure only can all four, *A*, *E*, *I*, *O*, forms be proved, and only in this figure can the conclusion be *A*. It is also the only figure in which the major and minor terms occupy the same position in their own premiss as in the conclusion; it is no doubt this characteristic which makes reasoning in figure I seem to be the most natural. In figure II the conclusion is always negative, and it is thus specially adapted to show that an individual (or set of individuals) must be excluded from a given class. Hence, it is sometimes

* For example, If every member of the class *airmen* has the property of *good-eyesight*, then these *volunteers* who lack the property of *good-eyesight* are excluded from the class *airmen*. It is quite easy to derive the special rules of the figures from their respective *dicta*, as in the case of the *Dictum de omni*. The fourth figure can be similarly dealt with, but we shall not include the statement of its *dictum* in this book. Anyone who is interested should consult *M.I.L.*, p. 97, or W. E. Johnson, *Logic*, Part II, p. 87.

called the *Figure of Exclusion*. The third figure, admitting only of particular conclusions, is specially adapted to show that not every member of a class has a certain property, or that two properties are compatible since both are possessed by a given individual or by a certain set of individuals. When the middle term is singular, denoting a single individual, this is the most natural figure to use. For example, *Stalin is a dictator, Stalin has a passionate love of his country* implies that to be a dictator is not incompatible with love of one's country. Again, *Staunton is a great chess-player, Staunton is eccentric* might suggest that there is an essential connexion between being a great chess-player and being eccentric. Accordingly, figure III is sometimes called the *Inductive Figure*. It must, however, be noticed that the conclusion cannot show us more than that the two properties are compatible (or, it might be, incompatible); it would then remain to discover some way of showing that the compatibility was due to an essential connexion, and the incompatibility to an essential disconnexion. To prove such conclusions as these we must go beyond the syllogism.

§ 4.* POLYSYLLOGISMS

A polysyllogism is a chain of syllogisms in which the conclusion of one syllogism constitutes a premiss of the next. The conclusions of all the syllogisms except the last are not stated; this is the sole peculiarity of this form of argument. The syllogism whose conclusion is a premiss (unstated) of the next syllogism is called a *prosyllogism*; a syllogism one of whose premisses is the (unstated) conclusion of the preceding syllogism is called an *episyllogism*.

The *Sorites* is a polysyllogism in which only the final conclusion is stated and the premisses are so arranged that any two successive premisses contain a common term. For example:

All dictators are ambitious.
All ambitious men are without compassion.

* This section and the next section may be regarded as concerned with examination tricks. Those who do not require to pass elementary examinations in logic, set by old-fashioned examiners, can disregard them.

All men without compassion are relentless.
All relentless men are feared.
All men who are feared are pitiable.
∴ All dictators are pitiable.

Two forms of Sorites are traditionally recognized:

(1) *The Aristotelian Sorites.* The minor premiss is stated first, and the term common to two successive premisses occurs first as predicate and then as subject; hence the form is

All A is B
All B is C
All C is D
All D is E
∴ *All A is E*

The special rules of this form are: (i) Only one premiss, namely the last, can be negative. (Violation of this rule would involve two negative premisses in one of the constituent syllogisms.) (ii) Only one premiss, namely the first, can be particular. (Violation of this rule would involve undistributed middle.)

(2) *The Goclenian Sorites* (so-called after Goclenius, who is said to have introduced this form). The major premiss is stated first, and the term common to the two successive premisses occurs first as subject and then as predicate; hence the form is

All D is E
All C is D
All B is C
All A is B
∴ *All A is E*

The special rules of this form are: (i) Only one premiss, namely the first, can be negative. (ii) Only one premiss, namely the last, can be particular. An example of a Goclenian Sorites is afforded by the following: *If those who lack friends are miserable, and those who are despicable lack friends, and those who betray their own country are despicable, and those who love power for itself betray their country, and Quislings love power for itself, then Quislings are miserable.* This is stated as a set of implications, not as asserted premisses.

§ 5. ABBREVIATED ARGUMENTS AND EPICHEIREMA

A syllogism with one proposition omitted is called an enthymeme, e.g. *Whales are not fish because they are mammals.* Here the major premiss, *No fish are mammals*, is omitted. This is called an enthymeme of the first order. If the minor premiss is omitted, the enthymeme is of the second order; if the conclusion, the enthymeme is of the third order. These names are quite unimportant. What is important is that we should be able to recognize an enthymeme for what it is, namely, an argument with an unstated premiss or conclusion. It is extremely rare for us to state our reasoning in full. We most often omit the major premiss, for we are apt to state that so-and-so has a certain characteristic *because* it is a *special case* without bothering to state the *rule* under which the case falls; but sometimes we state the rule and the result, taking for granted that we are dealing with a case which falls under the rule; less frequently, we state the rule and the case, leaving the result to be implicitly understood.

An *epicheirema* is a syllogism in which one or both of the premisses is stated as the conclusion of an enthymematic syllogism. For example:

No Marxist scientists are fair to Euclid's achievement, because they dislike its sociological background;
Professor H. is a Marxist scientist;
∴ Professor H. is not fair to Euclid's achievement.

This is a single epicheirema; when both premisses are stated as the conclusion of an enthymematic syllogism, the epicheirema is said to be double.

In a reasoned argument we frequently omit not only single premisses but even a whole syllogism, tacitly presupposed. Sometimes, indeed, an argument is merely hinted. It is often not difficult to supply the missing links but the omission of a connecting premiss may lead to a fallacy which would be detected if the argument were fully stated. It is for this reason that the brief examples given in logical textbooks are so obvious as to seem merely silly – the reader feels he would never make a mistake like that! Yet elementary mistakes in reasoning are of common occurrence.

An argument is sometimes put forward as a single premiss, on the assumption that the missing premiss and conclusion are too obvious to need explicit stating. For example:

(1) 'If that boy comes back, I'll eat my head' (*Oliver Twist*). The hearer supplies the premiss and conclusion required to complete the *tollendo tollens* argument.

(2) 'If we are marked to die we are enow to do our country loss; and if to live, the fewer men, the greater share of honour' (*Henry V*). This dilemma is faulty, since the alternatives *marked to die*, *marked to live*, are not exhaustive; more men might make the difference between victory and defeat.

CHAPTER V

Individuals, Classes, and Relations

§ 1. INDIVIDUALS AND CHARACTERISTICS

We have seen that the validity of inference depends upon the relations of implication and not at all upon the truth or falsity of the premisses. It is sometimes possible to know that an implication holds between propositions without paying any attention to the internal structure, or form, of the propositions themselves. For example, *If p and q, then r* implies *Either* ($\bar{p}$ *or* $\bar{q}$) *or r* implies *If* $\bar{r}$, *then either* $\bar{p}$ *or* $\bar{q}$, no matter what kind of propositions *p*, *q*, *r* are. Frequently, however, this is not the case. When we used *p*, *q*, *r* as illustrative symbols for the premisses and conclusion of a valid syllogism, we were able to represent the syllogism as an implicational form – *If p and q, then r*. But nothing in this form enables us to know that *No pets are ugly*, *All cats are pets*, *No cats are ugly* are so related that the first two of these propositions jointly imply the third. We know this only because we can analyse the propositions into *No M's are P's*, *All S's are M's*, *No S's are P's*; these forms show us that the first two do jointly imply the third.

Traditional logic is wholly concerned with propositions as analysed complexes the elements of which are not propositions. The terms of the *A*, *E*, *I*, *O* propositions are classes; it is these that constitute the subject-matter of the propositions. But not all terms are classes; there are also individuals. Terms thus fall into two groups: classes and individuals.

No attempt will be made here to define the word "individual"; it will be taken for granted that we all know *how to use* the word; thus, *Pius X is an Italian* is a proposition *about* a specified individual, viz. *Pius X*, and *being an Italian* is predicated of this individual. Whenever we make statements about individuals we say that they have, or do not have, certain characteristics – this Pope is subtle, that table is round, the sunset last night was beautiful, his attitude is intelligent, this feeling is pleasant, and so on. What we predicate of individuals is a *characteristic*, or, as it is sometimes called, a *property*. *Roundness* is an example of a characteristic; it is logically indifferent whether we say 'Roundness characterizes this table', or 'This table has the characteristic of being round', or 'This table is round'. The last is our normal mode of expression; we think of things as having definite characteristics without as a rule thinking what it is to be a characteristic or to characterize. But the three sentences given above all mean the same.

Characteristics are not always symbolized by single words, for example, 'dissolubility in water' expresses a characteristic of sugar; we might also have said 'the capacity of dissolving in water'. For certain philosophical problems it is important to distinguish between different kinds of characteristics and between degrees of complexity. For our present purpose this is not necessary. We must notice, however, that characteristics may characterize other things than individuals, e.g. *reducibility* is *highly abstract*, a certain *proposition* is *true*, a certain *relation* is *difficult to grasp*.

An individual has characteristics but does not characterize; it stands in relations but is not itself a relation. As contrasted with an individual a characteristic is abstract. Some logicians use the word *concept* for what is here called a *characteristic*. This has the advantage of not suggesting that a characteristic must characterize something; there may be characteristics that characterize nothing, for every characteristic has a contradictory characteristic, e.g. *perfect – imperfect*, *justice – injustice*, *animality – non-animality*. We use concepts with ease long before we begin to talk about concepts. Unfortunately when we, as philosophers, begin to talk about concepts we tend to ask nonsensical questions about them, e.g. 'What is a concept?' and expect an answer of *the same sort* as we should expect to the question, 'What is a centipede?' It is enough here to say that abstracting is not a highly difficult intellectual feat; whenever we think we are abstracting, attending to something and not to something else, recognizing similarities and differences without necessarily noticing *that we are recognizing* similarities and differences. As William James, the psychologist, has said, 'A polyp if it ever thought "Hallo, thingemabob again!" would thereby be a conceptual thinker.' The disadvantage of using the word 'concept' instead of 'characteristic' is that it tends to suggest that a *concept* is dependent upon being thought of. This is a mistake. Complex characteristics, e.g. *man*, are conveniently called concepts, provided that we remember that a concept is entirely identical with a characteristic or a specifiable complex of characteristics. When we fully understand a concept we are able actually to specify these characteristics. What I understand by a concept, e.g. *justice*, *home*, may be different from what you understand by it; we can then be said to have *different conceptions* of the *same concept*. Thus Newton certainly had a different conception of *force* from Einstein's, but, so to speak, they intended to think about the same concept. Advance in scientific thinking in part consists in clarifying our conceptions; we aim at abstracting from our personal habits of thinking, our private attitudes, hopes, and fears, and apprehending clearly what is constant in significance throughout repeated instances.

The converse of the relation of characterization is *exemplification*; an object, or entity, characterized by *red* exemplifies *redness*, i.e. is an *instance* of it. Thus Abraham, Aristotle, John Bunyan, James Clerk-Maxwell, etc., exemplify *man*; these individuals are *characterized by* the complex characteristic signified by the word "man".

A characteristic that could be exemplified even if in fact there are no actual instances of it is said to be *existent*. This is the use of the word "existence" in mathematics, as when we say, 'an even prime exists'. This sort of existence or being must be distinguished from the full-bodied (so to speak) kind of being which individuals have, namely being in time and space. Bertrand Russell calls the former *subsistence*, the latter *existence*. We shall not make use of the word "subsistence" in this book; when we say that a characteristic *exists* we shall simply mean that it is not inconsistent to assert that it has instances.

In the case of individuals we must distinguish between

what could consistently exist and what does in fact exist. For example, there could be a King of the United States but in fact there is not; there could be a King of Utopia but in fact there is no such country as Utopia and thus no King of Utopia. It is easy to indulge in much discussion on this point and to fall into apparently inextricable difficulties. But we do understand very well what is meant by saying that *God exists* and by saying that *God does not exist.* The distinction between what does exist (in the sense in which this, that, or the other, individual exists) is the distinction between fact and fiction.

Questions of existence are to be settled in two ways. If we ask, 'Do just men exist?' we may start from the assumption that certain men called *just* exist, e.g. Aristeides, but want to ask whether they are *really* just. This is a question about the *concept* just, i.e. it asks what the characteristic *just* is. The answer to this question is given by a definition of the word "justice", i.e. by clarifying the concept symbolized by "justice". But, given this clarification, we may still want to ask whether *justice* is exemplified in human beings. Such a question can be answered only by empirical investigation, just as the question, 'Do centaurs exist?', must be settled by looking everywhere to see whether there are any *centaurs.* Similarly, the questions, 'Does God exist?', 'Does the Devil exist?', might be meant in either of these two ways and must be settled either by clearing up what we mean when we use the word "God", or the word "Devil", or by appeal to our experience.*

§ 2. CLASSES

We often want to talk about all the instances of a certain characteristic, these instances being taken together. When we refer to all possible exemplifications of a given characteristic (simple or complex), we are speaking of the *class* determined by the characteristic. Those instances of the class which exist are called the *members* of the class, or sometimes, the *elements* of the class. The class is said to *contain* its members.

* It must not be assumed that *experience* is limited to what is given to sense. Whether this is so, or not, is a metaphysical question lying beyond our scope as logicians.

We are all familiar with the notion of class and, as we have seen, Aristotle's logic was primarily concerned with relations between classes and only incidentally with statements about individuals. The notions of *class*, *class-membership*, *class-inclusion* are presupposed by Aristotle's treatment and are not discussed by traditional Logicians except in the most perfunctory manner.

A class must be distinguished from its members for, as we shall see in a moment, a class has characteristics which its members lack. It must also be distinguished from the word or symbol used to refer to it. This is not peculiar to classes; we must always distinguish between a symbol and what it symbolizes, though in fact we do not always keep the distinction clear, especially when talking about classes.

There are two ways of selecting the individuals who constitute the membership of a class. One is to enumerate the individuals one after another, the order of enumerating being indifferent. For example, we might enumerate the individuals, *Stalin*, *Mussolini*, *Hitler*, and thus obtain the class whose members are Stalin, Mussolini, Hitler. The second way is to select a certain characteristic, e.g. *being a dictator in Europe in 1940*, which may belong to many individuals. In fact, the membership of this class consists of the three individuals named above; there is, however, nothing in the complex characteristic which determines that it should be limited to three members.* *World-dictator* is a characteristic determining a class which contains no members, though no doubt Hitler wishes that it contain one member and that he should be that member.

The enumerative selection of a class is possible only when the class contains a finite number of members; it is then called a *finite class*. An infinite class is clearly not capable of being enumerated; hence, such a class must be determined by a characteristic, whilst a finite class is usually but not necessarily so determined. For instance, a complete census, free from errors, of the inhabitants of Great Britain enumerates all

* Indeed this class probably contains more than these members, if General Franco and Dr Salazar are to be regarded as dictators in their own countries. The class could be limited to the three members specified if we altered the characteristic to *being a belligerent dictator in Europe in September 1942*.

the members of the class *inhabitants of Great Britain.* We might enumerate the class containing the following members: Pompey the Great, Falstaff's red nose, Cleopatra's Needle, Napoleon's emotion on first seeing St Helena. No one but a logician, or a fool, would want to select such a class, but we, for a purpose, have just done so, and the class – which contains four members – might be described as 'the class I have just selected', and these members each possess a certain property possessed by nothing else in the universe, viz. the characteristic of *being either Pompey the Great or Falstaff's red nose or Cleopatra's Needle or Napoleon's emotion on first seeing St Helena.* Such artificial classes are seldom useful for scientific purposes, but *this* artificial class has the use to which we have just put it.

A given characteristic is said *to determine* the class each member of which exemplifies that characteristic. Thus *men* determines the class containing the members Adam, Aristotle, Buddha, . . . Winston Churchill, where the dots indicate each of the other human beings whom in fact we could not enumerate though, it is assumed, God could do so; in a minute another item would have to be added to the enumeration, and so on, for every human being that is born. Thus *men* includes the dead, the living, and the yet to be born human being.

A characteristic which determines a class is said to be a *class-property.* This phrase is misleading, for a class-property is a property common and peculiar to all the *members* of a class; it is not a property of the class at all. It is a property of the class *men* that it has exemplification, but the class *men* has not the property of *being a rational animal.*

We could be, even if we are not, acquainted with the individual *Stalin*; but we could not be acquainted with the *class* determined by *being a dictator in Europe in 1940.* Accordingly, the way in which we refer to a class when we use a class-symbol is quite different from the way in which we refer to an individual when we use a proper name speaking to the person named. Class-symbols are descriptive; we can significantly use class-symbols although no members are presented to us, and even if we do not know whether the class has members or not. It is for this reason that we can significantly prefix to class-symbols such words as "all", "some", "any", "a", "the".

When we speak of *all* the members of a class the word "all" may be used ambiguously; we may mean "each and every one member" or "all the members jointly". Usually the context suffices to make the meaning clear, but we may sometimes be in doubt, e.g. "All the men could not move the cart" might mean that not *one of them alone* could move the cart or it might mean that *all together* could not. "The police routed the crowd" means all the members of the police jointly; "The police carried truncheons" means each member of the police did. When we use a term to signify each member severally, then we are said to use it *distributively*; when we use a term to signify all together, then we use it *collectively*. The distinction is a distinction *in usage*.

In the collective usage of "*all*", all the members of a class constitute its *collective membership*. For example, if the enemy army occupies a country, that which occupies is the collective membership of the class; it is clearly not each individual soldier who occupies the country nor the class for the class cannot carry arms nor shoot – it is only individuals that can act.

Finally, we must keep clear the distinction between *classes* and *associations*, or organizations, such as the Post Office organization, the T.U.C., the United States, the League of Nations. The class containing as members *the Nations* in the League of Nations must be distinguished from the League of Nations: being *a member of the League of Nations* is a class-property of Great Britain, and of each one of the other member-Nations, but *being-a-League-of-Nations* is not a property of any member. To say that it was would be to talk nonsense.

§ 3. RELATIONS

All deduction depends upon the logical properties of relations. Relation cannot be defined without using words that are more or less synonymous. We all recognize that individuals in the universe are not isolated; they stand in various relations. Physical objects stand in spatial and gravitational relations; human beings are related in numerous ways, e.g. by kinship, by enmity, or by friendship, by precedence, and so on. In short every individual object, of every possible sort, is related to some other individuals and also to the characteristics which they exemplify or which they fail to exemplify. Characteristics also stand in relations to other characteristics, e.g. implication, consistency, inconsistency.

Relations relate terms. The most elementary characteristic of a relation is the number of terms it requires in order to make sense. *Father of* requires two terms; *loving*, *governing*, *hurting* are also two-termed. Such relations are called dyadic. Relations requiring three terms are triadic, four terms tetradic, five terms pentadic, and so on. Relations requiring an indefinite number of terms are polyadic (e.g. among). Some logicians call any relation requiring more than three terms polyadic. In ordinary discussion we seldom talk about relations requiring more than four terms. *Giving* is triadic: *Tom gave a ball to Mark* relates *giver*, *gift*, *and recipient*. *Teaching*, *between*, are other examples of a triadic relation; *owing* is tetradic: *Jones* owes *Spencer £10* for *this watch*. Our discussion will be confined to dyadic relations.

Every relation has a sense, i.e. a direction in which it goes, e.g. *loving* goes from *lover* to *loved*, *father of* from *male parent* to *child*. The term *from* which the relation goes is the *referent*; the term *to* which the relation goes is *relatum*. In *Mary loves Darnley* (as the order of the words in English shows) *Mary* is referent, *Darnley* is relatum. We will substitute the illustrative symbols x, y for these respectively, and R for the relation; then we have xRy, which signifies *something having a relation to something*. It is sometimes convenient to write $R(x, y)$ instead of xRy, so that the same mode of symbolizing can be used for triadic relations, and those with more terms than three, e.g. $R(x, y, z)$, is a relational form into which we could fit the relational statement *Tom gives a penny to Mark*, provided that we have adopted some convention to show the order of the terms. As we are here concerned only with dyadic relations we shall use xRy. In what follows R will illustratively symbolize some one relation but not a specified relation.

Relations are said to *hold* or *fail* of given terms. When R holds from x to y, then there is some relation which holds from y to x, which will be the converse of the original relation. We might symbolize the converse of R by R^c. xRy is always equivalent to yR^cx but R and R^c are not necessarily the same relation. For example, *x loves y* is not equivalent to *y loves x* since the *loved* does not necessarily love in return, and is thus not also lover of the one who loves. The converse of R is sometimes written $\breve{R}$, as for instance by Bertrand Russell and A. N. Whitehead in *Principia Mathematica*. We shall use R^c for the converse of R since it is more directly suggestive of the *converse* of a relation. Which symbol we adopt is logically indifferent; it is a matter of notation to be decided on grounds of convenience or taste.

Logical properties of relations are properties which belong to relations without reference to the terms they may happen to relate. Many of these properties can be stated only if there are certain limitations to the possible referents and relata. Hence, it is convenient to distinguish between the domain, converse domain, and field of a relation.

If R is any relation, then the *domain* of R is the class of terms that have R to something, i.e. all possible referents of R. The *converse domain* is the class of terms to which something has R; i.e. all possible relata of R. The *field* of R is the sum of the domain and the converse domain of R. The domain and the converse domain may overlap, as, for example, is the case with the relation *ancestor of* limited to the field of the direct descendants of George I. The domain is the class of all those, in this field, who have descendants; the converse domain is the class of those who are his descendants. In this field, Edward VII is referent to George V, George VI, and is *relatum* to *Queen Victoria, George I.*

The relations holding between members of a family are familiar and can be used to illustrate important logical properties of relations. If the reader considers what is the converse of *married to*, *father of*, *uncle of*, *ancestor of*, he will easily notice that sometimes the same relation relates x, y (any two terms) as relates y, x, and sometimes a different relation. Again, the father of a father is not a father but a grandfather, but the ancestor of an ancestor is also an ancestor. These family relationships suggest to us the importance of distinguishing relations according to the properties they have. We shall now consider those properties of relations that are important for inference.

(1) *Symmetry.* A relation R is *symmetrical* when $xRy \equiv yRx$. Thus, if xRy, then yRx. For example, *spouse of*, *equal to*, *different from*, *brother or sister of*.

A relation R is *asymmetrical* when xRy is incompatible with yRx. Thus, if xRy, then never yRx. For example, *father of*, *darker than*, *greater than*, *preceding*.

A relation R is *non-symmetrical* when xRy is neither equivalent to nor incompatible with yRx. Thus, if xRy, then perhaps yRx and perhaps not yRx. For example, *implication*, *friend to*, *sister of*.

(2) *Transitiveness.* This distinction is based upon the consideration of pairs of terms with reference to some relation R. A relation R is *transitive* when, provided it holds from x to y, and also from y to z, it must hold from x to z. Thus, if xRy and yRz, then xRz. For example, *ancestor of*, *exactly contemporary with*, *parallel to*, *implication*.

A relation R is *intransitive* when it is such that if xRy and yRz, then never xRz. For example, *next to*, *father of*, *one year older than*.

A relation R is *non-transitive* when it is such that if xRy and yRx then perhaps xRz and perhaps *not* xRz. For example, *sister of*, *overlapping in time with*, *cheating*, *different from*.

The properties of symmetry and transitiveness, and their opposites, are logically independent. Hence, we can classify relations into the four following groups:

(i) *Symmetrical transitive:* equal to; matching in colour.
(ii) *Symmetrical intransitive:* spouse of; twin of.
(iii) *Asymmetrical transitive:* ancestor of; greater than; above; before.
(iv) *Asymmetrical intransitive:* father of; greater by two than.

Relations that are both symmetrical and transitive have the formal properties of *equality*. There is a third important property that belongs to such relations; this property is called *reflexiveness*. It may be defined as follows: a relation R is *reflexive* if it holds between x and itself, i.e. xRx. *Identity* is reflexive; *as tall as* is reflexive, and so on. A relation may be symmetrical without being reflexive, e.g. *spouse of*. The only relation that can be said to be reflexive without limitation is *identity*. Reflexiveness, symmetry, transitiveness are formal properties of *identical with*, and thus, *equal to*. Any relations that have these properties are of the formal nature of identity, e.g. *exactly matching*, *co-implication*, *coincidence*.

A relation that is both transitive and asymmetrical has also another property, called *aliorelative*. A relation R is *aliorelative* when it is such that no term x has R to itself, e.g. *successor of*. Asymmetrical relations are necessarily aliorelative, but the converse is not the case, since *spouse of*, *twin of* are symmetrical but also aliorelative. But if a relation is both transitive and asymmetrical, it is also aliorelative.

(3) *Connexity*. Given any relation R and the field of R, it is not necessarily the case that *any* two terms in the field are related by R or R^c. For example, given the field *human beings* and the relation *ancestor of*, it does not follow that of every pair of terms the relation must hold. When, however, this does hold the terms are said to be connected. *Connexity* may be defined as follows: A relation R is *connected* when, given any two terms of its field, viz. x, y, then either xRy or yRx (i.e. xRy or xR^cy). If this condition does not hold then R is said to be *unconnected*.

A relation that is transitive, asymmetrical and connected is a *serial relation*, i.e. it suffices to generate a series, e.g. an arithmetical progression. *Greater than*, limited to the field of natural numbers, is connected, since, of any two numbers one is greater than the other; *factor of* is unconnected. *Greater than* suffices to generate the series 1, 2, 3, 4 . . .

Relations may also be classified according to the number of terms to which the referent or relatum may stand in the given relation R. If Jones is a debtor to Robinson, it does not follow that Robinson alone stands in that relation to Jones, who may have many debtors; Jones may also himself have debtors. If Mary has sisters she is not the only daughter of David but she has only one father. In a monogamous country, if Mary is wife of James then no other man can be her husband and no other woman be James's wife. As these examples suggest, we can distinguish four groups of relations from this point of view:

(i) *Many-many relations:* R is *many-many* when both the domain and the converse domain can contain more than one member, and the selection of a term from either does not determine the selection of a term from the other, e.g. *1° of latitude north of*, *creditor to*, *sister of*.

(ii) *Many-one relations:* R is *many-one* when the selection of a term from the domain determines the selection of the term from the converse domain, but not reversely, e.g. *child of*.

(iii) *One-many relations:* R is *one-many* when the selection of a term from the converse domain determines the selection of the term from the domain, but not reversely, e.g. *father of*.

(iv) *One-one relations:* R is *one-one* if the selection of a given referent determines the selection of the relatum, and reversely. There may be many members of the domain and the converse domain of R, but the selection of any one of these terms as referent uniquely determines the selection of the relatum, and reversely. For example, *eldest son of a father*, *greater by one*.

It should be noticed that, for instance, *parent of* is not a *one-many* relation since, if x is parent of y, then x may be either father or mother of y; hence two terms stand in the given relation to y. If, however, the referents be limited to *males*, then the relation is *one-many*; if the relatum be now limited to *eldest son*, the relation is *one-one*. It is important to observe that mathematical functions result from one-many relations, e.g. the cosine of x, the logarithm of y. One-one relations are of great importance in the exact sciences; correlations are one-one relations.*

* It may be of interest to notice that relations can be combined. Suppose there is a relation R such that xRy, and a relation S such that ySz; then there is a relation between x and z compounded of the two relations R, S. This relation is called the *relative product* of R and S. Bertrand Russell symbolizes the relative product of R and S by writing R/S. The relative product of *sister of* and *father of* is *paternal aunt*. The order in which R, S is taken is significant; if their order be reversed a different relation may be obtained. For example, the relative product of *father of* and *sister of* is *father of*. The converse of a relative product is obtained by reversing the *order* of the factors and then substituting their converses: i.e. converse of $\check{S}/\check{R}$ is S/R (using $\check{R}$ for R^c), e.g. the converse of the

§ 4. CLASS-INCLUSION AND CLASS-MEMBERSHIP; SINGLE-MEMBERED CLASSES

We say, "All Marxists are determinists", and "Professor Hodd is a Marxist", and are thus led to suppose that *are* and *is* signify the same relation. This is a mistake. In "All Marxists are determinists" *are* signifies the relation of *inclusion*; in "Professor Hodd is a Marxist" *is* signifies *membership of a class*. These two relations differ in their logical properties: *inclusion* is non-symmetrical and transitive, whereas *class-membership* is asymmetrical and intransitive. *X* can be included in *Y* without its being the case that *Y* is also included in *X*, but it is also possible that where *X* is included in *Y*, *Y* also is included in *X*. Class-membership, on the other hand, is clearly not symmetrical, and is indeed asymmetrical. *Hodd* (in the example) is a member of the class *Marxists*, but the class *Marxists* is not a member of *Hodd*. All individuals are members of classes, but no class is a member of an individual. Class-inclusion is clearly transitive, but class-membership is not. For example, *Fido is a member of the class of my dogs; the class of my dogs is a member of the class of single-membered classes;* but Fido is not a single-membered class, for Fido, being an individual dog, is not a class of any kind. When we speak of *classes* as members of *other classes* we are indeed shifting the meaning of "member of". In this book we shall always understand by a *class-membership* proposition a *singular* proposition.

A singular proposition is a proposition about a uniquely specifiable entity, e.g. *David Hume is a philosopher. This is a pen.* A uniquely specifiable entity (e.g. *this pen*) may be regarded as the sole member of some class (e.g. *the pens now owned by me*). The traditional logicians treated every singular proposition as being a statement about a class containing only one member. On this view, *David Hume is a philosopher* is equivalent to *All David Humes* (*there being only one*) *are philosophers.* We mentioned this view earlier (p. 56) without criticizing it. We must now observe that, in adopting this view, the traditional

relative product of *husband of* and *daughter-in-law* is *father or mother-of*. The relative product of *R* and *R* is called the square of *R*. Thus R/R can be written R^2; the relative product of *father* and *father* is *grandfather*; the converse of the square of father is grandchild. The square of *ancestor of* is *ancestor of*.

D

Logicians did not see clearly exactly what they were doing nor why their analysis of categorical propositions required this interpretation of singular propositions.

It is obvious on reflection that a class-inclusion statement is different in kind from a class-membership statement. If we say *H.M.S. Hermes is an aircraft carrier* we are stating that a certain individual is a member of a class, viz. *aircraft carriers.* If we say *Aircraft carriers are warships* we are saying that *every* member of the class *aircraft carriers* is also a member of the class *warships.* A ship can, in the proper sense, sail the seas; a *class* cannot sail. We must then distinguish between a statement about a single-membered class and a statement that the class has only one member, and similarly we must distinguish a single-membered class from its sole member. *There exists one and only one number which is a factor of every number in a given finite collection of positive integers* is a statement that a certain class has only one member; this member is the H.C.F. of the given collection of numbers. The H.C.F. is the sole member of the class determined by the above formula when the finite collection is given. The class of even primes is a single-membered class, and its sole member is the number 2. The class of *most virtuous of dogs* necessarily contains only one member, for, if two dogs were equally virtuous neither could be said to be *the most virtuous.* The class of *my dogs* (on the assumption that I possess only one dog) is single-membered. This class contains fewer members than the class of *my books*, but it does not make sense to say that *my dog* has fewer members than the class of *my books*, or any other class.

We can see from what has just been said that anything which can be significantly stated about a class cannot be significantly stated about an individual. Logicians recognize this distinction by saying that an *individual* and a *class* are of different *logical types.* Accordingly "are" and "is" in the two sentences given at the beginning of this section differ in meaning.

§ 5. SUBCLASSES AND EMPTY CLASSES

A class α included in another class β is said to be a subclass of β. It is convenient to call the class β a superclass of α. The class *Frenchmen* is a subclass of *Europeans*; the class *Italians* is also a subclass of *Europeans*. For many purposes it is useful to be able to distinguish the subclasses of a class. In the next chapter we shall be concerned with this process of distinguishing subclasses. Sometimes we distinguish a subclass and subsequently find that it has no members. For example, in the summer of 1940 certain penalties were laid down by the British Parliament to be inflicted upon those who 'spread alarm and despondency'. It seemed good to the British Government to take this class into account. But it might well have turned out to be the case that *spreading alarm and despondency* was a complex characteristic having no exemplification, or, to use other words, the class determined by this characteristic was found to be empty. An empty class is a class that has no members. In Chapter II we noticed that there are no *dishonest immortal* politicians. Among a given class of school children there may be none who are both *hard-working and able*. We find no difficulty in seeing that complex characteristics may lack exemplification. In such cases it is convenient to say that the class determined by the characteristic is empty. This is a mode of speaking, or, as we may say, a convention. It seems strange to extend the meaning of "class" in such a way that we can speak of empty classes. But, as the above examples suggest, we shall avoid certain difficulties if we do so. For instance, if we admit that *A*, *E*, *I*, *O* propositions are statements about class inclusion and exclusion, we shall get into the sort of difficulties we noticed in the case of inversion unless we admit that a class may have no members. If we grant that a class may be empty, then we can bring out the fundamental difference in form between the universal propositions *A*, *E* and the particular propositions *I*, *O*.

Consider the two propositions: *All who spread alarm and despondency will be fined or imprisoned*; *All women between the ages of twenty and thirty will be called up for military service*. As understood by the people of Great Britain in the years 1940 to the present (September 1942), it would certainly be admitted that the significance of the first of these propositions does not depend upon there being any instances of the complex characteristic *spreading alarm and despondency*. Indeed, the British Government no doubt hoped that by threatening penalties the class determined by *spreading alarm and despondency* would remain empty. In the case of the second proposition we unhesitatingly assert *There are women between the ages of twenty and thirty*, i.e. we take for granted that the class constituting the subject-term is not empty. We do so because the proposition is asserted (if, indeed, anyone does assert it) in the context of our knowledge about the people in Great Britain. No one would have any interest in making this assertion if there were no women between the ages of twenty and thirty. Let us for a moment neglect what we *know*; we should have no difficulty in admitting that in *neither* case does the significance of the proposition depend upon there being members of the class constituting the subject-term of the proposition.

What, then, is the minimum interpretation that must be given to these propositions in order to render them significant? The minimum interpretation imports nothing into the proposition which depends upon knowledge not derived from the proposition stated. Clearly, then, it is advisable so to interpret these propositions that their significance should in no way depend upon there being any members of the class constituting the subject-term. This interpretation can be conveniently formulated in the sentence "If anyone spreads alarm and despondency, he will be fined or imprisoned", and analogously for the second proposition. This formulation brings out that the proposition asserts that a certain class is empty, viz. the class determined by the conjunction of characteristics *spreading alarm and despondency without being either fined or imprisoned*. Its significance is to deny that a certain class has members. Such a proposition is called existentially negative.

Now consider the propositions *Some young men are combatants*, *Some dishonest politicians are not mortals*. Ordinarily we should unhesitatingly assert that the significance of these propositions depends upon there being members of the classes respectively constituting the subject-term. We so use the word "some" in English that to assert any proposition of these two forms is to assert that there are members of the given class for which *some* is used as a quantifier. Thus, *Some trepangs are echinoderms* asserts that there are members of the class trepangs, i.e. the proposition is existentially affirmative. The proposition *Some trepangs are not pleasant to eat* is likewise existentially affirmative, whether true or false.

Granted then that the minimum interpretation of universal propositions does not require that the class constituting the subject-term should have any members but that particular propositions do require this, we can formulate the *A, E, I, O* propositions as follows:

A	Nothing is both *S* and *non-P*	$S\bar{P} = 0$
E	Nothing is both *S* and *P*	$SP = 0$
I	Something is both *S* and *P*	$SP \neq 0$
O	Something is both *S* and *non-P*	$S\bar{P} \neq 0$

The set on the right-hand side presents a convenient mode of symbolizing propositions from this point of view. SP, $S\bar{P}$ stand for the conjunction of two classes in each case: SP stands for the class constituted by combining *S* and *P*, $S\bar{P}$ for the class constituted by combining *S* and *non-P*; "$= 0$" signifies that the class has no members, i.e. is empty; "$\neq 0$" signifies that the class has members, i.e. is not empty.* This symbolism is convenient, but it must not be supposed that it gives us any more, or less, information than is given by the corresponding English sentences on the left-hand side.

It should be observed that if it is true that nothing is both *S* and *P*, then, provided that *S* has members, $\bar{P}$ also has members, or – as it may equivalently be stated – either *S* has no members or *non-P* has members.† For example, if it be true that *nothing is both human and infallible*, then either the class *human beings* has no members or there are *fallible beings*.

The above formulations bring out very clearly that the universal propositions are fundamentally different in form from the particulars, whereas the difference between negative and affirmative propositions is not fundamental.

* This symbol must of course be distinguished from the number 0.

† This can be formulated: *Either* $S = 0$ *or* $\bar{P} \neq 0$.

If we assume that the subject S has members, we can formulate these propositions as follows:

$$\begin{array}{lll} A & SaP & S \neq 0 \text{ and } S\bar{P} = 0 \\ E & SeP & S \neq 0 \text{ and } SP = 0 \\ I & SiP & SP \neq 0 \\ O & SoP & S\bar{P} \neq 0 \end{array}$$

Here, again, the difference in form between the universals and the particulars is made manifest. On the assumption that in the particular propositions the class constituting the subject-term is not to be interpreted as necessarily having members, the formulation is:

$$\begin{array}{lll} I & SiP & \text{Either } S = 0 \text{ or } SP \neq 0 \\ O & SoP & \text{Either } S = 0 \text{ or } S\bar{P} \neq 0 \end{array}$$

§ 6. THE UNIVERSE OF DISCOURSE AND THE UNIVERSAL CLASS

In the preceding section it was said 'we unhesitatingly assert'. For whom does "we" stand? Presumably moderns of European culture who are able to read English. The context in which this book is written and read enables us to take the reference of "we" as understood. In any discussion that proceeds without serious misunderstanding or ambiguity the context is understood by all the speakers. If I say, 'Hamlet killed Polonius, not Polonius Hamlet', I shall be understood to refer to the realm of Shakespeare's plays. If I say, 'Cromwell was not really like what Scott makes him out to be', I shall be understood to be contrasting Scott's fictitious presentment *of* Cromwell in *Woodstock*, with Cromwell who actually lived and was Lord Protector of England in the middle of the seventeenth century. We contrast the 'world of fiction' with the 'world that actually is'. But frequently we want to put some limitation upon the context of our discourse so that what we are saying shall not be understood to refer to everything that has happened or happens everywhere. For example, 'Women have the right to vote' would usually be understood to be limited in reference to the country under discussion or in which the speakers are living; it would also ordinarily be understood to be limited to a fairly recent period of time. The context thus understood may be called the *universe of discourse*.*

In the language of classes we can say that the universe of discourse is the class such that all classes discussed are subclasses of it. Since every member of a subclass is a member of its superclass, it follows that every member of a class under discussion is a member of the one universal class. But just as we can have a different universe of discourse on one occasion (e.g. fictitious entities) from the universe of discourse on another occasion (e.g. actual world), so we can have a different universal class on different occasions. But, granted the context of the discussion, there is only *one* universal class. In a given universal class we can distinguish subclasses which would have no place in another universal class.† For example, in the universal class of *men throughout the history of the world* it makes sense to distinguish between *men acting freely* and *men not acting freely*, even if we subsequently decide that one of these classes is empty; in the universal class of *physical entities such as electrons* the distinction between *acting freely* and *not acting freely* may be without sense.

When we are not clear with regard to the limitations placed upon the universal class (constituted by any discussion) we are apt to talk nonsense without noticing that we do so.

§ 7. RECONSIDERATION OF THE TRADITIONAL TREATMENT OF OPPOSITION AND IMMEDIATE INFERENCES

Once we have admitted that the universal propositions *SaP*, *SeP* are to be interpreted as existentially negative, we can see

* This phrase was introduced by A. de Morgan (*Formal Logic*, pp. 41, 55) and G. Boole (*Laws of Thought*, p. 166). It was thus explained by de Morgan: 'If we remember that in many, perhaps most propositions, the range of thought is much less extensive than the whole universe, commonly so-called, we begin to find that the whole range of a subject of discussion is, for the purpose of discussion, what I have called a *universe*, that is, a range of ideas which is either expressed or understood as containing the whole matter under discussion.'

† In Pirandello's play *Six Characters in Search of an Author*, the worlds of fiction and of reality are deliberately brought together, with dramatic effect, but the *real* characters in the play and the 'six characters' are, in *fact* (as we say), both fictitious.

that we must reconsider the validity of the inferences allowed by the traditional Logicians. For we have also agreed that particular propositions are existentially affirmative, so that *Some explorers are intelligent* implies that there are explorers and, consequently, also intelligent beings.

Confining our attention to the traditional 'square of opposition', we find that *A* and *O*, *E* and *I*, respectively, are contradictories; for, $SaP \equiv S\bar{P} = 0$, and $SoP \equiv S\bar{P} \neq 0$. But the inference from *SaP* to *SiP*, and from *SeP* to *SoP* is not valid, since *SaP* implies only that nothing is $S\bar{P}$ (i.e. $S\bar{P} = 0$), whereas *SiP* implies something is *SP*, and this means that the class *S* is not empty. Again, *SaP* and *SeP* are not contraries since it is not inconsistent to assert $S\bar{P} = 0$ and also $SP = 0$, on the assumption that nothing is *S*. The force of asserting both of them is to deny that there are any members of *S*. This may seem absurd, but it is not difficult to give significant examples: *All disinterested leaders are trustworthy*, *No disinterested leaders are trustworthy*, taken as both true, constitute a denial that there are any disinterested leaders.* The inference of *SiP* from *SaP*, and of *SoP* from *SeP* does not hold good, since the particulars imply that the class *S* is not empty, whereas the universals do not imply this.

In general, on the assumption we are making, a universal proposition can be validly inferred from another universal proposition, and a particular proposition from another particular; but a particular cannot be inferred from a universal. Hence, the following traditional immediate inferences are invalid, unless the assertion that *S* is not empty be added: (i) conversion of *A*; (ii) contraposition of *E*; (iii) inversion. Likewise, a syllogism with two universal premisses and a par-

* Mrs Ladd-Franklin gives an example in the following quotation: '*All x is y*, *No x is y* assert together that *x* is neither *y* nor not-*y*, and hence that there is no *x*. It is common among logicians to say that two such propositions are incompatible; but that is not true, they are simply together incompatible with the existence of *x*. When the schoolboy has proved that the meeting-point of two lines is not on the right of a certain transversal and that it is not on the left of it, we do not tell him that his propositions are incompatible and that one or other of them must be false, but we allow him to draw the natural conclusion that there is no meeting-point, or that the lines are parallel' (*Mind*, 1890, p. 77 *n.*). This example assumes that *on the right* and *on the left* are contradictory terms; granted this assumption, then the two propositions are of the form *No S is P*, *No S is not P* (i.e. *All S is P*).

ticular conclusion is invalid, since the conclusion will imply that the class S is not empty, whereas this is not guaranteed by the minor premisses in the cases under discussion. Consequently the weakened moods are invalid, together with *Darapti*, *Felapton*, *Bramantip*, *Fesapo*, each of which contains a strengthened premiss. The valid syllogisms, therefore, reduce to fifteen: four in figure I, four in figure II, four in figure III, three in figure IV.

These results confirm our contention in Chapter II that the validity of inversion depends upon the assumption that the classes S, $\bar{S}$, P, $\bar{P}$ are not empty, i.e. have existence in the universe of discourse.

At this point we can return to the two questions raised on page 26. The assumption that S, P, $\bar{S}$, $\bar{P}$, all exist in the universe of discourse can be represented diagrammatically by

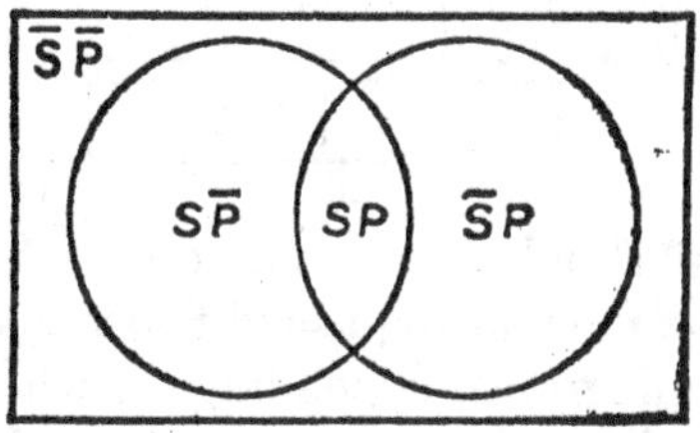

saying that the area outside the circles, in each case, represents everything that is neither S nor P. Let a rectangle represent the universe of discourse, within which any of the five diagrams given on page 25 can be drawn. It will suffice to take one example: we select diagram 4. The compartments are labelled with the four possible combinations. We could substitute any diagram instead of 4; hence, in every case *Some non-S is non-P*. If this is correct, then every proposition of the four traditional forms has an inverse, and, indeed, the same inverse. This is absurd. We must, then, conclude that there is not always some area *outside* the circles but included in *the universe of discourse*. We need, then, *ten* not *five* diagrams.

These ten may be conveniently given in the form of rectangles:

(i)	SP	$\bar{S}\bar{P}$		
(ii)	SP			
(iii)	SP	$\bar{S}P$	$\bar{S}\bar{P}$	
(iv)	SP	$\bar{S}P$		
(v)	SP	$S\bar{P}$	$\bar{S}\bar{P}$	
(vi)	SP	$S\bar{P}$		
(vii)	SP	$S\bar{P}$	$\bar{S}P$	$\bar{S}\bar{P}$
(viii)	SP	$S\bar{P}$	$\bar{S}P$	
(ix)	$S\bar{P}$	$\bar{S}P$	$\bar{S}\bar{P}$	
(x)	$S\bar{P}$	$\bar{S}P$		

These diagrams* should be compared with Euler's diagrams (p. 25). We have now distinguished two ways of interpreting each of Euler's diagrams, depending on whether or not the class $\bar{S}\bar{P}$ has members. Thus diagrams (i) and (ii) correspond to Euler's No. 1, and so on.

How do we deal with the case when a term, significant in the universe of discourse, nevertheless signifies nothing in the actual world? Consider our original example, *Ghosts are not always draped in sheets.* This is a particular negative proposition. We shall represent it by

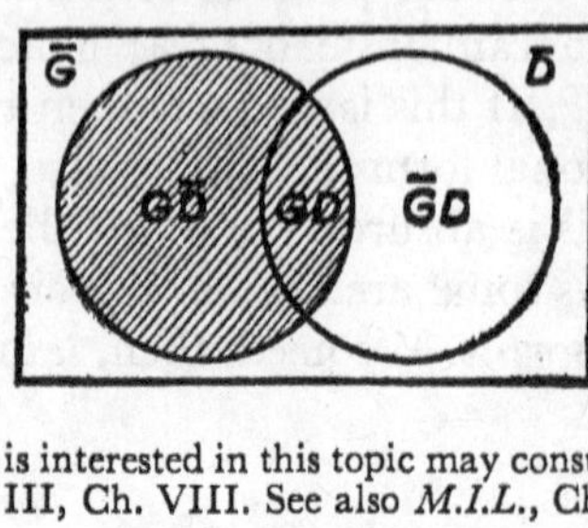

* The student who is interested in this topic may consult J. N. Keynes, *F.L.*, Pt. II, Ch. VIII, Pt. III, Ch. VIII. See also *M.I.L.*, Ch. V, §§ 4, 5.

The circle that is shaded may be regarded as blacked-out; it is empty, i.e. no ghosts exist in the actual universe; *non-ghosts* ($\bar{G}$), *things draped in sheets* (D), *things not draped in sheets* ($\bar{D}$) all exist both in the actual universe and in the universe of discourse; ghosts (G) exist only in the universe of discourse: the class *ghosts* is empty, but, in the given proposition, it is falsely assumed not to be empty. Hence, the proposition *Ghosts are not always draped in sheets* is false; so too is the proposition *Ghosts are sometimes draped in sheets* (i.e. an *I* proposition).

§ 8. THE LOGICAL PROPERTIES OF RELATIONS AND THE VALIDITY OF INFERENCES

In discussing the traditional immediate inferences (in Chapter II) we found that in some cases the inferred conclusion was equivalent to the premiss from which it was inferred but that in some cases it was subimplicant to it. We can now see that this difference follows from the logical properties of the relations involved. The *A*, *E*, *I*, *O* propositions are statements of class-inclusion or exclusion. Since inclusion is non-symmetrical we cannot tell from the fact that *X* is included in *Y* whether *Y* is included in *X* or not. Hence from *SaP* (interpreted as meaning *All S's are P's*, i.e. *the class S is included in the class P*) we can infer only *PiS*. Thus the converse of an *A* proposition is not equivalent to the original proposition. But partial inclusion and total exclusion are both symmetrical; hence *SiP* and *SeP* both have simple converses. The traditional Logicians did not study the properties of relations, so that their treatment of immediate inferences is untidy and unpleasing. The conversion of *A*, *E*, *I*, *O* propositions depends entirely upon the symmetry or non-symmetry of the relation asserted to hold between the class taken for subject and the class taken for predicate.

The validity of categorical syllogisms depends upon the transitivity of the relation of class-inclusion. Using α, β, γ as illustrative symbols for three different classes, the *Barbara* syllogism can be represented by *If* α *is included in* β *and* β *is included in* γ, *then* α *is included in* γ. That the compound antecedent implies the consequent is manifest from the fact that *included in* is transitive.

The case is different in a syllogism where one premiss is singular, e.g. if *All Marxists are determinists and Professor Hodd is a Marxist, then Professor Hodd is a determinist.* As we have seen, class-membership is an intransitive relation. The validity of this syllogism depends upon a modified form of the *axiom de omni*, which can be stated as follows: *Whatever can be affirmed or denied of every member of a given class can also be affirmed or denied of any specified member.* This principle has been called the applicative principle;* it may also be called the principle of substitution.

Consider the following inferences, where *a*, *b*, *c* are illustrative symbols for individuals:

(i) $a = b$ and $b = c$, $\therefore a = c$.
(ii) *a* is richer than *b* and *b* is richer than *c*, ∴ *a* is richer than *c*.
(iii) *a* precedes *b* and *b* precedes *c*, ∴ *a* precedes *c*.

No one will doubt that these inferences are valid, whilst the following are clearly invalid:

(iv) *a* loves *b* and *b* loves *c*, ∴ *a* loves *c*.
(v) *a* annoys *b* and *b* annoys *c*, ∴ *a* annoys *c*.
(vi) *a* is father of *b* and *b* is father of *c*, ∴ *a* is father of *c*.

The relations in (i), (ii), (iii) are, in each case, transitive; the relations in (iv) and (v) are non-transitive, in (vi) intransitive. In (i) the relation is symmetrical, so that the relation and its converse are the same; in (ii) and (iii) the relation is asymmetrical. But the validity of the inference depends upon the property of transitivity, not upon symmetry. In each case the conclusion establishes a relation between the first and third of three terms; the second term stands in the given relation to one of the terms and in the converse relation to the other term. Since the relation is transitive the intermediate term can be eliminated.

Whenever premisses are connected by transitive relations, *chains of deduction* are possible. Given that the premisses are

* W. E. Johnson, *Logic*, Pt. II, p. 10.

true, the intermediate term, or terms, can be eliminated and the conclusion can be asserted. William James has expressed the principle in virtue of which such elimination is possible as 'the axiom of skipped intermediaries'; he says, 'symbolically we might write it as $a < b < c < d \ldots$ and say, that any number of intermediaries may be expunged without obliging us to alter anything in what remains written'.* It is in accordance with this principle that the conclusion of a *Sorites* is obtained, and that the middle term in the categorical syllogism is eliminated. The property of transitivity, as we have defined it for dyadic relations, is indeed a special case of the conditions that make elimination in general possible.†

The traditional Logicians by failing to single out the property of transitivity as essential to such inferences fell into absurd difficulties in dealing with arguments such as (ii) and (iii) above. An argument of this kind was called the *a fortiori argument*. Absurd attempts were made to restate the argument in traditional syllogistic form, i.e. in propositions containing between them three and only three terms, the terms being connected by the copula *is*. These attempts were bound to fail.‡

* *Principles of Psychology*, Vol. II, p. 646.

† Any student who wishes to consider this topic further should consult G. Boole, *Laws of Thought*, Ch. VII; cf. also, J. N. Keynes, *F.L.*, pp. 489–94.

‡ For a discussion of these attempts, see J. N. Keynes, *F.L.*, pp. 384–8.

CHAPTER VI

Classification and Description

§ 1. TERMINOLOGICAL CONFUSIONS

The topics to be discussed in this chapter can be approached from various points of view; the emphasis placed upon one topic as contrasted with another varies in accordance with the point of view adopted. Extension and intension, connotation and denotation, classification and division, definition and description – all these are more or less interconnected topics, important not only for the formal logician but also for the purposes of scientific investigation. The traditional Logicians approached the discussion of these topics from the metaphysical standpoint of the classical doctrines of Aristotle's works on logic, modified by the contributions of the Schoolmen. We shall not attempt to follow this treatment, and, with one exception,* we shall not keep to the traditional terminology. The topics to be discussed in this chapter are involved in all systematic thinking both at the level of common-sense reflection and of scientific thought.

The discussion of interconnected topics is often confused; it is difficult to distinguish in thought what is not separated in fact, whilst the adoption of an unsatisfactory terminology at the outset hinders further advance. Of these difficulties extension and intension, connotation and denotation present an example. These two pairs of words have been used sometimes as synonyms, sometimes to indicate different meanings. We shall distinguish between extension and denotation and between intension and connotation. We shall further have to make clear to ourselves what it is that has extension, denotation, intension, and connotation respectively. It is only too

* See § 5, below. The topics included in this chapter are dealt with more fully, and with more detailed reference to traditional doctrines, in *M.I.L.*, Ch. II, §§ 3, 4; Ch. IX, § 2; Ch. XXII. For a good discussion from a strictly Aristotelian point of view, see H. W. B. Joseph, *Introduction to Logic*, Chs. IV, V, VI.

easy* to confuse, in this discussion, the symbol and what is symbolized.

In earlier chapters we have frequently used the word "term"; it is to be hoped that we have done so without ambiguity. "Term" is, however, ambiguous though not as a rule inconveniently so, since the context usually suffices to show whether we mean by "term" a word or an element in a complex, such as the terms of a proposition, of the syllogism, or of a relation.† In this chapter the word "term" will always be used to mean a word, or set of words, i.e. what *signifies*, not *what is signified.*

The resemblances between individuals and their differences from one another are recognized in ordinary speech by our use of class-terms. No one has the slightest difficulty in using many class-terms; numerous instances of them appear on every page of this book. A class-term signifies a class-property, e.g. the *word* "book" signifies the complex characteristic which determines the class of individuals each of which is a book; the word "steel" signifies a certain constant conjunction of characteristics.

If I say 'Give me that book', then "that book" is used in the hope of referring you to a certain individual object which you will be able to identify because you understand the words used. If you do not understand "book" reference fails; if you do understand "book" but no book is findable reference again fails. We are clearly using the word "reference" here with a double usage. This double usage is so familiar that it requires some effort on our part to notice that it is double. On the one hand words are used to refer to individuals; on the other hand words are used to refer to characteristics, simple or complex; these modes of reference are very different. We can refer to an individual by using words because, and

* As the author knows to her cost; it is not improbable that the reader also falls into this insidious confusion.

† Curiously enough the traditional Logicians unwittingly illustrated the ambiguity of "term", by giving as one of the rules of the syllogism that 'the middle term must not be ambiguous'. Violation of this rule was known as the fallacy of *quaternio terminorum* (of four terms). But this was already provided against by the rule that there must be *only three terms*. Ambiguity is a characteristic of *language* (i.e. the symbols), not of what language refers to (i.e. the symbolized).

only because, individuals exemplify characteristics which also characterize, or could characterize, other individuals. An individual and its characteristics are distinguishable in thought but not separable in fact. To keep clear the double reference of words we need as precise a terminology as we can devise, for we are going to talk about a distinction which everyone makes with ease but often without paying attention to the distinction. Our present concern is with words from the point of view of their logical functions.

§ 2. CONNOTATION, DENOTATION, AND INTENSION

We have seen that a class is determined by a characteristic, simple or complex; conversely, any characteristic determines a class. We *mention* the characteristic, simple or complex, by using a word or a combination of words. We shall now use "term" as a synonym for "a word or combination of words signifying a characteristic or set of characteristics". A term is thus an element in the triadic relation *signifying*; thus a term (as we are here using the *word* "term") is a term (in the other sense) going along with the other two terms required for *signifying*, viz. what is signified, and the interpreter. To ask 'What does such and such a term mean?' is to ask 'What does the term signify?' These are synonymous interrogative sentences.

We noticed (in Chapter V [see p. 77], § 1) that, for example, the complex characteristic signified by "man" is exemplified by Abraham, Aristotle, . . ., where dots are used to indicate each of the other individual objects that could correctly have the term "man" applied to it. How are these objects determined? The answer is clear: because each of these objects has the characteristic, simple or complex, which "man" signifies. What "man" signifies is technically called the *connotation of "man"*. Words or terms have connotation. The *connotation of a term* is the characteristic, or set of characteristics, which anything must have if the term can be correctly applied to it. What the term applies to is the members of the class determined by the characteristic, simple or complex. This constitutes what is called the *denotation* of the term. It should be noticed that the denotation is not the *class* but the *collective membership* of the class. Hence, the denotation of a term is the collective membership of the class determined by the characteristic signified by the term. Thus connotation determines denotation.

"Man" connotes "rational animal"* and denotes *men*, i.e. the collective membership of the class determined by *being a rational animal*. "Triangle" connotes *plane figure bounded by three straight lines* and denotes the collective membership of the class determined by the connotation of "triangle".

A term signifying a characteristic lacking exemplification has no denotation, since the class determined by the characteristic is empty, and thus has no collective membership; e.g. "centaur", "house made of gold", "house made of plastics". If, in the future, a house is made entirely from plastics, then the term "house made of plastics" will have denotation. There is nothing in the least mysterious about this once we have granted that a class may be empty.

The reader may not be willing to agree that "man" connotes "rational animal"; he may object either: (i) 'men are not rational anyhow', or (ii) 'rationality isn't a good characteristic to select for the purpose of distinguishing *men* from *other animals*'. These objections we might be willing to admit, but must first point out that anyone who does raise them has clearly understood what is meant by "connotation", which is the sole point under discussion. The objections, however, serve to call our attention to two important points: (i) a characteristic cannot belong to the connotation of a term if any member of the term's denotation lacks it; (ii) what characteristics are signified by a term (and must therefore characterize anything denoted by the term) is by no means always easily settled. It is a sheer mistake to suppose that most words have fixed and quite determinate meanings, so that anyone who *uses* the word correctly knows *exactly how* he is using it. To this point we shall need to return.† But, as the second objection emphasizes, one function which we want

* "Man" can also be said to connote *man*, i.e. the characteristic or concept signified by the term "man".

† See § 6, below.

the words we use to perform is to mark off what we are talking about from anything with which it might easily be confused. There may arise a moment in a discussion at which we find ourselves compelled to ask: 'Well, what exactly do you mean by this word?' One answer to this question would be to state the connotation of the word.

At this point a third objection might be raised: (iii) 'Do not different people mean different things by the same word?' The answer is that often they do but sometimes they do not. It must be remembered that a term signifies something to someone; it is the signifying element in the relation and requires an interpreter. When *I* use the words "tiger", "montbretia", "home", "intelligent" (to select examples almost at random), what I happen to think of as the characteristics that must be possessed by anything denoted by one of these words is very likely to differ to some extent from the characteristics *you* think of when you use the word. We say, for instance, ' "Home" doesn't mean the same for him as it does for me, or for you.' We want to distinguish the 'meaning of a word' in *this* sense from the 'meaning' in the sense of 'connotation'. Hence, the convenience of using as a technical term a word not very often used in common speech, and to which we (in our activity as logicians) have given a precise meaning. What the word makes me, or makes you, think of is distinguished from connotation, and is usually called *subjective intension.* We can define "subjective intension" as "the characteristics which a given user of the term thinks of as possessed by the members of the class signified by the term". The phrase just given in inverted commas tells us the connotation of "subjective intension" (unless the author of this book is in error on this point).

"Intension" has been used as a synonym for "connotation" but, as the above objections indicate, this is an unhelpful usage. The "intension of a term" connotes characteristics possessed by the denotation of the term, but we must distinguish these characteristics into three sets: (1) all the characteristics possessed by all the members of the class – whose collective membership constitutes the term's denotation; (2) the characteristics which anyone may happen to think of when using the term, and which, therefore, vary from time to time and from one person to another; (3) the characteristics which must be possessed by the denotation of the term. It is convenient to call (1) the objective intension, or the comprehension, of the term; (2) the subjective intension; (3) the connotation. Hence, (1) comprises all that could be meant, (2) all that you or I may happen to mean, when the term is used. The connotation includes some only of the characteristics in fact possessed by the denotation; this selection of a minimum of meaning is, we shall find, useful for certain purposes, as, for instance, in defining.

§ 3. EXTENSION AND CONNOTATION

We saw that the traditional Logicians failed to distinguish the relation of an individual to the class of which it is a member from the relation of a subclass to a class which includes it. Accordingly they said that, for instance, the class *Europeans* 'extends over' or 'includes in its extension' the class *Frenchmen* and also that the class *Frenchmen* includes in its extension all individual Frenchmen. Now that we have seen that the membership relation is quite different from the class-inclusion relation we must also see that we cannot use the same word both for the term signifying the relation of a class to its subclasses and for the term signifying the relation of a class to its members. Accordingly, we shall distinguish in meaning between "extension" and "denotation". The extension of a term signifying a class-property of a given class is all the subclasses collectively. For example, "Man" is a term signifying a certain class; it denotes each individual man; the extension of "man" is the collective membership of all subclasses of the superclass *man*, e.g. it comprises *white men, black men, brown men, yellow men, red men*. Another way of saying the same thing is: the extension of a term signifying a class-property is all the varieties distinguished as subclasses. The extension, therefore, are *classes*, not individuals; the denotation is *the membership of the classes*, not the classes. Hence, when a certain man dies, the extension of "man" is in no way affected. The subclasses need not have members although it must be possible that there should be members. Thus *centaurs* is an empty class, but there is no logical inconsistency in supposing that there may be *centaurs*; since there are none, "centaur" lacks denotation, but its extension comprises *wise centaurs* and *foolish centaurs*.

It has been held by many logicians that extension and intension vary inversely. This doctrine is worth discussing because the discussion should reveal the confusions which have been caused by failure to distinguish clearly between denotation and extension.* Jevons, for instance, says:

> When we pass from one term to another by merely adding some quality or qualities to the connotation, the denotation of the new term is less than the old, and when we pass from one term to another by merely removing some quality or qualities from the connotation, the denotation of the new term is greater than that of the old.†

In his *Principles of Science*, he states the doctrine as follows: 'When the intent or meaning of a term is increased the extent is decreased; and vice versa, when the extent is increased the intent is decreased.'‡ This he calls an 'all-important law'. He cites as examples: *planet, exterior planet.* But, he points out, there must be 'a real change in the intensive meaning, and an adjective may often be joined to a name without making a change. *Elementary metal* is identical with *metal*; *mortal man* with *man*.'§ These quotations suffice to show that there is considerable confusion in this doctrine. It is not surprising to find that logicians who have accepted it have worried themselves over the question whether the intension of man can be said to increase when a man dies and decrease when a human baby is born. Obviously not. The question is so absurd that we may suppose the whole doctrine is nonsense. If so, it is not downright nonsense, for it suggests something

* We have *defined* "denotation" and "extension" in such a way that we could not attempt to use them as synonyms; that they have frequently been so used is due to the failure to notice the distinction upon which we have insisted.

† *Elementary Lessons in Logic*, p. 40. Jevons is careful to point out the decrease is not in *exact* proportion to the increase. One wonders why, in that case, the *precise phrase* 'inverse variation' should have been used.

‡ op. cit., Ch. XXX, § 13.

§ ibid.

true but in so confused a manner as to lead to nonsensical questions.

As the *connotation* of a term is increased, the *extension* is decreased. It is connotation and *extension* that vary in this way, not connotation and *denotation*, nor *intension* and extension. Since the extension of "ship" is all the subclasses of *ship*, it follows that by enriching the connotation, e.g. adding *steam-* and thus obtaining *steam-ship*, the extension is decreased, for all subclasses of *ship* not propelled by *steam* are now ruled out. Conversely, by changing the connotation of "plays" so as to comprise *cinema plays* the extension is increased as the connotation has been decreased, for the term "plays" will have less richness of connotation if it is to comprise dramas not witnessed by eyewitnesses than the word "plays" formerly had.*

These examples suggest that the so-called 'inverse variation of extension and intension' relates to terms arranged in a classificatory series, i.e. that it relates to *classes* arranged in a certain order, namely, in which a subclass is grouped together with other subclasses under a superclass, which is in turn a subclass of another superclass, and so on. Such an arrangement of classes constitutes a *classification.*

§ 4. CLASSIFICATION AND DIVISION

The process of distinguishing the subclasses of a class is called *logical division*; the reverse process is *classification.* The process of classifying presupposes the grouping of individuals in classes; it is useful only when the classes to be arranged in an orderly manner have important characteristics. *Importance* is relative to a purpose. All men have needs which necessitate the making of classifications, e.g. of people into enemies and friends, of plants into edible and poisonous – which itself presupposes a distinction between edible and non-edible – of materials into inflammable and not-inflammable, and so on. The earliest classifications are made to

* It should be noticed that I have not written "plays" and "cinema plays" but "plays" and *cinema plays*, i.e. the term "plays" is supposed to include in its connotation *cinema plays*. If this is not noticed the reader may think that I 'increased' the connotation of "plays".

satisfy some practical purpose; in using class-terms it is hardly possible not sometimes to notice that certain classes are closely associated with certain other classes. The earliest stage of a science is the classificatory stage: it is not long since botany passed beyond this stage and sociology has hardly done so yet.

A class, then, can be assigned a place in different systems of classification. The arrangement of vehicles, for instance, in classes and subclasses would be very different if carried out for the Ministry of Transport from what it would be if done to satisfy the needs of the Chancellor of the Exchequer.* An unscientific person is likely to choose obvious characteristics for the determination of which subclasses are to be associated, but obvious characteristics are often not important ones because they are not connected relevantly. Thus a landlady arranging a student's books is very likely to be guided by such characteristics as size, colour, style of binding rather than by the subject-matter or authors of the books. If the books must be fitted into shelves of different heights, then size is certainly a characteristic important for *that* purpose, but it remains irrelevant for the purposes of the student who uses the books. Consider the example on page 110.

This arrangement of aeroplanes in subclasses, and subclasses of subclasses, can be looked at either as a classification or as a division; if the former, then we begin with the smaller classes and include them in wider classes; if the latter, we begin with the widest class and subdivide into smaller classes. Classification and division are fundamentally the same so far as the logical principles are concerned. These principles can be most conveniently stated in terms of the process of division. Subclasses on the same level are called *co-ordinate*; on a level above super-ordinate to the subclass below; on the level below sub-ordinate.

The basis of the division, that is the characteristic by reference to which co-ordinate subclasses are differentiated one from another, is usually known by its Latin name – *fundamentum divisionis*. The principles in accordance with

* See *M.I.L.*, pp. 433–4, where the classification of vehicles, from the point of view of transport, is worked out.

which a sound division should proceed can be summed up in the following rules:

1. There must be only one *fundamentum divisionis* at each step.
2. The co-ordinate classes must be collectively exhaustive of the superclass.
3. The successive steps of the division must proceed by gradual stages.

From Rule 1 there follows the corollary that co-ordinate classes must be mutually exclusive. Violation of this rule results in the fallacy of *cross-division*, i.e. there are overlapping classes. This corollary together with Rule 2 secures that every member contained in the classes is contained in one class only and no member in a superordinate class is omitted in the next level. Hence, the sum of the subclasses must equal the whole class divided, or classified.

Rule 3 secures that each stage of the division should be in accordance with the original *fundamentum divisionis*. If, for example, we were to divide *university students* first into *science* and *arts* students, and were then to subdivide *science students* into *polite* and *impolite*, and *art students* into *dark*, *fair*, and *medium-complexioned*, the division could serve no useful purpose.

The fallacy of *cross-division* is of common occurrence. If we divide the *languages of mankind* into *Aryan*, *Semitic*, *Slavonic*, *Hamitic*, and *Ancient Egyptian*, we commit this fallacy, since *Ancient Egyptian* falls into the *Hamitic group*, and *Slavonic* into the *Aryan*. This division is also not exhaustive.

Any given class can be subdivided into two mutually exclusive and collectively exhaustive subclasses on the basis of a given characteristic which is possessed by every member of the one class and is not possessed by any member of the other class. Thus we can divide civilians into those doing work of national importance and those not doing work of national importance. It would be a contradiction to assume that any member of the one subclass could also be a member of the other subclass, whilst every civilian must fall into one or other of the two classes – granted that the criterion – work of national importance – is sufficiently well-defined. Such a division is called division by dichotomy (i.e. *cutting in*

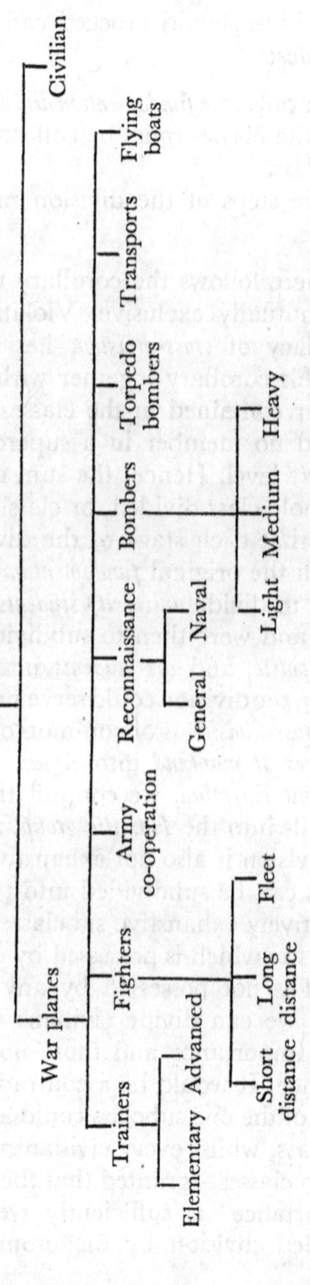

* It is not claimed that this classification is complete. Any student who can correctly emend it shows (i) that he has *knowledge about* aeroplanes, (ii) that he understands how to classify.

two). The following is an example of a dichotomous division.

This division formally secures that the subclasses are mutually exclusive and collectively exhaustive, but this formal simplicity is attained only by a multiplication of classes negatively characterized, and it obscures the simpler relationships that appear only when classes are arranged on the basis of positive characteristics. In the natural sciences

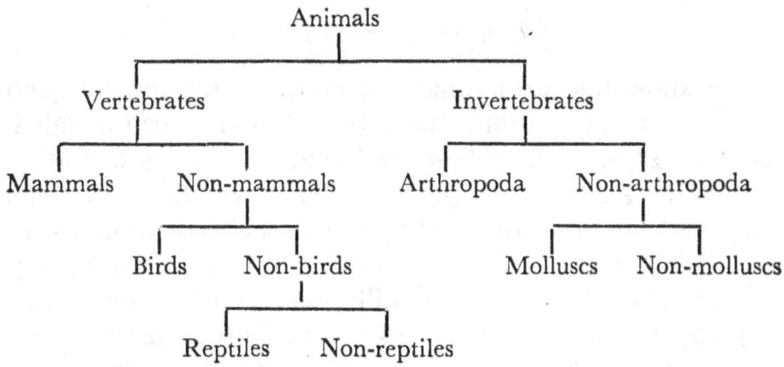

dichotomous division would be of little use. The above subdivision of vertebrates into mammals and non-mammals, and so on, which results in placing *birds* on one level and *reptiles* on another, obscures the relation that holds between mammals, birds, reptiles, amphibians, and fishes as together exhausting the class vertebrates.

Traditionally, division has been regarded as the division of a *genus* into its *species*; the *genus* from which the division starts is called the *summum genus*; the species with which it ends are called *infimae species*, intermediate species *subaltern genera*; an intermediate genus is called the *proximum genus* of its constituent species. These names are not of importance; what is important is to recognize that the distinction between genus and species is relative, and depends for its significance upon the given table of division.*

* In biological classification genera and species are used in a sense fixed by the hierarchy of classes: subclasses of species are called *varieties*; superclasses of genera are *families*; then come the *order* and *class*. It should be observed that in the dichotomous division of *animals*, given above, the negative class must be taken as strictly a subclass of the proximum genus at each stage, thus *reptiles* are non-birds, non-mammals, and vertebrates.

We have insisted that a division or a classification is relative to a purpose – classes are subdivided, or are grouped together in a wider class in order to bring out connexions between classes that are fruitful for some purpose. In the sciences the classes we select for orderly arrangement are natural classes, i.e. classes whose members are characterized by *connected* properties.

§ 5. THE PREDICABLES

If we know that an animal is a mammal we know a good deal about it, e.g. that it has a backbone, is warm-blooded, and has some kind of hair, and that the female has milk-producing glands with which to suckle her offspring. Some mammals, the marsupials, bring forth their young in a very undeveloped stage and carry them in pouches; another group of mammals lay eggs but still suckle their young. This example serves to suggest to us to classify the characteristics possessed by the members of a class into three groups: (1) those which every member possesses and only the members of the given class possess; (2) those which every member possesses but which are also possessed by members of other classes; (3) those which some only of the members possess. Let us take as an example the class *man*. Every member of the class *man* has the property of *animality*, also the properties of *being mammalian*; every member of the class man has also properties peculiar to man, e.g. a larger brain relatively to size of body than any other animal, and along with it *rationality*. *Animality* and *being mammalian* are generic properties of man, *rationality* is a specific or differentiating property. "Generic" is here used in the logical, not the biological sense; if we regard *animal* as the genus of *man* (neglecting the genus *mammals*) then we can say that the species (in the logical sense of "species") *man* is differentiated from co-ordinate species of *animal* by the property of being *rational*. This is to follow Aristotle's classification. We shall all agree that along with the property of *being rational* there go other properties peculiar to *man* within the genus *animal*, e.g. *capable of seeing a joke*, or – to take one of Aristotle's favourite examples – *capable of learning grammar.* We feel that, even if a parrot and a budgerigar can speak (i.e. utter verbal sounds), only a man *could* learn grammar. Such a property, common to every member of a species (i.e. a subclass of a genus) and connected with the property that differentiates this species from co-ordinate species, is called a *proprium.**

There are also properties which every member of a subclass of *man* has but which are not possessed by members of other subclasses, e.g. white-skinned, black-skinned, curly-haired, straight-haired, dolichocephalic, brachycephalic, and so on. Such properties are called *accidents.*

These names – genus, differentiating property or differentia, proprium and accidents – are known as the 'predicables', for Aristotle first distinguished them when he attempted to answer the question: What different sorts of predications can be made about a species? His reply was that we are *able to predicate* of the species *man* (for instance) the *genus* – animal, the *differentia* – rational, a *proprium* – able to learn grammar, an *accidens* – white-skinned.† The genus and differentia taken together constitute the *definition,* which is *per genus et differentiam.*‡

The words *genus, species, differentiate, property, accidental* characteristic – all come down to us through Aristotle's treatment of this topic. Professor R. M. Eaton has said, 'Aristotle's genius for clear analysis, which enabled him to give to logic a terminology and form that persisted for two thousand years, is nowhere better exemplified than in his theory of the predicables.'§ It is rare to find a modern

* The Latin word *proprium* (translation of Aristotle's word ἴδιον) is retained because in this context it is used with a narrower sense than "property" which is often used as a synonym for "characteristic". The plural of *proprium* is *propria.*

† It should be noticed that the *subject* of predication was the *species* (e.g. man, or triangle) not the individual (e.g. Socrates or *this* scalene triangle). Porphyry (A.D. 233–304) hopelessly muddled Aristotle's doctrine by putting the *species* in place of the *definition*, and taking the subject to be the individual, e.g. Socrates. He, and later logicians, wasted their time in making further distinctions, utterly trivial and needlessly elaborate.

‡ This means 'by assigning the genus and the distinguishing characteristic'.

§ *General Logic*, p. 273. Professor Eaton gives by far the best account of Aristotle's theory of the predicables, from the point of view of the elementary student of logic, who wishes to know in more detail what Aristotle's theory actually was.

logician according such praise to Aristotle's work in logic, but the praise is – in the opinion of the present author – well deserved. At the same time we must insist, as Professor Eaton also admits, that Aristotle's theory of the predicables is rooted in his metaphysic. That metaphysic we reject. It may indeed be urged that the influence of Aristotle's metaphysic upon his logic was very unfortunate, and the traditional Logicians' adherence to it and their retention of every mistake Aristotle made has been disastrous in hindering the development of logical doctrines. Aristotle's theory is now mainly of historical interest to those who are not studying metaphysics. It would, however, be worth while to follow it in some detail – did space permit – because it provides a good example of a rigorous attempt to analyse the sort of statements we can make, and to pay serious attention to the important distinction between essential and non-essential characteristics.

We may sum up Aristotle's list of predicables by exhibiting them in the form of a dichotomous division, the basis of which is the convertibility or inconvertibility of the predicate with the subject. A predicate is convertible with the subject if it is common and peculiar to the subject. This statement does not make sense unless we remember that, in this context, subject must be taken to mean *species*:

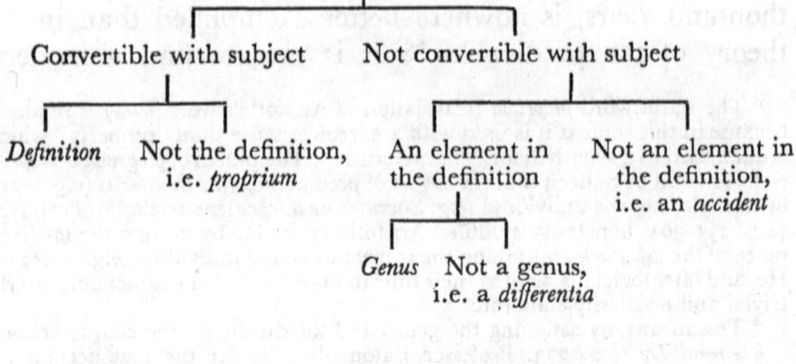

The italicized words are the predicables. The definition is not a fifth predicable distinct from the others but is the predication of genus and differentia together. We add an example taken from geometry:

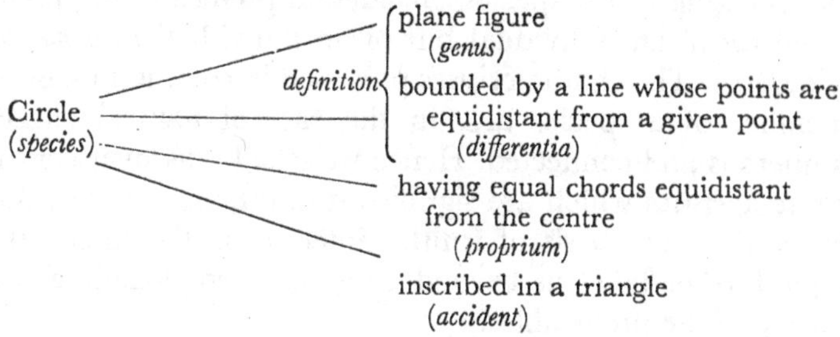

Artistotle held that each species had a fixed and determinate essence; this was set forth in the definition. The proprium, although not part of the essence, was nevertheless regarded as *essential* to the species; it is derivable from the essence, i.e. follows from the definition. Thus the distinction between definition and proprium was taken to be absolute. This view we must completely reject. The distinction is absolute only relatively to a given system of concepts. It is most easily seen in the case of geometry. Euclid regarded geometrical figures as given in intuition by construction of the figures in space. This view is now abandoned, hence we cannot hold that there is one and only one definition of, e.g. a "circle", which will set forth its essence. If the definition of "circle" given above be accepted, then it is a proprium of a circle that with a given perimeter its area is maximum; if, however, we *define* a circle as the plane figure which has a maximum area with a given circumference, then it *follows* that all its points are equidistant from a given point, and thus this is a proprium. Which we choose as definition is determined by non-logical considerations; once chosen, then, whatever can be deduced from the definition is a proprium. It is easy to see that the propria are the theorems implied by the axioms and definitions. They are essential in the clear sense that to accept the definitions and reject the propria would be self-contradictory.

The distinction between propria and definition, and between propria and accidents, is much less easy to draw in the case of natural species, e.g. man, cow, snake. It must suffice to say that a characteristic or property is essential if, lacking it, the thing in question could no longer be regarded as belonging to the species. Accidental predicates are predicated *not* of an individual but of an individual *as a member of a species*. The characteristics possessed in common by every member of a species are, in the case of natural classes, numerous and connected. Hence we seek to discover certain characteristics which are significant of others, and can thus be used as the basis of fruitful inferences. To pursue this topic further takes us beyond anything recognizable as the theory of the predicables.

§ 6. DEFINITION

We have seen that the traditional rule for definition is that it should be *per genus et differentiam*. This is unduly narrow. What, we must ask, is the purpose of definition? When do we want a definition, and, if successful, what does a definition achieve? The student, for instance, who is beginning the study of logic may want to know what logic is. Is this a request for a definition? If so, how is it to be met? The answer to this latter question will depend upon the needs of the questioner. Is he entirely ignorant of the meaning of the word "logic", i.e. has he just met it for the first time? Or does he know that logic is somehow or other concerned with reasoning and he wants to know *further* how logic is to be distinguished from psychology? If the former, then the answer, 'Logic is concerned with the principles of reasoning', should meet his case, provided he understands how to use the words in the defining phrase. If the latter is his case, then the answer must indicate characteristics differentiating a logical treatment of *reasoning* from a *psychological* treatment. The most satisfactory answer will probably take the form of a set of statements with illustrative examples. It is seldom enlightening to be given a definition in a short, crisp statement. Occasionally such an answer will suffice. Suppose A asks B: 'What does "whatnot" mean?' B replies, 'A "whatnot" is an article of furniture with open shelves, rather wide, designed for the purpose of putting objects of various kinds on it.' Then A's question is satisfactorily answered provided that (i) A knows the words B uses in the defining phrase, (ii) the defining phrase does indeed present the characteristics that things *called* 'whatnots' have. Perhaps (iii) should be added: A wanted an explanation of "whatnot" and not of "what not", i.e. something added at the end of a list to mean "and all sorts of things". The context alone can decide whether A did mean the sort of thing which B understood him to mean. If he did not, then communication has failed.

Usually our requests for definitions are not so easily dealt with. We seek definitions as a means of thinking more clearly about something; we want to think more precisely, to know exactly what it is that we are saying. For instance, 'What is the policy of appeasement, as understood by Neville Chamberlain and his supporters between, say, 1936 and 1939?' Clearly something more than a dictionary definition of "appeasement" is needed to answer this question. But, we may feel, "appeasement" as used in the question must have some reference to the dictionary definition of "appeasement". Or again, 'Are you a Communist?', to which the reply may be 'that depends upon what you mean by "Communism".' The student has probably taken part in conversations such as the above. At this point he should ask himself what sort of answer he would find satisfactory. There is not one and only one way of explaining how words are used; any answer that enables us to use the word – for a definition of which a request is made – is so far a satisfactory definition. The answer generally takes the form of a sentence, i.e. we explain a word by using other words. Will this leave us in the uncomfortable position of one who endlessly chases his own tail?

A proper answer to the questions and difficulties suggested by the preceding paragraph would require a book, not a brief section in a chapter.* All that can be done here is

* I should very much like to write such a book, but neither space (owing to war-time scarcity of paper) nor time is available. The student who is interested in these topics would find I. A. Richards' *Interpretation in Teaching* both interesting and enlightening. A logician may be pardoned for thinking that Professor Richards is unduly narrow in his apprehension of specifically logical problems and perhaps unnecessarily dogmatic. But his books are worth careful study.

to suggest a very few of the pertinent questions we need to ask and to indicate, in the case of a few only of these questions, the lines along which answers to them should be sought.

We use words to talk about things; we use words to ask for definitions and most commonly we use words in giving the definition. But there must be an attachment of the words used to life, i.e. to the rest of reality. We cannot here attempt to give any account of the ways in which a child begins to learn the language he hears spoken by those who tend him; we take the miracle for granted. Verbal expressions must, at certain points, link up with other things than words unless definition is to remain merely a set of verbal manipulations. Such linking up can be given by *pointing*, i.e. by what has been called *ostensive definition*. For example, 'What does "wink" mean?' The most satisfactory answer to this is given by 'Doing this' – *and*, the speaker *winks*. The questioner will then surely know what "wink" means; he may very well not know if he cannot observe someone winking but has to rely only on his dictionary.* Again, someone asks, 'What is an epic poem?', and is answered, '*The Iliad*, *The Odyssey*, *The Æneid*, *Paradise Lost*, and anything like these.' The difficulty is to know 'like in what respects'. Shall we include *The Dynasts*? The answer does not take us very far, but it is a beginning. It is an ending also in the case of words such as "red", "sound of A♯ on a violin". We must ultimately explain the meaning of many words by giving *samples*, as in the case of "epic poem" above.†

The treatment of definition by most logicians has been too much divorced from the consideration of how we come to

* At this point I consulted the *Shorter Oxford English Dictionary*, which gives "A glance, or significant movement of the eye (often accompanied by a nod) expressing command, assent, invitation or the like", adding that this (meaning) is obsolete except in proverbs; it gives under the verb "to wink" – "to close one eye momentarily in a flippant or frivolous manner, especially to convey intimate information or to express good-humoured interest". The reader who knows that the Latin "connivere" means "to wink" will find the derivation of "connive" interesting.

† The sampling method is quite indispensable, but to learn by means of it is not as easy as it may sound, as anyone who has tried to learn, or to teach, Latin by the direct method is likely to admit. Here we can only remind the reader that we can *sort* and *distinguish* without knowing *how* we have sorted and distinguished.

use words, how we learn to *understand*. Attention has been concentrated upon what is, from the scientific point of view, of great importance, namely, what conditions must a satisfactory definition fulfil? In answering this question we need to remember that 'satisfactory', like 'importance', depends upon the point of view. Let us first consider the traditional rules, which presuppose that what is needed is an explanation in words of how a given word is to be understood. The word to be defined is traditionally called the *definiendum*, the defining phrase is called the *definiens*.

A. *Rules concerned with the nature of definition.*

1. The definiens must be equivalent to the definiendum. From this rule two corollaries follow: (1·1) * The definiens must not be wider than the definiendum. (1·2) The definiens must not be narrower than the definiendum.

B. *Rules concerned with the purpose of definition.*

2. The definiens should not include any expression that occurs in the definiendum or that could be defined only in terms of it.

3. The definiens should not be expressed in obscure or figurative language.

4. The definiens should not be negative in significance unless the definiendum is primarily negative in significance.

Granted that the purpose of giving a definition is to make clear the limits within which a word, or phrase, can be rightly used, these rules seem obvious enough to require but little comment. The point to be stressed is that the definition and the defining phrase must be equivalent, from which equivalence it follows that the one can be substituted for the other without alteration in meaning. A definition *per genus et differentiam* fulfils the conditions laid down by these rules, provided that the expression used for the differentiating property be not obscure. What is obscure is relative to the questioner's knowledge; the futility of using in the defining phrase words more obscure to the questioner than the word to be defined is too obvious to need further comment. A

* The corollaries are numbered in this way to emphasize their connexion with rule 1; the decimal point is used to distinguish the two corollaries.

circular definition also defeats the purpose of defining, e.g. ' "Physical force" means "the power which produces motion" ' is circular if "force" and "power" are taken to be synonyms and if, further, the request was for a definition of "force" rather than of *physical force*. "Justice is giving to every man his due" is circular if "what is due to a man" is defined as "what it is just he should have".

The definition of "orphan" as "one with no father or mother" is not faulty because it is negative but because it is unclear whether an orphan thus defined is a Melchizedek. "One deprived of father and mother" is affirmative in statement and negative in significance, which fits the concept *orphan*. The student will easily think of words the primary significance of which is to deny the possession of an attribute, e.g. "alien", "bachelor".

A question that has been much discussed is whether definition is of *words* or of *things*. The question is badly put; words are used to refer to something; we define the *word*, but there is a word to define only because we want to talk about what the word stands for; we talk *with* words *about* something.

A distinction has been made between *verbal* and *real* definition. A verbal definition gives in the definiens a word or set of words that can be used to symbolize exactly what the definiendum symbolizes. In real definitions the definiens represents an analysis of the definiendum. A definition is always an equation: one word, or set of words, is equivalent to another word or set of words. The definiens may be analytic, i.e. it may show an analysis of the definiendum. Analysis in this sense must be contrasted with physical analysis. For example, in chemical analysis there is both the unanalysed whole (e.g. *water*) and the set of constituents into which it is analysed. In logical analysis there is not first one thing and then a set of things, but there are *two* expressions which mean the same. For example, given the definition: "danger" means "exposure to harm", there is not a complex property symbolized by "danger" *as well as* the set of properties symbolized by "exposure to harm"; on the contrary, there is *one* set of properties which both "danger" and "exposure to harm" symbolize.

§ 7. DESCRIPTIONS

Logicians have often defined "definition" as "the explicit statement of the connotation of a word". The objection to this definition is that it suggests that the connotation of a word is fixed, and all that needs to be done is explicitly to state this. In the case of abstracta this is so, e.g. the terms used in geometry have definitely delimited meanings. Thus "chiliagon" means "a thousand-sided regular polygon" on every occasion of its use. The words we have most trouble in defining are those whose meaning shifts in different contexts; such words can only be defined relatively to a given sort of usage, and with reference to explanatory examples of the word *used* in some sentence.

We are naturally tempted to ask whether every word can be defined. If "to define" means "to explain how the word is used", the answer is that every word can be defined but few can be defined shortly. If "to define" means "to state explicitly the connotation", then the answer is that some words cannot be defined, either because they have no connotation or because the connotation cannot be made clear (to one who does not already know it) by means of other words alone. To consider the second case first. "Red" connotes *redness*, but "redness" can only be understood by knowing that *redness* is the quality of those objects which "red" denotes, and *this* can be known only by *seeing* red objects. Hence, a man blind from birth cannot know what "red" means.

The other case is that of words which have no connotation. Whether there are any non-connotative words is a matter of dispute among logicians. J. S. Mill held that proper names have no connotation. Let us begin by very briefly considering how we use a proper name, for example, "Franklin", as contrasted with a phrase such as "the man in the moon" or "the man whom you spoke to just now".

Most of those who hear the name "Franklin" in 1942 would think of the present President of the United States or of the younger son of the present Duchess of Kent or of Benjamin Franklin, the American scientist and statesman; some may think of some other personal acquaintance. The name "Franklin" does not give us any information with regard to the objects so named; there is no reason to suppose that the four objects (assumed to have been referred to by "Franklin") have in common anything except (i) being called by the name, (ii) having properties of sufficient interest to someone to have been given that name. But (ii) is shared by those called 'John', 'Cordelia', 'Smoodger', and does not, therefore, suffice to mark out those called "Franklin" from the rest. Thus "Franklin" lacks connotation in so far as the name does not signify any characteristics common and peculiar to the individuals called by the name, for "Franklin" may be the name of a poodle or a motor-car. If this had been all that Mill meant by saying that proper names are non-connotative he would have been right. Possibly this is all he meant, but he certainly spoke as though he denied any kind of meaning to a proper name.*

A proper name has a meaning because it is given to an individual to distinguish him (or it) from other individuals. Its significance is thus known only to those who are personally introduced to the individual and to those who know a proposition of the form, ' "Franklin" is the name of the present President of the United States', ' "Cordelia" is the name of the girl over there in the red dress' – where it is assumed that 'the girl over there in the red dress' uniquely identifies an individual. In practice we give proper names only to individuals in whom we have a special interest which makes us desire to refer to them frequently. We ask for 'my hot-water bottle', not for 'Aristarchus' unless we have notified that the hot-water bottle in question has been thus named.

"The man in the moon", "the present President of the United States", "the author of *Adam Bede*", "the author of *Ecclesiastes*" resemble proper names in one respect, namely, that each refers to only one individual. They are known as definite descriptions, for, unlike proper names, these phrases are descriptive and can be understood by anyone who knows English. Some logicians have held that definite descriptions are names but very complicated names. This view is certainly

* See J. S. Mill, *A System of Logic*, Bk. I, Ch. II, and see further *M.I.L.*, Ch. III, §§ 3, 4.

mistaken. If "the author of *Adam Bede*" were simply another name for the person called "George Eliot", we could refer to this person as "the person called 'the author of *Adam Bede*' ", just as we can refer to this person as "the person called 'George Eliot' ". Now Mary Ann Evans was called "George Eliot", and the fact that she so called herself constitutes a sufficient title for her to be spoken of as 'George Eliot'. But however much she called herself or any one else called her "the author of *Adam Bede*" she would not have in fact been the author unless she had actually written *Adam Bede*, and that she did write it is what we mean by saying she is 'the author of *Adam Bede*'. Likewise, the President of the United States is not made President by being called so but only in virtue of his actually holding the office.

"The man in the moon" raises another difficulty against the view that definite descriptions are names, for there is no man in the moon, and it seems absurd to say that a non-existent individual has a name. So, if we use the description, "the present King of France" or "the crock of gold in the well" – when there is no such crock of gold – we are using significant phrases, but there is, in each case, nothing answering to the description. Philosophers have been puzzled to explain how we can use descriptions that describe nothing, and if these descriptions were in fact names the puzzle would be insoluble.

We owe to Bertrand Russell an account of how descriptions are used that shows us exactly how it is that we can significantly make use of descriptions that describe nothing. The account is given in terms of the theory of classes. A definite description is analysable into an identification of a class together with the implication that the class in question has only one member. Thus "the author of *Adam Bede*" identifies the class determined by the characteristic *having written 'Adam Bede'* and implies that the class has only one member. Since we have reasons for asserting that *Adam Bede* was written by one author the description describes him (or in this case her). Since we have reasons for believing that *Ecclesiastes* was written by two authors, the description describes no one. "The man in the moon" and "the present

King of France" are also descriptions describing nothing. Since the significance of these descriptions is entirely independent of there being any exemplification of the characteristic determining the class in each case, their significance is unaffected by the discovery that the class in question is empty. This theory also shows how two, or more, different descriptions can be different even though they describe nothing, or, what is the same thing in different words, even though the classes corresponding to the descriptions have no members; it is not upon the denotation that their significance depends.

On this theory we can analyse what it is exactly that a proposition such as *The author of 'Adam Bede' is George Eliot* asserts; it is equivalent to the conjoint assertion of three propositions:

(i) At least one person wrote *Adam Bede*.
(ii) At most one person wrote *Adam Bede*.
(iii) There is nobody who both wrote *Adam Bede* and is not identical with George Eliot.

If any one of the three constituent propositions is false, then the original proposition is false.

The proposition *The author of the 'Iliad' exists* can be similarly analysed into the conjoint assertion of:

(1) At least one person wrote the *Iliad*.
(2) At most one person wrote the *Iliad*.

If either of these constituent propositions is false, then the original proposition is false; hence, if more than one person wrote the *Iliad*, or if no such book was ever written, then *The author of the 'Iliad' exists* is false. Since (1) and (2) are of the same form as (i) and (ii) above, it is clear that *The author of 'Adam Bede' is George Eliot* asserts that the author of *Adam Bede* exists. Thus any statement attributing a property to *the author of 'Adam Bede'* is false unless there really was such a person.

The analysis of *The present King of France is bald* asserts conjointly:

(i) At least one person reigns over France now.
(ii) At most one person reigns over France now.

(iii) There is nobody who both reigns over France now and is not bald.

Since, of these three constituent propositions (i) is false, it follows that the original proposition is false.

The definite descriptions we have so far been concerned with are *singular* descriptions; they are often expressed by the form "the so-and-so". We must, however, be on our guard against supposing that grammatical similarity is a safe guide to similarity of logical form. "The lion is carnivorous" does not express a singular proposition; it expresses a proposition equivalent to *All lions are carnivorous*, since this latter proposition implies and is implied by *The lion is carnivorous*. Accordingly, the proposition is a universal affirmative proposition.

Definite plural descriptions are used in stating such propositions as *The members of the House of Commons are elected*, *The members of the Committee have been notified of the complaint*. In these propositions a statement is made about every member of a certain class specified by the description.

Indefinite descriptions are used in stating such propositions as *A member of the King's household was killed*. This is equivalent to 'There exists at least one member of the King's household and he was killed'. Such propositions are often expressed by the verbal form 'A so-and-so is such-and-such', but we must again notice that the same verbal form may be used to express a proposition different in kind, e.g. 'A dog likes bones' means 'Every dog likes bones'.

CHAPTER VII

Variables, Propositional Forms, and Material Implication

§ 1. VARIABLE SYMBOLS

Frequently in the preceding chapters we have used illustrative symbols.* The use of such symbols is not logically essential but it is convenient and is probably psychologically indispensable to enable us to concentrate our attention upon the form of propositions. Illustrative symbols are by no means confined to logic and mathematics. They are employed in ordinary speech when we use pronouns. For instance, suppose you are listening to the news on the wireless and are in a room with several people, some of whom are not anxious to hear what is said. There is a murmured buzz of low-toned conversation. You say: 'I can't hear; someone is saying something; it may be important but can't it wait till after the news?' Here "I" stands for the speaker and is definitely specified for anyone who knows who is speaking; "someone is saying something" does not specify *who* says *what*; these pronouns are illustrative symbols standing for *one person* in the class of persons in the room but an unspecified one. Suppose now you say, 'Jack, it is you who are talking', then "*Jack*" names an *individual*, i.e. the illustrative symbol "someone" has been replaced by a specified individual's name "*Jack*". In contrast with the indefinite pronoun "*someone*" we call "*Jack*" a constant, for it signifies the same individual throughout every occasion of its use (provided we make the assumption that there is only one person named "Jack" in the set to which reference is being made). Personal pronouns may also be used indefinitely when the person to whom reference is made is not specified. In this book "I"

* At this point the student may find it convenient to re-read Ch. I, §§ 4, 5.

and "you" have been thus used to stand for any *one* person (the speaker, questioner, etc.) and for any one *other* person (the hearer, answerer, etc.), respectively.* "He" is often so used to stand for some unspecified murderer (at least by detectives in fiction), also in legal documents and in various expositions, and in some places in this book, where "he" could be interpreted *in some contexts* as standing for a female. We are so used to these conventions that we find no difficulty in understanding what is meant. ("We" in the preceding sentence is used in an illustrative way even though *one* person denoted by "we" is *I, Susan Stebbing.*) There is no more difficulty in understanding variable symbols than in understanding how pronouns are used. Statements in which pronouns are used will be ambiguous unless the context specifies the range of their application; this is usually the case, but sometimes difficulties arise through failure in specification.

Consider the following remarks:

(1) 'Someone is saying something.'
(2) 'He is saying something.'
(3) 'Jack is saying something.'
(4) 'Jack is saying that he does not want to hear him.'
(5) 'Jack is saying that he does not want to hear Gram Swing.'

As we proceed from (1) to (5) specification is becoming more and more complete, i.e. at each step one more element previously referred to without specification is now specified. In accordance with the ordinary conventions of the English language (5) may be taken as completely specified since "he" unambiguously stands for "Jack".† It is a question of interpretation whether we say that (1) states a proposition; if it be regarded as either true or false, it is a proposition. Some logicians may consider that (1) is a propositional form and that to obtain a proposition the indefinite 'someone', 'something' must be replaced by a definitely specified element. On this view (2) and (3) must also be regarded as propositional forms; it is, then, perhaps hard to draw a line between (3)

* See Ch. II, § 2, where warning was given that this procedure would be followed.

† Cf. the use of *se* and *ille* in Latin.

and (4), since "him" is not specified, and "he" is specified as referring to *Jack* only on the convention that whoever made statement (4) would have used a proper name instead of "he" if there had been risk of understanding that *Jack* was speaking of, say, *Tom* as not wanting to hear. Then, on reflection, we may begin to be doubtful about (5). But I (the author of this book) regard (5) as completely specified within the context supplied by the *illustration* at the beginning of this section, viz. a set of people some of whom are listening to the wireless. There are thus good reasons for holding, *in the given context*, that (1) to (5) are all propositions since (it is assumed) each one of them might be stated by a definite person on a definite occasion, and the statement so made will be true or it will be false, i.e. it is a proposition. Hesitation on this point – namely whether any or all of (1) to (4) are propositions or only schemas (so to speak) for propositions – may help us to see clearly the difference between a proposition and a propositional form (or schema for a proposition).

Consider the following expressions:

(1) Jack loves Jill.	(6) Someone hates Dick.
(2) Jack loves Ben.	(7) Someone hates someone.
(3) Tom loves Ben.	(8) *A* hates someone.
(4) Tom hates Ben.	(9) *A* hates *B*.
(5) Tom hates Dick.	(10) *x* hates *y*.

Clearly (1) to (5) are examples of propositions; (6) is a form of expression which might certainly be used to put forward a proposition by, say, someone who is trying to account for the happening of frequent disasters to Dick. (7) is an expression that would hardly be used except in some such context as the above. (8) and (9) are not propositions since it does not make sense to assert that a letter of the alphabet *hates*, and we had not adopted a convention that "*A*" was shorthand for *Ann* or "*B*" for *Ben*, or for any other proper name. (10) is a propositional form; if a constant be substituted for *x* and another constant for *y*, then the result would be a proposition – true or false according to the facts of the case stated in the proposition. In (10) we have an empty propositional form in which one constant, *hates*, is given along with two variables, *x*, *y*.

A variable – or more strictly a variable symbol – is a symbol which may be replaced by any one of a set of various constants, each of the constant symbols standing for a different individual. Thus, if we suppose ourselves to be limited to five persons whose names appear in propositions (1) to (5), and if, further, we suppose that these five propositions state truly the relations holding between them, then, if in (10) we replace *x* by one of these names and *y* by another until we have tried all the possibilities, the result would be in some instances a true, and in others, a false proposition. The constants thus replacing the variables are called *values of the variables.*

We may go a step further than in (10); we can let "hate" vary, and write '*xRy*'. This is a pure propositional form; it is wholly abstracted from particular persons, emotions, and so on; nothing is *specified*, but something is *represented*, namely, the form common to all propositions that state that two terms are related. *xRy* is a dyadic propositional form. *Tom is taller than Ben, Dante lived before Mazzini, David worshipped God* are instances of this form *xRy*, and the symbolization *xRy* may be regarded as symbolizing all such propositions.

A propositional form is a schema: symbols are used to show empty places waiting, as it were, to be filled; when all the places are filled the result is a proposition. Logically there are no restrictions with respect to the symbols we can use provided that the symbols do the work required of them. But it is convenient to make use of symbols that will be as easily grasped and remembered as possible. For this reason logicians use *x*, *y*, *z* (and other letters taken from the end of the English alphabet when more than three are required) to show the empty places for *values* of the variables. *R* is often used to stand for an unspecified relation; sometimes Φ, or other Greek capital letters are used, and the relational form is written $\Phi(x, y)$, $\Phi(x, y, z)$ according to the number of variables required, i.e. the number of terms needed to make sense of the relation. Φ may be regarded as an illustrative symbol.*

* Φ can itself be taken as a variable, e.g. Φ can be used to stand for any serial relation; it will then require two variables, so that we should write Φ (x, y).

§ 2. PROPOSITIONAL FUNCTIONS AND GENERAL PROPOSITIONS

Propositional forms are called by Bertrand Russell *propositional functions*, for they are in some respects analogous to mathematical functions. Whether we speak of 'functions' or 'forms' is not important. One use of propositional forms is to enable us to give an analysis of propositions involving the notions of *all of a class* and *some of a class*; in this connexion it is more convenient to speak of *functions* than of *forms*, but it must be emphasized that a propositional function is a propositional form – a schema which requires specification in order that a proposition may be obtained.

The propositions, *Ann is sad*, *Ben is sad*, *Tom is glad*, may all be regarded as having the same form – a characteristic is predicated of an individual; other examples are, *This is red*,* *That is square*. If we replace the subject-term, in any of these propositions, by x, then we have a propositional form, e.g. 'x is sad', containing one variable. The values substitutable for x are called *arguments* of the given propositional function.† The arguments are determinate entities; in the cases we shall be considering they are individuals, and the symbols used to name these individuals are called *constants*. Sometimes we use a, b, c, or other letters taken from the beginning of the alphabet, as illustrative symbols for definite specifiable individuals which are not, in fact, specified.‡ Thus Φa, $\Phi(a, b)$, each represent an unspecified but *constant* value of their respective functions.

* It is possible to argue that the five propositions given above are not *subject-predicate* propositions, and that, for example, *This is red* is a relational proposition, since (it may be contended) *red* is a term in an irreducible polyadic relation. I, myself, take this view of *red*; but the understanding of such a view presupposes that we understand what is *meant* by saying that *red* is a non-relational quality and *This is red* a simple subject-predicate proposition. As such we shall regard it here.

† This is a technical use of the word "argument", which has nothing to do with "argument" meaning a connected reasoning.

‡ Such symbols as a, b, c used in this way are analogous to *parameters* in mathematics. For example, in $ax + by - c = o$ (which symbolizes any linear correlation), a, b, c stand for variables denoting *any* numbers, just as x, y do: but they are to be distinguished from x, y, because a, b, c retain unchanged values throughout the same set of operations with x, y. Since, however, a, b, c were not given determinate values, the result is established for *any* numbers, so that a, b, c are properly variables (see, on this point, A. N. Whitehead, *Introduction to Mathematics*, pp. 68–9, 116–17).

There is a further point about notation with regard to which we may as well be clear, for the sake of accuracy. Sometimes we want to indicate the number of variables required by a given function: thus we distinguish $\Phi\hat{x}$* from $\Phi(\hat{x}, \hat{y})$, since the former requires one, the latter two, variables. If we were to write Φx, we should be indicating a variable value of $\Phi\hat{x}$, i.e. of the *function* represented by Φ. We shall not, in this book, need to make use of Φx, but we must notice the distinction. We might say that Φx represents *something that has the property* Φ, whereas $\Phi\hat{x}$ represents the *property that something has*. Φa indicates a constant but unspecified value of the function $\Phi\hat{x}$. We use Φa, as we used *Ann is sad*, in the preceding paragraph, merely illustratively; we were not talking about an actual person named 'Ann' whom we knew to be sad; we used 'Ann' as an example. Thus in 'Φa', 'Φ' stands for a definite but unspecified property, 'a' for a definite but unspecified individual that has the property.

The class of all possible arguments of a given propositional function is called the *domain* of the propositional function. A possible argument is one which, when used to complete the propositional form, makes sense. Consider, for instance, '$\hat{x}$ is French', and a set of possible values for x, viz. Voltaire, Cervantes, General de Gaulle, Pétain, Franklin Roosevelt. Relying upon our extra-logical knowledge, we can say that the substitution for x of any one of these five names would yield a significant proposition, but only the first, third, and fourth would yield a true proposition. Those arguments which yield a true proposition are said to *satisfy* the function – a convenient word taken from the terminology of mathematics; the others do not *satisfy* the function but they make *sense*, and must, therefore, be included in the domain. If we were to substitute for x, in '$\hat{x}$ is French', the word "wittiness", the result would be a nonsensical set of words. The significant propositions which are obtainable by substituting values of the variables are called the *range of significance* of the propositional function.

Suppose that in a certain class of university students

* "$\Phi\hat{x}$" may be read "Φx-cap".

reading logic in a given year there are twelve members, denoted respectively by the letters *a*, *b*, . . . *l*. On investigation it is found (we shall suppose) that *a* is a chess-player, *b* is a chess-player, and so on to *l* is a chess-player. This information could be given by the conjunction of twelve component propositions: *a is a chess-player, and b is a chess-player . . . and l is a chess-player.* This takes a long time to write or to say if we mention each of the twelve component conjuncts separately; the same information could be given by saying *All these logic-students are chess-players.* This proposition is equivalent to the conjunctive proposition with twelve conjuncts, for 'all these' shows not only that each of the students is a chess-player, but also that we have left none out. Such a proposition is enumerative, for each of the individuals about which the statement is made has been separately taken into account. Clearly this is possible only in the case of a limited class with all the members of which we can be acquainted. A class containing an infinite number of members could not even theoretically be thus enumerated, and a class containing an indefinitely large number of members cannot in fact be enumerated. At present we shall neglect these difficulties and consider only our limited domain.

We must notice that in using the expression "all these logic-students are chess-players" we have not stated a properly universal proposition, since "these" is nothing but shorthand for the names of the twelve students. Let us then say, "For all values of x, if x is a logic-student, then x is a chess-player." This expression is unrestrictedly general, but we claim to assert the proposition thus expressed only because we know that *a*, *b*, . . . *l* are each arguments satisfying the propositional functions, "$\hat{x}$ is a logic-student" and "$\hat{x}$ is a chess-player", and we assume we have left no one out.

Let us now suppose that we know further that among these students there are some who are musical. We can state this information in the form '*Either a is a chess-player and also musical or b . . .*', where the dots show that we need to write down the remaining ten alternants. We can express this by "For some value of x, x is a chess-player and is musical."

This is equivalent to *Some chess-players are musical*, where "some" has its usual meaning "at least one".

It will easily have been recognized that we have been using expressions which are suitable for expressing the universal and particular propositions of the traditional schedule. These are *general* propositions. It may seem odd, at the first glance, that a statement made about *some* members of a class should be a *general* proposition; it will not seem odd, however, as soon as we reflect that, in our example of the class of logic-students, the statement refers to some members in the domain, and it refers to them *quite generally*, i.e. it is not necessary to *specify* any one member. The assertion is that *somebody* in the domain is both a chess-player and musical. This is a general statement.

So far we have been considering a domain limited to twelve possible arguments for the propositional functions, '$\hat{x}$ is a chess-player', etc. Let us now forget this limitation and consider any two characteristics, which we shall symbolize respectively by "Φ" and "Ψ", and thus obtain the two propositional functions, $\Phi\hat{x}$, $\Psi\hat{x}$. Let a be some constant value for $\Phi\hat{x}$ and for $\Psi\hat{x}$. We can assert, *If* Φa, *then* Ψa. If it did not matter whether we chose a, or b, etc., but *any* argument in the domain would satisfy both functions, we can write *For all* x, *if* Φx, *then* Ψx. It is usual to abbreviate this to $(x) \,.\, \Phi x$ implies Ψx. An example that would fit into this form is *If an animal is ruminant, it is horned*, i.e. (x) . 'x is a ruminant animal' implies 'x is a horned animal'. This is a proposition and is thus either true or false.

We have seen that x is used for a variable symbol. There is an important difference between the way in which x is used in $(x) \,.\, \Phi x$ *implies* Ψx and in $\Phi\hat{x}$. We saw that $\Phi\hat{x}$ represents the property that something has; it is analogous to the traditional notion of an abstract term, e.g. "$\hat{x}$ is red" is roughly equivalent to *redness*, a property that something has. The form "$\hat{x}$ is red" is not a proposition; it asserts nothing until a value is substituted for x, in "$\hat{x}$ is red". The proposition yielded by the substitution of a value for x will depend for its truth or falsity upon *which* value is substituted. If *the* *page on which this is printed* were substituted for x, in "$\hat{x}$ is red", the resultant proposition would be false; if *the colour of blood* were substituted, the resultant proposition would be true. Hence, the nature of the term substituted is all-important for determining the truth or falsity of the resultant proposition. But in (x) . 'x is a flash of lightning' implies 'x is followed by thunder', the resultant proposition will be true *no matter what value is substituted for* x. Hence, in the latter expression, x is called *an apparent variable** because we do not need to give a specific value to x in order that the resultant proposition should be true; in "$\hat{x}$ is red" we do need to give a specific value, and the x is here called *a real variable.*

It is important to notice that (x) . 'x is a flash of lightning' implies 'x is followed by thunder', does not apply only to those terms which are *a flash of lightning*; what is asserted is that *if* x is a flash of lightning, x will be followed by thunder. We can *express* the same point by using the traditional symbolism: *All S is P*. This makes an assertion about what is *non-S* as well as about *S*; if this were not so, we could not use the method of *reductio ad absurdam*, which consists in using implications where, as it turns out, the antecedent is false. All that is required is that in (x) . '*x is an S*' *implies* '*x is a P*', we should know what can be *significantly* substituted for x in the propositional form. What can be significantly substituted depends upon the *meaning* of "*S*" and of "*P*"; or, if we use the Φ, Ψ symbolism, upon the *meaning* of "Φ" and "Ψ".

There is a point about which it is easy to be confused. The propositional form, or function, is *not* a proposition but, as we have seen, it is an empty schema, which does not assert anything. But if we can say that the propositional function holds for *any*, or for *some*, of its possible arguments, then we obtain a proposition. Thus the difference between a *real* and an *apparent* variable is extremely important; with the former we assert nothing, with the latter we assert a true or a false proposition.

We shall conclude this section by writing down the four traditional propositions in the symbolism associated with this

* The term "apparent variable" is due to Peano.

doctrine of propositional functions. Let *S* stand for the terms which satisfy $\Phi\hat{x}$, and *P* for the terms which satisfy $\Psi\hat{x}$. Then we obtain

'*SaP*' means $(x) \, . \, \Phi x$ implies Ψx.
'*SeP*' means $(x) \, . \, \Phi x$ implies not-Ψx.
'*SiP*' means $(\exists x) \, . \, \Phi x$ and Ψx.
'*SoP*' means $(\exists x) \, . \, \Phi x$ and not-Ψx.

The new symbol '∃' here introduced will be easily read, since we are already acquainted both with the traditional symbolism (given on the left-hand side) and with the analysis of particular propositions as asserting 'For at least *one* value of x, Φx and Ψx'. Thus '$(\exists x)$' can be read 'There is an x such that . . .' or 'For some value of x . . .'

These different forms of symbolism are merely *notationally* different. But, as anyone acquainted with the history of musical notation or of mathematical notation knows, a good notation brings out the essential points in a way that makes them easier to grasp. The advantage of the notation with x is that it shows us clearly that what we *assert* in these general propositions is a connexion of properties and that the assertion is significant even when we do not know the individuals characterized by them. Like the notation used in Chapter V ($S\bar{P} = 0$, etc.) this notation once more emphasizes that the difference between affirmative and negative propositions is unimportant, whereas the difference between particulars and universals is fundamental. Finally, it reminds us that the *A*, *E*, *I*, *O* propositions are by no means *simple* propositions.

§ 3. MATERIAL IMPLICATION AND ENTAILING

In our illustration of the class of logic-students, we felt confident in asserting that (x) . '*x is a logic-student*' implies '*x is a chess-player*', for we were dealing with a very limited domain. Knowing (as we do long before we began to study logic) that it is, as we say, 'a mere matter of chance' that all those who studied logic were chess-players, we shall not wish to assert that it *follows* from the fact that someone studies logic, that he is also a chess-player. But, within our domain, we could assert that *If x is a logic-student, then x is a chess-player*; this is equivalent to *Either x is not a logic-student* or *x is a chess-player.* In writing out the *A* and *E* forms above, we used "implies". We saw (in Chapter II) that a proposition of the form *If p, then q* can be interpreted as meaning *p implies q*, in the sense that *p* cannot be true and *q* false. This fits in with our assertion about the logic-students.

But "cannot" might mean "could not" or it might be interpreted as meaning "cannot, the facts being what they are". The second gives a much weaker meaning to "*p* cannot be true and *q* false". To this interpretation of *If p, then q*, Bertrand Russell has given the name *material implication.* This can be defined as follows:

"*p* materially implies *q*" means "either *p* is false or *q* is true".

We shall contrast material implication with a stricter relation illustrated in the following examples: (1) *If a triangle is isosceles, then its base angles are equal*; (2) *If this is red, this is coloured*; (3) *If A is father of B, then B is a child of A*; (4) *If B and C have the same parents and C is male, then C is brother of B*; (5) *If all detectives are quick-witted and no quick-witted people are easily hoodwinked, then no detectives are easily hoodwinked.* The relation that holds between the antecedent (i.e. the implying proposition) and the consequent (i.e. the implied proposition) in each of the above examples is a relation of necessary implication. It is, it will be observed, the relation that holds between the premiss (whether simple or compound) and the conclusion of a valid inference. In all the examples except (1) the antecedent alone suffices to necessitate the consequent; the latter follows logically from the former alone. In (1) there is presupposed the axioms of Euclidean geometry; this being understood, we can say of (1), as of the other four examples, that the antecedent *could not* be true and the consequent false. For this relation Professor G. E. Moore has used the word '*entailing*', and this word is now used by many logicians to signify the relation that holds between *p*, and *q* when *p could not be true and q be false.* But this is what we most often mean when we say '*p* implies *q*', and we so used "implies" in Chapter I. Hence, in order to distinguish *entailing* from the weaker relation, we shall follow Bertrand

Russell, and shall call the matter-of-fact relation *material implication.*

It should be noticed that *If . . . then . . .* is ambiguous, since it may be used to signify *materially implies* or it may be used to signify *entails*. Such a sentence as 'If it is cold to-morrow, I shall stay indoors' is quite naturally used to state that I shall not as a matter of fact go out if it is cold; this sentence would not normally be understood to mean that *its being cold tomorrow* necessitates *my staying indoors*, however firm my resolution may be. On the other hand it is not unnatural to say, 'If Mary and Jane are second cousins, then at least one parent of each are first cousins', and here the antecedent does necessitate the consequent, for the former could not be true and the latter false; i.e. the antecedent entails the consequent. It is, accordingly, not surprising that there should have been a good deal of confusion with regard to the interpretation of *If . . . then . . .*, and a failure to see clearly that *entailing* and *material implication* are different relations. Material implication is the weakest of all relations in virtue of which one proposition can in any sense be said to imply another; it does, indeed, lay down one *essential* condition of implication in every sense in which we could say that one proposition *implies* another, namely, that if p is true and q false, then in no sense can p imply q.

At this point it is notationally convenient to introduce some shorthand symbols. In defining "p materially implies q" we used the logical notions of *either . . . or*, and of the *negation* of a given proposition; to say "p is false" denies, or negates, p; hence, we can write the contradictory of p as *not-p*. Hitherto we have used the bar-symbol and have written "$\bar{p}$" to mean "p is false". We shall now use the symbol introduced by Bertrand Russell in *Principia Mathematica*; thus "not-p" is written "$\sim p$". This is merely notationally different from "$\bar{p}$", as "IV" is notationally different from "4". The notion expressed by "either . . . or . . ." will be written "v", so that "either p or q" will be written "$p \vee q$".* We shall now

* The symbol "v" is derived from the letter *v*, which is the first letter of *vel*, Latin for "or". It is unfortunate that Russell and the symbolic logicians generally call this relation *disjunction*.

rewrite the definition of material implication in the linguistic form:

$$p \supset q \,.=.\, \sim p \vee q \; df.$$

The symbol $\supset$ is shorthand for "materially implies"; ". = ... *df*" is shorthand for "is the defined equivalent of". The student should have no difficulty in reading this expression. It must be remembered that the expression on the right-hand side, the definiens, states the meaning given *by definition* to the expression on the left-hand side. Whenever we define an expression we must, if we are to be consistent in our usage of words, keep to the definition; hence, when we say "p materially implies q", or write "$p \supset q$", we mean exactly what "$\sim p \vee q$" expresses, viz. that "*either* p is false *or* q is true"; the *either . . . or* is non-exclusive.

Bearing this definition in mind, we shall see that material implication holds between propositions of which neither would ordinarily be said to imply the other; ordinarily, we understand by "implies" a relation that holds between propositions which are relevantly connected; by *relevant connexion* we probably mean a connexion in the *meaning* of the propositions. To this consideration we shall return after we have examined some examples of material implication. In stating these examples we take for granted that we *know* (independently of anything we have learnt from logic) which of the propositions is true, which false; we also know that every proposition either is true or is false.

(*a*) 2 + 2 = 4.
(*b*) Italy is an island.
(*c*) A cat has ten legs.
(*d*) Columbia University is in New York.
(*e*) A triangle has three sides.
(*f*) Rome is in England.
(*g*) 6 + 41 = 57.
(*h*) The Pope is a woman.

The examples have been indexed by small letters of the alphabet in parentheses, for the purpose of summing up the results in a small space; hence (*a*), etc., will be used to *name* the propositions.* We can see:

(*a*) $\supset$ (*e*); (*b*) $\supset$ (*f*); (*c*) $\supset$ (*g*); (*d*) does not materially imply (*h*), since (*d*) is true and (*h*) false. But in the other

* In reading the statements that follow the student should mentally substitute for (*a*), the proposition *2 + 2 = 4*, and so on for each index letter.

three cases cited *either* the first is false *or* the second is true, and, since *either . . . or . . .* is not exclusive, we can admit the case when *both* the first is false *and* the second is true. The excluded case is when the *first* is *true* and the *second* is *false*, for anything implied by a true proposition is true: this condition, we saw, is essential to every possible meaning assignable to the word "implies".

It is easy to see that the eight propositions given provide other examples, e.g. $(a) \supset (d)$; $(b) \supset$ each of the other propositions and so on.

We can state these considerations in another way. Every proposition has two possibilities with regard to truth and falsity, namely, *truth*, *falsity*. These are called the *truth-values*. There are, with two propositions, four combinations: (1) both true; (2) both false; (3) and (4) one true, the other false. Using T for *truth*, and F for *falsity*, we will write them down as follows:

p	q
T	T
T	F
F	T
F	F

Using this notation we will write down the compound propositions, obtained by combining p *with* q, (i) by $\supset$, (ii) by v, (iii) conjunctively, which we shall symbolize by a dot (.), so that "$p \cdot q$" means "p and q".

p	q	$p \supset q$	$p \vee q$	$p \cdot q$
T	T	T	T	T
T	F	F	T	F
F	T	T	T	F
F	F	T	F	F

From this table we can see at a glance that the conjunction of p with q (i.e. $p \cdot q$) excludes three of the possibilities; but $p \supset q$ excludes only one possibility, viz. p *true* with q *false*;

$p \vee q$ also excludes only one possibility, viz. *both p and q false*. We are interested in the interpretation of $p \supset q$, with regard to truth or falsity; we see that any proposition, true or false, is *materially implied* by any other false proposition, whilst any true proposition is *materially implied* by any other proposition, true or false. This is in accordance with the results we found when considering the eight significant propositions given in the list above.

This result has been called paradoxical; indeed, the conclusions we have just summed up have been called 'the paradoxes of implication'. There is, however, no paradox, for a *paradox* is a statement apparently absurd or self-contradictory but possibly well-grounded. *Provided we keep in mind the definition of "material implication"*, these results do not even seem absurd. What is there absurd in saying that, given the compound proposition *either p is false or q is true*, then this compound proposition is itself true if (i) p is false and q true, (ii) p is true and q true, (iii) p is false and q is false? Clearly this is not in the least absurd. What is absurd is to define *materially implies* as we have done and then to forget the definition, drop out the qualification indicated by "materially", and thus think of *implies* as equivalent to *entails*. These so-called 'paradoxical' consequences, as Professor G. E. Moore has pointed out, 'appear to be paradoxical, solely because, if we use "implies" in any ordinary sense, they are quite certainly false'.* It is difficult to use a very familiar word in a wholly unfamiliar and technical sense without at times falling back into the familiar meaning which has been *excluded by definition*. This is the simple mistake committed by those who allow themselves to be puzzled by apparent paradoxes resulting from the definition of "material implication".

For certain technical procedures in mathematical logic it is convenient to define "implication" in terms of *negation* and *either . . . or . . .*; thus, for these purposes, "implication" means "material implication". It should be noticed that whenever it is true that *p entails q*, then it is true that $p \supset q$, for $\supset$ is a weaker relation than *entailing*; it holds whenever *entailing* holds, but the converse is not true.

* *Philosophical Studies*, p. 295.

It is not essential to define $\supset$ in terms of *either . . . or*; it can be equally well defined in terms of negation and conjunction; thus:

$$p \supset q \,.\!=.\, \sim(p \,.\, \sim q) df.$$

This may be read: "p materially implies q" is the defined equivalent of "It is false that p is true and q is false."*

The following equivalences are worth noticing:

$$p \supset q \,.\!\equiv.\, \sim p \vee q \,.\!\equiv.\, \sim(p \,.\, \sim q).$$

It should be observed that these three equivalences have already been stated, in Chapter III, § 1, as normal equivalents of composite propositions. These equivalences are in no way affected by our definition of $\supset$, for the relation of material implication suffices to yield the equivalent alternative and disjunctive propositions with which we are already familiar. It is convenient for certain purposes to use the shorthand symbols that appear above, but it is not essential.

§ 4. EXTENSIONAL AND INTENSIONAL INTERPRETATIONS OF LOGICAL RELATIONS

Our discussion of material implication should have made clear that knowledge of the truth or of the falsity of p, q is alone relevant to determining whether $p \supset q$: provided p is false, q can be any proposition; provided q is true, p can be any proposition. Hence, we are entirely unconcerned with what p, q may be about; thus, we pay no attention to what is commonly called the meaning of the proposition. Hence, we saw, *Italy is an island* $\supset$ *The Pope is a woman* because both these propositions are false. (*The Pope is a man* $\supset$ *Italy is an island*)† is a false statement; the first proposition is true, the second false; hence the first cannot be related by $\supset$ to the second. *The facts being what they are* we discover that *The Pope is a man* does not materially imply *Italy is an island.* If a

* The fact that we can give alternative definitions of $p \supset q$ illustrates the fact that no one of these definitions is fundamental. We can take our choice whether we shall regard *either . . . or* or *both . . . and* as fundamental; then, combining with *negation* we get the definitions given above.

† Parentheses are used here to show that the two propositions are combined into a single statement which is asserted, as a whole, to be false.

geological convulsion broke off Italy from the continent, then either of these two propositions would imply the other. Thus, it is what is actually the case that determines whether a material implication holds. Another way of saying this is to say that whether a proposition is true or is false depends upon what the facts are. It is a fact that Italy is a peninsula; hence, *Italy is an island* is in discordance with, *Italy is a peninsula* is in accordance with, this fact. Looking at a proposition merely from the point of view of whether it is true or false is said to be taking the proposition *extensionally*. We are supposed to know (*how* does not matter for our purpose) whether the truth-value of a given proposition is *truth* or is *falsity*. That is all we need to know.

Suppose, meditating upon the frailty of human nature, we say 'To err is human'. Let us now make the somewhat rash assumption that this is equivalent to 'All men err'. What does this proposition assert?

(1) We attempt to analyse it as follows: *Either A is not human or A errs; and Either B is not human or B errs . . . and Either X is not human or X errs.* The dots show that we have left out many cases. Now, *Either A is not human or A errs* is equivalent (by definition) to *A is human* ⊃ *A errs*; and so on, in each of the cases cited. Now *A*, *B* . . . *X* belong to the class *human beings*; hence, we can drop out our reference to the individuals *A*, *B*, etc., and say *x is human* ⊃ *x errs, whatever x may be.* This is an instance of generalized material implication, i.e. a conjunction of singular statements asserting that a material implication holds. Russell calls this '*formal implication*', in order to contrast it with the conjunction of singular propositions, true or false, which fulfil the condition required for material implication. No new concept of implication is involved in passing from material implications to formal implications (as thus understood); a formal implication is simply a collection of material implications, in which the truth or falsity of the resultant statement depends entirely upon the truth-values of the singular statements constituting the components of the compound proposition.

At this point we are forced to ask ourselves whether we were justified in saying that, since *A*, *B*, . . . *X* belong to the class *human beings*, we can omit further reference to them and assert that *whatever x may be, x is human* $\supset$ *x errs*. For this procedure rests upon the assumption that what is true of a collection of individuals which are members of a given class is true of *all* members of the class, including those not in the subclass which constituted the original collection. Clearly this does not hold. For instance, to say 'whatever is true of a subclass of humans is true of all humans' is clearly false; Russians are a subclass of humans, Frenchmen are another subclass, and there are many things true about Russians that are false about Frenchmen, and conversely. It is not necessary to multiply instances.

(2) We thus attempt another analysis. 'Although it is not true', we may urge, 'that all human beings have all the characteristics true of all Russians, this is irrelevant since the characteristic we are concerned with is the *liability to make mistakes*; there is an essential connexion between *human nature* and *liability to make mistakes*; it follows from the fact that human nature is what it is that human beings err.'

If we give this answer, then we are taking an intensional view; we are asserting that there is a connexion between *being human* and *erring* which can be apprehended without examining vast collections of human beings and finding out in each case that *this*, *that*, and *the other* human being errs. We may be willing to admit that we should not have noticed this connexion unless we had been confronted with actual instances of it; but that is true also of, say, the connexion between *being an angle in a semi-circle* and *being a right-angle*. But, once we have noticed it, we are asserting a connexion that is not merely a statement of the coincidence of true singular statements.

This second answer suggests that we might reformulate our original proposition thus: '*To be human*' *implies* '*to err*'. This reformulation has the advantage of showing that we are *abstracting* the characteristics *being human*, *erring*, from the instances which exemplify them; thus, we are considering these characteristics in a contemplative way, not taking note of their exemplification in actual cases. Or, as we said just now, we are regarding the proposition *intensionally*, as asserting a *connexion of meaning*. Clearly, then, "implies" will not be interpreted as "materially implies". Are we, then, to interpret "implies" in '*To be human*' *implies* '*to err*' as *entails*?

This question raises a problem of great importance to which no decisive answer can be given, and of which no adequate discussion is possible within the limits of this book. Enough, perhaps, may be said to make clear the sort of questions this problem raises.

Let us go back to the examples of entailing, given at the beginning of § 3. We observed in the case of each of the five examples, that the antecedent *could* not be true and the consequent false; further, that the antecedent alone sufficed to necessitate the consequent. The word 'observed', used in the last sentence, is appropriate. We could not claim to have done more than to adduce examples which the reader would admit were examples of a relation entirely different from material implication. We can now add that the truth of the compound propositions adduced as examples is entirely independent of the make-up of the actual world. That the consequent followed, in each case, from the antecedent could be known without knowing whether the component propositions were true or false. Consider example (5), for instance: the entailing relation holds between the compound antecedent and the consequent; the whole proposition is an example of a syllogism in *Celarent*. Thus one example of entailing is the relation of the premisses to the conclusion in a valid syllogism. Example (2) – *If this is red, this is coloured* – is quite different. This is an example of connected *meanings*; we so use "red" that to say 'this is red' and to deny 'this is coloured' is to say what is self-contradictory.

It can hardly be maintained that this is true of the connexion between *being human* and *erring*. We conclude that we cannot hold that 'To be human' *entails* 'to err'. Nevertheless, we need not rest content with the view that *All human beings err* can be adequately analysed into a set of material implications stating *Either it is false that A is human or it is true that A errs*, and so on, throughout the remainder of the individuals *B . . . X*. There is another alternative left us. We shall be bold enough to maintain that the characteristic of *being human* is relevant to the characteristic of *erring*, in a way in which *The Pope is a man* is not relevant to $2 + 2 = 4$, although – since they are both true – these two propositions materially imply one another, and are thus materially equivalent.

What the relation of material implication demands is solely truth-values; what the relation of entailing requires is a necessary connexion between that which entails and that which is entailed. We are now insisting that there is another connexion that may be found between propositions intensionally interpreted, namely, a connexion of relevance: the *meaning* of the premiss must be *relevantly connected* with the *meaning* of the conclusion.

And what, it may be asked, do we mean by being *relevantly* connected? Some attempt to answer this question will be made in Chapter VIII. We shall scarcely be able to claim that we have done more than to pose the problem; certainly we shall not solve it. But to see that there is a problem to solve is to have taken the first step essential to solving it. So far as the author of this book is concerned, this first step is likely to be also the last.

CHAPTER VIII

Logical Principles and the Proof of Propositions

§ 1. THE TRADITIONAL LAWS OF THOUGHT

In every chapter of this book we have been engaged in reasoning; we have – to use a popular phrase – 'put two and two together and obtained four'. We have judged that, if certain propositions are true, others are also; if certain propositions are false, others are also; again, if certain propositions are false, others are true. We have not only judged that these conclusions *are* so, but that they *must* be so. In Chapter I we pointed out that to judge in this manner is characteristic of rational beings; it is the mental activity we call reasoning. When we reason correctly, our reasoning is in accordance with logical principles.

Three of these principles were formulated clearly by Aristotle.* They are traditionally known as the 'three Laws of Thought'. They may be stated as follows:

1. *The Law of Identity:* Everything is what it is.
2. *The Law of Contradiction:* A thing cannot both be and not be so and so.
3. *The Law of Excluded Middle:* A thing either is or is not so and so.

This statement of the Laws is appropriate to the consideration of the singular proposition *This A is B*; Aristotle was thinking of the most elementary and fundamental characteristics of predication, in its purely formal aspect. They can be reformulated as they concern propositions, implication, and truth and falsity:

(1) Every proposition is equivalent to itself (i.e. every

* See *Analytica Priora*, 47*a*, 9; *Metaphysica*, 1006*a*, 7; *De Interpretatione*, 18*b*, 1–5 Cf. *M.I.L.*, Ch. XXIV, § 2. For a detailed discussion of the traditional laws see J. N. Keynes, *Formal Logic*, Appendix B, pp. 450–67.

proposition implies and is implied by itself), *Principle of Identity*.*

(2) No proposition is both true and false.

(3) Every proposition is either true or false.

This formulation brings out the essential relation of the three laws; they cannot, however, be reduced to a single principle, since the deduction of, for instance, (3) from (1) or from (2) requires the independent notions of *falsity*, or of *negation*, which cannot be defined without using the principles themselves. Both (2) and (3) are required in order to define the *relation of contradiction* between propositions, since contradictory propositions are defined as propositions which cannot *both* be true but *one* must be true.

These "three laws of thought" have been subjected to severe criticism by modern logicians; these criticisms may be summed up in the somewhat Pickwickian formula: 'They are not *laws*, they are not laws of *thought*, and they are not *the* laws of thought since there are others no less essential.' We shall examine these criticisms briefly. The first two points may be taken together. Certainly, the 'laws of thought' are not statements of psychological laws, i.e. statements of the ways in which we do think. Unfortunately, we often contradict ourselves, we often think (or behave as though we believed) that there is a mean between truth and falsity. The "laws" are not made true by the way in which men think; they are statements of how men *ought* to think, and will think if, and in so far as, men are thinking rationally. Accordingly, it is far better *not* to use the description 'laws of thought'; it is better to call them 'logical principles'. "Laws" suggest at best *uniformities* in mind and nature, at worst *commands*. Unfortunately, no one has the power to command us to think logically; even were this not so, we have not always the power to obey such a command. Our thinking is in part determined by our emotional attitudes and our deep-seated prejudices.

Certainly 'the three Laws' are not sufficient for regulating our thinking; it is undoubtedly true that 'consecutive thought and coherent argument are impossible' without these laws,

* For reasons given later on this page, it is better to call these *Principles* and not *Laws*.

but the traditional Logicians were mistaken in singling these out as though they were in any sense more fundamental than other logical principles. We cannot here attempt to state all those other principles which are clearly exemplified in ordinary reasoning; it must suffice to mention only three:

(4) *Principle of Syllogism:* If p implies q, and q implies r, then p implies r. This is the principle which underlies the *dicta* of the traditional syllogism, but it has a much wider application.

(5) *Principle of Deduction* (sometimes called the *Principle of Inference*)*:* If p implies q, and p is true, then q is true. This principle permits the omission of an implying proposition (the antecedent) provided that the implying proposition is true; it is in accordance with this principle that conclusions are drawn from true premisses in valid arguments.

(6) *The Applicative Principle* (or *Principle of Substitution*)*:* Whatever can be asserted of *any instance however chosen* can be asserted about *any given instance.* W. E. Johnson has said of this principle that 'it may be said to formulate what is involved in the intelligent use of "every" '.*

The last three principles are exemplified in all chains of reasoning, whilst the first three are also exemplified in all coherent reasoning. These principles do not *suffice* but they are all essential to sound reasoning.

Various special criticisms have been made of the three principles known as 'the traditional laws of thought', most of which rest upon extraordinary muddles. Thus it has been argued that '*A* is not necessarily *A*, for *A* is changing all the time, and anyhow, everyone knows that *A* is always *B*'. The point probably intended in this comment is that *things* change and that every *thing* has various different properties. The principle is not in the least in conflict with these contentions. Unless *A* were identifiable *as A*, it would make nonsense to say that *A is B.* In the form in which this principle concerns propositions, it is clearly true, since, unless p implies p, p could be both true and false. This takes us to the principle of contradiction, so that the principle of identity stands or falls with it.

* W. E. Johnson, *Logic*, Pt. II, p. 9.

More serious criticisms have been made of the principle of excluded middle. We shall first, however, consider an objection that is so easily refuted that it should never have been made by competent logicians.

(i) It is argued that 'things change insensibly', so that sometimes it is not possible to assert that the thing has, or has not, a given characteristic; e.g. *this tomato is ripe*, *this tomato is not ripe* may neither be true, and yet these propositions are formal contradictories. The point lies in the last statement. Are the propositions contradictories, or only *apparent* contradictories? That will entirely depend upon what we *mean* by "ripe". Is there a criterion of *ripeness*? If so, then the propositions are contradictory, and there seems no reason to deny that both cannot be true. If there is no criterion of *ripeness*, then "ripe" is like "bald", namely, a word used to signify any *one* of a range of degrees in which a characteristic may be present. Some words are properly *vague*, i.e. are used to signify a characteristic capable of a continuous series of intermediate degrees. It is illogical to demand that a sharp distinction should be drawn between that which possesses and that which does not possess such a characteristic. We may not know where 'to draw the line', and in some cases *no line can be drawn*. But, if it be granted that "bald" can be precisely defined in terms of number of hairs, then *bald* and *not-bald* are proper contradictories; if it cannot be thus precisely defined then these are not proper contradictories.*

(ii) The most serious objection to the principle relates to its use with regard to *propositions*. It is argued that in addition to the *true* and the *false* there is also the *doubtful* (or the *undecided*).

We may begin by noticing that this looks like a cross division. The division of propositions into *true*, *false* is dichotomous, i.e. *true*, *false* are mutually exclusive and collectively exhaustive. It is possible to argue that much discussion still centres round the exact meaning of "true" and "false". This is so, but it is at least clear that in every ordinary usage the division is dichotomous. We can easily

* I have discussed this point in more detail in *Thinking to Some Purpose*, pp. 138–42 (3rd edition).

obtain a four-fold division of propositions into: (1) true and known to be true, (2) false and known to be false, (3) true but not known to be true or known to be false, (4) false but not known to be false or known to be true. Now we can certainly say that (3) and (4) yield *the doubtful* (or *the undecided* in the sense that *we* are not able to decide whether the proposition is true or is false). But it is clear that (3) and (4) both fall under our original dichotomous division. A proposition is true if in accordance with the facts; false if not in accordance. We may very well not yet know, or never be able to know, which of these possibilities is the case, but that we can be thus ignorant of the facts has not the slightest tendency to show that any proposition can be neither in accordance with the facts (i.e. true) nor not in accordance with the facts (i.e. false).

It must not be supposed that the above remarks are an attempt to *prove* the principle of excluded middle; if what has been said had been offered as a proof it would certainly be circular. All that has been attempted is to show that the objection has no point, and is, in fact, guilty of the fallacy of cross division.

It may, however, be further argued that, even if the assertion that a proposition is true if in accordance with the facts, and false if not, be accepted, the principle of excluded middle still fails, since the *facts* may be undecided. This contention rests upon a sheer mistake. It has been argued most strongly in connexion with facts about the future. Let us consider the proposition, *Hitler will be a prisoner in London on March 10, 1943*. This proposition is asserted today (September 27, 1942) by the author of this book (who would like it to be true but is afraid it is false). The comment in parentheses is the sort of comment we all of us make at times with regard to propositions about the future. The view we are now considering is that the proposition about Hitler (henceforth to be symbolized by *p*) is neither true nor false. There seem to be two different reasons urged in favour of this view.

(1) *p* is not known to be true and is not known to be false. This must be granted, but as we have just seen, this does not imply that it is neither.

(2) If we argue that p is either true or false, we are asserting that it either is the case that Hitler will be a prisoner in London on March 10 of next year or it is not the case; and this presupposes that there are past and future facts which necessitate that he will be a prisoner in London next March, if p is true; or it presupposes that there are past and future acts which necessitate that he will not be a prisoner in London next March, if p is false. But, it is argued, this assumes the truth of what is called 'determinism', namely, that everything that happens is necessarily determined by past events. Determinism, it is urged, is open to dispute.

This argument entirely fails to establish the required conclusion. Whether Hitler's future movements are, or are not, determined by past and present facts, the statement that he will be in London on a certain date is a *factual* statement. If determinism is correct, then it is factually (or causally) necessary that he will be in London on the given date; *or* it is factually (or causally) impossible that he will be in London on the given date. Now, whichever of these is the case, either the facts necessarily determine *that p is true* or the facts necessarily determine *that p is false*; if, however, determinism is false, then past and present facts in no sense determine Hitler's future movements, so that he may, or may not, be in London on the specified date. But whether p is *true* or is *false* is not in any way affected by the answer to the question: 'are there facts *now* which determine future facts?' To suppose otherwise is to confuse (i) causal necessity with logical necessity, (ii) truth with our knowledge of the truth.

Certain logicians have argued that if there is no available method of determining whether a given proposition is true or is false, then it is neither. Examples of such undecidable propositions are: *Julius Caesar sneezed as he entered the Senate for the last time. All numbers of the form* $2^{2n+9} + 1$ *are factorable.* This contention again confuses *truth* with *knowledge of truth.* Some who have taken this view with regard to undecidable propositions have, it seems, wished to maintain that unless the truth of a proposition can be verified or falsified, then it is neither true nor false. To maintain this is simply to substitute for the notion of *truth* the notion of *verifiability*. Here it must suffice to assert that this is a question of terminology, and nothing in the contentions of these logicians suggests that anything is to be gained by this change in the meanings of these words.*

§ 2. NECESSARY AND FACTUAL PROPOSITIONS

We saw in the last chapter (§ 4), that we can regard propositions from an extensional or from an intensional point of view. When we adopt the latter point of view we pay attention to the *meaning* of the proposition, that is, to what the proposition states; from the former point of view we consider only its truth or its falsity. The mere fact that two propositions are both true (or both false), which entitles us to assert that one materially implies the other, does not give to the combination thus made any unity of meaning. That is why it surprises us to discover that *Italy is an island* ⊃ *The Pope is a woman*, or that *2 + 2 = 4* ⊃ *A triangle has three sides*. We cannot easily bring the two component propositions together in thought; the truth of the implying proposition does not in any way limit the truth or the falsity of the implied proposition; only, *if it so happens* that the implied proposition is false and the implying proposition is true, then the former does not materially imply the latter. Whether ⊃ holds or not we discover only after we know the truth-values of the component propositions. As we saw in the last chapter, a certain geological change in the structure of the continent would make it true that *Italy is an island* no longer materially implies *The Pope is a woman*, since the latter proposition is false. We shall, accordingly, say that *material implication* is a *factual relation*; whether it holds or not depends upon the actual constitution of the world. *Entailing*, on the contrary, is a necessary relation.

* This position is that of most Logical Positivists. The questions raised are more properly philosophical than strictly logical, and cannot be discussed here. The objections to the principle of excluded middle, discussed above, have been dealt with in a masterly fashion by Professor C. A. Baylis, in an article entitled, 'Are some Propositions neither true nor false?' (*Philosophy of Science*, Vol. 3, No. 2, April 1936). This article is so clearly and beautifully written that even elementary students may be able to profit from reading it.

Consider the following propositions:

(1) Every body continues in a state of rest or of moving uniformly in a straight line, except in so far as it is subject to external forces.
(2) All planets move in elliptical orbits.
(3) Men must die.
(4) Cows are ruminants.
(5) This red rose is not red.
(6) Water freezes at 0° Centigrade.
(7) An angle in a semi-circle is a right angle.
(8) Prices are regulated by the law of supply and demand.
(9) Hitler entered Prague on March 15, 1939.
(10) It rained in Tintagel on September 28, 1942.
(11) An igloo is an Eskimo dome-shaped hut.

It is easy to see that these propositions are of very different kinds. Should any one of them be disputed, the evidence required to justify its assertion would be entirely different from the evidence required in the case of some of the others. Let us examine them from this point of view. Our first step should be to sort them out, so as to bring together those which require the same sort of evidence in order to justify their assertion. For this purpose we need a principle of division.*

Ought we not first to inquire in the case of each proposition whether it is true or false? This is not essential. Consider (10) for instance: the evidence required to establish its truth (if it is true) is of *the same sort* as the evidence required to establish its falsity (if it is false). I, the author, who am now writing this sentence, assert that proposition (10) is true. The evidence I offer is (i) today is September 28, 1942, (ii) I see rain falling each time I look up from my desk, (iii) I remember seeing the rain falling this morning. Now both (i) and (ii) may be questioned, i.e. evidence in support of these assertions may also be asked for. There is not space to pursue this illustration in detail here. It must suffice to say that my evidence for (i) is based upon my acceptance of

* The student is recommended to pause at this point, and to sort out the propositions for himself.

my calendar as being correctly marked; my evidence for (ii) is sense-experience. I quite literally *see* rain falling. It is not to be denied that people sometimes *think* it is raining when it is not, but the final, and only evidence that can be offered is – seeing and feeling rain falling. (iii) may seem to be more dubious, but in fact it is not. My reliance about so recent a memory is not less great and is not (so far as I can introspectively judge) different in kind from my reliance upon the direct evidence of my sense-experience. It is characteristic of the sort of evidence constituted by both (ii) and (iii) that it is available only for myself. (Here "*I*" could, under suitable conditions, stand for some other person who is having the *same sort* of experience.) If this be granted, then the truth of proposition (10) cannot, at a subsequent date, be established by exactly the same sort of evidence, or rather, there would be *needed in addition* evidence of another sort, e.g. an entry in someone's diary, the report of the meteorological office, and so on. The entry in the diary could be regarded as reliable evidence only if the testimony of the writer could be established as acceptable. And *his* statement is based (if correct) upon such evidence as that offered in (ii) and (iii). It is not unlikely that no entry in anyone's diary, no sufficiently detailed report from the meteorological office, will be able to be cited in evidence of proposition (10) by the time this book is printed; detailed daily reports of the weather in a small Cornish village are not likely to be made. But, whether this is so or not, that is the sort of evidence that would be required to establish the truth of (10) at some date subsequent to the present.

This is an example of a singular factual proposition; so, too, is proposition (9). The event stated in (9) is an event of considerable importance in the history of Europe, and consequently, of the world today. It is reasonable to suppose that there will be an abundance of testimony which can be used as evidence of its truth. If I (the author*) have made a slip in the date, exactly the same sort of evidence will establish

* No apology should be needed for the author's intrusion into the text at this point. The purpose is to call the reader's attention to the need (when occasion demands) to *verify* the statements made to him, and to point out to him that certain propositions need more careful scrutiny than others.

its falsity. In the case of both (9) and (10) the sort of evidence required can be summed up under the three heads: (*a*) direct experience, (*b*) reliance upon testimony which involves (α) *someone else's* direct experience, (β) some method of testing the reliability of such testimony, (γ) general principles of inference. Propositions (9) and (10), different though they are, resemble each other in one important respect, namely, the evidence for their truth includes, in each case, someone's direct experience at a specified date. It is probable that for years to come the indirect evidence of testimony will be available to establish (9), but not available to establish (10). This difference has nothing to do with the logical nature of these propositions; both are singular factual propositions; their difference has to do with the relative importance of their truth for the affairs of men. With that difference the logician is not at all concerned.

Propositions (2), (3), (4), (6) are also factual propositions but they are not *singular* propositions; each of them involves generalization. Without generalization no science is possible. In the next chapter we shall examine what is involved in generalization; here it is enough to point out that generalization involves an inferential leap: it is the passage from direct observation that certain observed instances of the class *C* each have the property *f*, to the conclusion that every member of *C* has *f*. The four propositions now being discussed are the results of such an inferential process. But they are not all on the same level. *Cows are ruminants*, taken thus in isolation from any context of discussion, may be regarded as a statement that *cows* fall within a certain superclass in a biological classification; or it may be regarded as a generalization from the observation of particular cows. The latter interpretation takes the proposition to be at a more primitive level than the former; by the time we are able to assign a biological class to its place in a classification a certain amount of systematization has been achieved. (2), (3), and (6) may be taken together, so far as our present purpose is concerned. Of each it is true that (i) it involves generalization from direct observation of particular instances, (ii) the evidence for its truth is in large part derived from its place within the system of the special science to which it belongs.* (8) is also a factual generalization but, as every student of economics will readily admit, it cannot be truly asserted without considerable qualification. For example, in Great Britain today, the price of many commodities is regulated by governmental fiat. Even apart from this complication, questions peculiar to the so-called 'social sciences' will force themselves upon our attention once we begin seriously to examine what is the evidence upon which the assertion, *Prices are regulated by the law of supply and demand*, rests.†

Proposition (1) would at one time have been regarded as a generalization from the observed behaviour of bodies extrapolated to fit ideal (i.e. imagined) conditions in which no actual body can ever be. The way in which this statement has been formulated suggests, what is in fact the case, that proposition (1) is, as used by physicists, no generalization from experience; it is a mixture of conventions and records of observation. This proposition is Newton's *First Law of Motion*; the evidence for it is to be found in the whole body of Newtonian science. Once granted, then proposition (2) can be deduced from it together with certain premisses about planets derived by generalization from particular instances. It must be emphasized that the 'evidence' for Newton's Law is so fundamentally different in kind from the evidence upon which a natural law (such as *water freezes at* 0° *Centigrade*) is based that we feel compelled to put 'evidence' in inverted commas – a symbolic device commonly adopted to show that we are using a word in an unusual sense.

Proposition (7) is entirely different from the other propositions we have been considering; nothing that happens in the world is relevant to its truth or falsity. That *an angle in a semicircle is a right angle* follows from the definitions and axioms of Euclidean geometry; it is a necessary consequence of these.

Proposition (11) may be regarded as the statement of a definition. We say 'may be regarded' because it depends upon the context in which it is asserted what exactly the words used

* On this point, see further, Ch. IX, § 5.

† I much regret that lack of space prevents me from raising, and attempting to answer these questions. The student should ask himself, in *what* sense of "law" is there a *law of supply and demand*.

to express it are intended to convey. Here it is given apart from a context; it was in fact taken from the *Everyman Dictionary*, at random. "*Igloo*" *means* "*an Eskimo dome-shaped hut*" has the form of a definition of "Igloo". Even so, it contains a factual element, since it is an assertion which involves the statement that "igloo" is the word used by Eskimos to refer to what in English can be described as "a dome-shaped hut". The evidence for the truth of this proposition is factual.

Proposition (5) is a self-contradictory proposition, or, as it is sometimes called, 'an inconsistency'. It is necessarily false, and its contradictory, *A red rose is red*, is necessarily true. To know that this proposition is true it is necessary and sufficient to know the meanings of the words used to express it. Such propositions are usually called *tautologies.*

If we review our prolonged discussion of the eleven propositions given at the beginning of this section, we shall see that we can divide them into two mutually exclusive and collectively exhaustive classes, the principle of division being the nature of the evidence required to establish their truth or falsity; the two classes may be denominated: factual propositions, non-factual propositions. The latter may be subdivided into: necessarily true propositions, necessarily false propositions, or self-contradictories.

Factual propositions are sometimes called *contingent propositions*, because they can be known to be true (or false) only by investigating what happens in the world, i.e. their truth (or falsity) is contingent upon what the world is like, and cannot, accordingly, be discovered by any careful examination of the structure of the propositions. The contradictory of a contingent proposition is also contingent. We have seen that contingent (or factual) propositions differ among themselves with regard to the way in which their truth or falsity can be established. All alike, however, are ultimately based upon direct observation of particular instances; that is to say, there must be an appeal to sense-experience. Facts that can be known only by sensible observation are called 'empirical facts'. Such facts constitute the original data of the natural sciences. Upon them, in the last resort, is built the imposing structure of the physical sciences.

Necessarily true propositions are usually called 'necessary propositions', for necessarily false propositions are self-contradictory and thus impossible. Many modern logicians hold that all necessary propositions are tautologies (i.e. resemble *This red rose is red*). Thus $2 + 2 = 4$ is regarded as a tautology on the ground that the truth of the proposition follows from the definition of the terms involved. On the same grounds such propositions as *An angle in a semi-circle is a right angle* are regarded as tautologies. These logicians usually make distinctions within the class of *tautologies*. For example, *Wealth is riches*, *Courage is bravery*, are called *synonymous* propositions. It is not possible for us to examine these views. It must suffice to point out that, given that a proposition is such that its truth is a consequence of the nature of the terms involved in it, then the proposition is necessary and its contradictory is self-contradictory. It is impossible for a necessary proposition to be false. This statement is itself tautologous.

§ 3. THE NECESSITY OF LOGICAL PRINCIPLES

Some contemporary logicians (including those known as 'Logical Positivists') hold that all necessary propositions, including logical principles, are conventions. Some go further and maintain that such Laws of Nature as the gravitational laws are conventions.* To discuss this view properly it would be necessary to examine the various meanings of the word "convention", and to show how gradually we pass from the meaning of "convention" as used in the forms of social intercourse (e.g. 'Mrs Johns is not at home') to its use in connexion with scientific laws. We not only have not the space to attempt this here; it must be admitted that a rigorous analysis of the concept *convention* has not yet been carried out. We mention the view simply in order to point out that here is something for the student to investigate if, and when, he can. We shall not adopt the conventional view of logical principles in this book.

It is not easy to make clear exactly in what sense of

* This view is specially associated with the writings of Professor A. S. Eddington on philosophy of science.

"necessary", logical principles are necessary.* It is simple enough to assert that their truth is *self-evident*, and that a self-evident truth must be necessarily true. But self-evidence is a dangerous notion; it seems to combine obviousness and logical priority. What is obvious to one person is not to another; it depends in part upon keenness of mental vision and in part upon familiarity. Unfortunately, we have learnt that a proposition which has long been regarded by competent thinkers as self-evident turns out to be false. What is indubitable is not necessarily true; our capacity to doubt depends upon our previous knowledge and our mental agility.

Modern logicians have devoted considerable skill and energy to the construction of deductive systems, in the sense in which, for example, Euclidean geometry is a deductive system. Setting out from carefully stated definitions and postulates, theorems are deduced by a rigorous step-by-step deduction. Some of these systems have been specially devised in order to offer proofs of the principles of logic. The most elaborate construction of the kind is the *Principia Mathematica* of Whitehead and Russell.† In this system the principle of contradiction, for instance, is not included among the postulates; it is deduced comparatively late in the system. But this by no means shows that the principle has not in fact been *used* throughout the demonstration. What such a system shows is that logical principles are so closely knit together that any one principle can be deductively derived from a finite set of other principles, and can be shown to imply itself. This procedure may strengthen us in our belief that logical principles are indispensable for all rational thinking, but it cannot be regarded as offering an independent proof of the principles themselves. We must be content to assert here that logical principles are so fundamental to our thinking that without presupposing them we could not think at all, and could not, therefore, construct systems.

* The difficulty is by no means due solely to the need for brevity, although this limitation does increase it. The difficulty is, however, in large part due to unclearness on the part of the author herself.

† See *M.I.L.*, Ch. X, § 4. An excellent introduction to the study of *Principia Mathematica* is provided by Part III of R. M. Eaton's *General Logic*.

§ 4. PERSUASION AND PROOF*

To believe a proposition and *to believe it to be true* are one and the same thing; nevertheless, we often believe propositions which are false. We should like our beliefs to be knowledge; sometimes we entertain a belief *knowing* that it is believed and not known. We can *know* our conclusions to be true only when we *know* both that the premisses are true and that they imply the conclusion. For this purpose we *reason*. Unfortunately, in our haste to resolve our doubts we may be persuaded to believe by other methods than by reasoning. A sharp distinction is here to be drawn between *persuasion* and *conviction*; they are to be distinguished by the nature of the process whereby doubt is resolved. The orator frequently uses the method of persuasion; his aim is to induce belief at all costs rather than to prove his contentions; his art consists in persuading his readers (or hearers) to accept conclusions for which he may have offered no evidence, and which may even be false. The orator's appeal is not to reason but to uncontrolled emotion, not to considerations logically relevant but to prejudice. We are not infrequently orators to ourselves.

The method of rational conviction consists in reasoned proof. A well-constructed argument, designed to convince the intellect, exhibits the characteristics of clearness, connectedness or relevance, freedom from contradiction or consistency, demonstrativeness or cogency. If I seek thus rationally to convince myself or others that a certain proposition is true, I must be careful to ascertain whether the premisses are true and I must aim at constructing a rigorously valid argument. An argument is valid if the conclusion is drawn in accordance with the logical rules, e.g. of the syllogism or of the compound arguments. We may be honestly mistaken in supposing that our argument is valid; there may be unsuspected ambiguities in our language; we may use as a premiss a proposition which we erroneously believe to have been proved. There are many ways of going wrong. In the ordinary discussions of practical

* Some of the paragraphs in this section have been taken in part from *M.I.L.*, Ch. XXIV. A fuller treatment will be found in that chapter.

life, concerning politics, art, education, religion, careful attention to the form of our arguments is not sufficient to ensure that our conclusions are true. We make tacit assumptions, which do not always hold; we have often to rely on but slight probabilities. Formal logical rules cannot afford us a certain guarantee that our arguments are conclusive, but a keen awareness of them, combined with the desire to reason correctly, undoubtedly helps us to detect fallacies and to put the rules we have learnt into practice.

It is customary in elementary textbooks on logic to include a chapter (sometimes more than one) on fallacies. We shall content ourselves with a brief indication of the commonest kinds of fallacy, and shall make no attempt to classify them.*

To commit a fallacy is to break one of the rules of logic which are regulative of sound reasoning. An argument in which one (or more) of these rules is broken is said to be *fallacious*. In learning the rules we must have also learnt the fallacy that arises from their violation. It will suffice here to remind the reader of formal fallacies due to violation of the rules of immediate inference and the syllogism. These may be briefly listed as follows: (1) the fallacy of wrong distribution, e.g. by simple conversion of an *A* proposition, by illicit major or illicit minor, and the fallacy of undistributed middle term; (2) the fallacy of affirming the consequent, and the fallacy of denying the antecedent; (3) the so-called 'fallacy of four terms', which consists in using ambiguous language so that the *term* indicated by the words used in the premiss is not the *term* indicated by the words used in the conclusion, or a similar mistake with regard to the language used to indicate the middle term.

(3) differs from (1) and (2) in the important respect that the fallacy is due to the language used in stating the propositions entering into the argument, so that, unlike the case of

* It would be a serious mistake if the student supposed that the treatment of fallacies given here is at all adequate. In my opinion fallacies cannot profitably be dealt with shortly; they need to be illustrated at length. Space does not permit this, nor should it be necessary. The student ought, after studying the preceding chapters, to be able to make out his own list. I have given many examples of fallacious reasoning in my *Thinking to Some Purpose*, see especially Chs. XII and XIII.

(1) and (2), attention to the formal rules alone will not suffice to guard us from falling into this fallacy. By the nature of the case this fallacy cannot be illustrated briefly.*

Fallacies of irrelevant conclusion are extremely common. A conclusion is irrelevant if it is not the conclusion we set out to prove and does not imply it. Such a fallacy is called by logicians '*ignoratio elenchi*' (i.e. the mistake of disregarding the opponent's contention). An example is afforded by the contention that post-primary education is useless because some highly educated men and women are not good citizens.† The 'appeal to authority' (called *argumentum ad verecundiam*) is sometimes fallacious, namely, when a point in dispute is supposed to be settled by showing that some respectable person has held the disputed view. If, however, the authority in question is an expert in the subject and the opponent is ignorant, the appeal to authority is justifiable. Logicians, however, might notice that progress in logical theory was delayed for centuries because logicians were too ready to suppose that what Aristotle had said was both true and the whole truth of the matter. Another form of this fallacy consists in trying to argue that a certain person's contention must be false because he is a disreputable fellow. A converse error is to credit someone's opinion on, say, theology or education, because he (or she) is in the public eye in some other capacity wholly unrelated to the topic, e.g. a popular novelist or a film star. The fallacy consists in assuming a relevant connexion between public fame in one capacity and expertness in quite another. It does not, of course, follow that the novelist or the film star is incompetent in these other affairs, but it must not be taken for granted.

The fallacies of composition and division are converses of each other: both rest upon the confusion of the collective and the distributive use of a term or upon the confusion of an alternative with a conjunctive proposition. Thus the extravagant man argues that, since he can afford to buy *A*, or *B*, or *C* he can afford to buy *A* and *B* and *C*; the niggardly man

* For a fuller treatment see my *Thinking to Some Purpose*, pp. 127–38, and also, *M.I.L.*, Ch. II, §§ 2–4.

† I take this example from a discussion at which I was a participant, and also the next example, illustrating a circular argument.

argues that since he cannot afford to buy *A* and *B* and *C* he cannot afford *A*, or *B*, or *C*.

Fallacies of circular argument consist either in flatly assuming the point at issue or in using as a premiss a proposition which can itself be proved only by using the conclusion for which it has already been used as a premiss. The arguer goes round in a circle. For example, it is argued that higher education is useless because it does nobody any good to study once he has left school. The premiss simply repeats the conclusion, but usually in a more subtle and disguised form. If the 'diameter of the circle' is very large, the fallacy may be hard to detect. Descartes fell into this fallacy (in a small circle) when he argued, 'There cannot be a vacuum, because if there is nothing between two bodies they must touch'.

A fallacy of this sort is known as *petitio principii*, i.e. begging the question. One form of it consists in using question-begging words, usually in the form of unpleasant epithets. As Mr A. P. Herbert has said, 'give your political dog a bad name and it may do him more harm than many sound arguments'.*

§ 5. IS SYLLOGISTIC PROOF CIRCULAR?

Some logicians have contended that all deductive arguments involve the fallacy of *petitio principii*, because the conclusion could be deduced from the premisses only if these premisses somehow 'contained the conclusion'. There may be some confusion if we use the word "contained" in this context; it must mean that the premiss *implies* the conclusion. This is certainly a condition of all valid deductive argument, but it does not necessarily involve a circle. It is true that if p implies q, p cannot be true unless q is also true; but there will be a circular argument only if the truth of q has been used as a premiss in establishing that p is true. That this is not necessarily the case will be recognized when we examine the way in which we do use deductive arguments, and more especially the syllogism, in order to obtain a conclusion. If Newton's physical theories are true, then it follows that, for example,

* *What a Word!* p. 229. Ch. VIII of Mr Herbert's book contains many amusing and instructive examples of this fallacy.

a pair of double stars will revolve around their common centre of gravity in elliptical orbits. Now this statement concerning the pair of double stars formed no part of the evidence upon which Newton's physics is based. But the conclusion can certainly be validly deduced from premisses afforded by Newton's physics. We may know that everyone to whom a V.C. is awarded has performed an act of conspicuous gallantry, and subsequently discover that *A*, whom we had not supposed to be specially courageous, is a V.C. and we *thence* conclude that he has performed an act of conspicuous gallantry.

It may be objected to this last example that we cannot be certain that the V.C. is always rightly awarded. Even if this were true, the objection would be irrelevant. The falsity of a premiss in no way tends to show that the argument is invalid, still less that it commits the particular fallacy of *petitio principii*. It is important to notice that universal premisses may be accepted on the basis of evidence which is not conclusive but has considerable weight; new cases can be subsumed under this universal premiss and a conclusion deduced which certainly did not constitute part of the original evidence.

J. S. Mill raised this question in its best-known form. He argued that 'in every syllogism, considered as an argument to prove the conclusion, there is a *petitio principii*'.* The point of this contention lies in what we mean by '*proving* the conclusion'. Mill looked at it in this way: *Every X is Y*, *This A is an X*, *therefore This A is a Y*. How do we know that every *X* is *Y* unless we have already used *this A* as part of the evidence for establishing the generalization stated in the major premiss? As Mill clearly saw, the answer to this question involves an account of how we come (i) to form, (ii) to justify, empirical

* *System of Logic*, Bk. II, Ch. III, § 2. Space is lacking to examine Mill's doctrine here. It is discussed, but not very clearly, in *M.I.L.*, Ch. XII, § 3, and to that the student may be referred. In that chapter also I have discussed the question whether *we* can obtain 'new knowledge' from syllogistic reasoning. By far the best account of Mill's theory of the syllogism is contained in R. Jackson's *An Examination of the Deductive Logic of John Stuart Mill*. The student cannot do better than read this book, if he is interested in this problem; he must, however, be warned that it is not an easy book to read and was not written for the elementary student.

generalizations. This question cannot be discussed here, but it may be pointed out that our inferences, when they are fruitful, are made within a context of knowledge. To prove a proposition is to find true premisses by which it is implied. When our premisses are factual propositions the evidence for their truth is never conclusive, but this does not imply that all factual generalizations are of equal value. There are various sources of knowledge and various criteria for determining what weight may *validly* be attached to a conclusion that has not been demonstrated. Mill wanted to use as premisses only propositions that are *known* to be *certainly* true. We never can know this when our premisses relate to matters of fact. It is, however, a mistake to suppose that we must wait until the evidence is – so to speak – 'all in' before we can assert a proposition and use it as a premiss for deducing conclusions that we should not have known otherwise. We cannot by deductive inference guarantee the material truth of factual propositions, but we can show that conclusions follow from such premisses and have such probative force as belongs to the premisses themselves.

CHAPTER IX

Methodology of Science *

§ I. INDUCTIVE REASONING

If we were confined to deductive reasoning we should be gravely inconvenienced. To say this is indeed to speak too mildly. We should not be able to reach any conclusion concerning matters of fact that went 'beyond the present testimony of our senses, or the records of our memory'.† Generalization (i.e. going beyond the evidence) is essential to carrying on the affairs of our daily lives; it lies at the very foundation of all the empirical sciences. All the sciences except logic and mathematics are empirical; they are based upon observation, experiment and generalizations from experience. Generalization from a number of observed instances of a certain class, which are assumed not to constitute *all* the instances of the class, is called 'Induction by simple enumeration'. Its logical form is: *All the observed S's are P's; therefore all S's are P's.* This inference is clearly not valid, for, in inferring from a premiss about *some S's* a conclusion about *all S's*, there is an illicit distribution of *S*. Consequently, the premiss may be true although the conclusion is false. This is an essential characteristic of inductive reasoning. All *valid* reasoning is deductive, but it does not follow from this that inductive reasoning is unreasonable, unworthy of a clear thinker. What does follow is that we must find other criteria with which to check and control our reasoning than the criteria provided by the rules of deductive reasoning. It is far more difficult to discover these criteria, to make them explicit, and to formulate rules than is the case with deduction. To do so

* Within the limits of a short chapter it is impossible even to indicate all the topics that must be included in any study of scientific method. It is essential for students who are reading for university examinations to consult other textbooks on scientific method. See *M.I.L.*, Pt. II; Cohen and Nagel, *Introduction to Logic and Scientific Method*, Bk. II.

† Hume, *An Enquiry Concerning Human Understanding*, Sect. IV, Pt. I.

constitutes one of the main problems of what is known as the 'methodology of science', i.e. a systematic investigation of the logical character of the methods employed in the empirical sciences. It must be admitted that this investigation is still in a stage that may be described as rudimentary.

It is impossible within the limits of a single chapter to do more than to indicate some of the chief questions that arise in connexion with the methodology of science, and in this way to suggest to the reader how wide is the field for study.*

Everyone makes inferences by simple enumeration. The statement just made is itself an instance of such a mode of inference. It is vital to simple enumeration that there should be no conflicting evidence, that is, no instances of the class in question which lack the characteristic which has been found to belong to all the observed instances. A single contradictory instance at once disproves the conclusion. Many Europeans who have observed a few instances of the class *Japanese*, and have found them all to be dark-eyed, have drawn the conclusion: *All Japanese people are dark-eyed.* A single example of a blue- or a grey-eyed Japanese would disprove this conclusion. But it might still be reasonable to hold that the percentage of dark-eyed people among the Japanese is very high. It would not be very surprising to find that among a nation, which for centuries did not intermarry with other nations, there should be a tendency towards one colour of eyes.

Consider the following statements:

Artists with dark hair and blue eyes almost always paint landscapes, while short artists with dark hair and dark eyes paint figures.

Blue-eyed painters with relatively broad heads tend to figure painting, and those with long heads to landscapes.

An exceptionally short head means artistic versatility and the ability to paint both landscapes and figures.

Women tend more to paint figures than do men.

These statements were made in a short article in the *News Chronicle* (Sept. 7, 1938). Perhaps the reader will agree with the author of this book that the statements are surprising. If

* I have dealt at considerable length with methodological problems in Part II of *M.I.L.* The student must consult some textbook about these problems, for the account in this chapter is nothing but a sketch. He is recommended to read also J. S. Mill, *System of Logic*, Introduction, Bk. III, Chs. I–X, XIV, XXI.

so, we should ask ourselves why they are surprising. Variation in the colour of hair or eyes, in height, and in width of head do not strike us as likely to be correlated with artistic ability or with the sort of pictures an artist paints. Especially is this the case with regard to colouring. If we ask why this should be so, the answer is not far to seek. We are accustomed to seeing hens of various colours, and cows, roses, and rabbits; we think of *colouring* as an *accidens* of a species. That there should be a correlation between colouring and the kind of picture an artist is likely to paint seems hard to believe.* On the other hand, we are not surprised to learn that a specific glandular deficiency is correlated with a specific mental defect, that a deficiency in vitamin C is correlated with the disease known as scurvy. We expect the waves to dash against the rocks after a gale has been blowing. As these illustrations show we have found in our experience that characteristics often go together in groups. It is for this reason that we find class-names indispensable, e.g. *artists*, *cows*, *politicians*, *Americans*, *measles*. Such classes as these differ from the artificial classes we make at will, such as *square scarlet things*, *black-haired archdeacons*. Cows, for example, possess in common characteristics which differentiate them from other classes, such as *horses*, *buffaloes*; whereas *black-haired archdeacons* probably have no characteristics in common, except the colour of their hair, which are not also possessed by other black-haired men or by other archdeacons. We feel that *being black-haired* is not a characteristic in any way relevant to the performance of archidiaconal functions. This 'feeling' has a respectable basis in our past experience and in the recorded experience of generations of men, as handed down to us in their class-names, and in records of their observations. Such classes as these may be called natural kinds, to adopt a name from J. S. Mill.

The nature of induction by simple enumeration can be stated as follows: *Such and such instances of Φ have the property Ψ*; *no instances of Φ lacking Ψ have been observed*; *therefore, every Φ has*

* The statements quoted from the *News Chronicle* are given in a report of 'the conclusions reached by Dr Mostyn Lewis' after four years of investigation; his work is described as 'research in racial psychology'. The number of artists analysed was said to be 1,000.

Ψ. The instances of Φ constitute a class having the properties connoted by "Ψ".

Inferences of this sort belong to a very early stage of man's thinking; without a considerable accumulation of the results of such inferences science would be impossible. Class-names enable us to abbreviate and to connect; it is the connexion of properties that is essential not only to scientific thinking but also to the ordering of our daily lives. Although some things 'just happen so', we all believe that there are dependable regularities in the world. Everyone believes that if he is hungry and eats food, his hunger will be satisfied; that water will quench his thirst; that fire will warm him; that heat will melt snow and butter; that day will alternate with night. Such beliefs as these are held with varying degrees of strength. They may be mistaken. The thirst of fever is not quenched by water; a dying man is not warmed by the fire. Nevertheless, without believing in some dependable regularities we should not act as in fact we all do. That our expectations are sometimes fulfilled shows that we have learnt that natural happenings can be regarded as having some kind of order; that they are sometimes disappointed reveals our partial ignorance.

We are, then, accustomed to distinguish between occurrences which we regard as being *regularly connected* and occurrences which we consider to be only accidentally, or casually, conjoined. Occurrences of the first type we shall call *uniformities*, of the second type *multiformities*. Simple enumeration leads us to discover such minor uniformities as the connexion between *flames and warmth*, *drinking water and quenching thirst*, *being a negro and having curly black hair*. The last example differs from the first two in that it is a uniformity of co-existing characteristics, whereas the other two are uniformities of successive occurrences. The latter may be called *causal connexions*. For the analysis of causal connexions simple enumeration does not suffice.

§ 2. CAUSAL LAWS

The earliest stage of a science consists in distinguishing multiformities from uniformities and in recognizing in some multiformities characteristics relevantly connected in such a way that uniformities of higher generality and abstractness may be discovered. Hence, the first task of the scientist is to describe and classify. As was suggested in the last section everyone engages in this type of scientific activity; we pass insensibly from common-sense knowledge through organized common sense to knowledge that can be called strictly scientific. There is no sudden break.* Primitive savages have to make some effort to control their environment; certainly knowledge gives power.

The scientist is not interested in singular statements such as *This water has just boiled*, *I am feeling hot now*, *This man is angry*, except in so far as the fact each describes can be regarded as an instance of some type of order. The sciences are branches of orderly knowledge: the scientist aims at seeing the connexions between things of certain sorts, natural happenings (i.e. events in nature), and organizing them into systems. The scientist takes note of the particular occurrence, *This water has just boiled*, only in order to determine the conditions under which it has boiled, the temperature at boiling-point, the change which occurs as it passes into steam, and so on. "Water" now signifies a *constant conjunction of characteristics*, which we call *properties* of *water*. To say 'this thing has such and such a *property*' is a way of saying that 'this thing *under certain conditions* behaves in such and such a way'. For example: *Iron has the property of expanding with rise of temperature* means *Iron expands when heated*; *Sugar has the property of solubility* means *Sugar dissolves in fluids*.

As the above examples suggest and our daily experiences abundantly show, the way in which something behaves (e.g. a lump of sugar, a poker) depends both upon the sort of thing it is and the situation in which it happens to be placed. This lump of sugar dissolves in water; this poker does not. The poker thrust into a fire becomes hot; taken out and put

* Consider, for instance, how often the result of a complicated set of psychological experiments (e.g. the formulation of 'practice curves') strikes the layman as just a statement of what 'everyone knows' about the improvement of ability to perform something as a result of practising. Nevertheless, the scientific investigation prepares the way for formulating more precise and generalized statements about human behaviour than is possible at the common-sense level.

in the fender it becomes cold again and reverts, approximately, to its former condition. After frequent recurrences of being heated and left to cool its shape gradually changes: eventually it may be hardly recognizable as *that poker*. Each of these things we recognize as an *instance* of what we have called a *natural kind*, i.e. a thing having characteristics of a certain sort which make it *the sort* of thing it is. Whenever a certain kind of thing is in a certain definite situation it will exhibit certain characteristic modes of behaviour; these are recurrent modes of change. Causal laws are the laws of these recurrent modes of change.

The recognition that kinds of things behave characteristically leads us to the discovery of causation and conditions. Similar modes of change recur in situations that differ in certain respects. Iron becomes red-hot in a furnace, in a fire in a cottage, in a burning factory, in the muzzle of a cannon when many cannon-balls have been fired. Thus shortly to indicate widely different situations in which something very familiar to us is happening (iron becoming red-hot) will not serve our present purpose unless we can forget what we are familiar with. (Think, for example, of Charles Lamb's story of the Chinaman's discovery of roast pork.) We discover that there are occurrences to the happening of which much else that is also happening in the same spatio-temporal situation is irrelevant. If this were not so there could be no causal laws and no science. The discovery of a causal law is the discovery of what is *relevant* to a given mode of behaviour. It is for this reason that the discovery of causal laws requires observation of particular situations. It is only from observation that we know that sugar dissolves in water and pokers become red-hot in a fire. Thus causal laws cannot be *deduced* from a single situation which is passively observed; they are discovered by analysis of different situations in which things are brought into relations with other things; we observe their behaviour in *varying* situations. By eliminating factors present in different situations we can discover which factors are irrelevant to a given mode of behaviour. In the next section we shall be concerned with methods by which causal laws can thus be ascertained.

It is important to distinguish causal laws from the particular causal propositions which state exemplifications of the laws. A particular causal proposition states a definite causal occurrence happening once only. For example, *This shot through his heart caused this man's death.* In asserting that his death was *caused* by the shot we are asserting more than the historical fact that two particular occurrences were conjoined. When anything is happening there are always multitudes of other things happening simultaneously and in close succession. To say that the man's death was caused by the shot must mean that whenever a bullet passes through a man's heart there follows the cessation of the beating of his heart, i.e. he dies. The form of such a causal law is: *Whenever an occurrence having the characteristic Φ happens at a time t_1 to a thing of the kind k_1, then an occurrence having the characteristic Ψ happens at a time t_2 to a thing of the kind k_2.* It may be the case that (i) Φ and Ψ are the same sort of characteristic, k_1 and k_2 are the same thing; (iii) t_1 and t_2 are the same time. It is the causal law that is fundamental, not the particular causal proposition stating an instance of causation.

When we ask for *the cause* of an occurrence, e.g. the breaking of *this* window, we expect an answer that would hold good in other cases. On reflection, at least, we should agree that whatever caused *this* window to break would also cause other windows to break. But we are not always thinking at the same level when we ask questions about the breaking of the window. 'What broke the window?' is a question which would probably be satisfied by the answer, 'An air-raid', or by 'A bomb'. The first answer is extremely abstract, but it does indicate one important element in any satisfactory answer to the question, for it cites an occurrence without which (it is presumed) *that* particular window would not have been broken when and as it was. The second answer cites an essential factor in the particular situation. But it would unhesitatingly be admitted that the mere presence of a bomb in the neighbourhood would not have sufficed to do the damage. An unexploded bomb might be harmless. A third answer might be, 'The explosion of a bomb'. However, there are (we assume) other windows in the same neighbourhood which are not broken. A fourth answer, 'The impact from the blast of an exploded bomb', approaches the scientific level of thinking. In ordinary life, 'What broke the window?' is probably asked at the level of thought of the first or second answer; the last two state the circumstances more carefully.

This example may suffice to show that 'the cause of an occurrence, *A*', is an ambiguous expression. The reader should ask himself what sort of answer would satisfy a medical officer of health who inquires, 'What is the cause of *this* outbreak of typhoid in my district?' He does not want an answer in terms of bacilli; he knows that wherever people have contracted typhoid a bacillus is present; his interest is in the source that carried the bacilli; is it the water, or the milk, or the meat, or what? But this knowledge had to be gained by long and patient research. This involved at the beginning a careful examination of complicated situations in which people were ill with typhoid; their circumstances had to be carefully noted and one type of situation compared with another. The form of the question that controls this activity of thinking is: 'What factor is present in these situations which is such that *whenever* it is present typhoid occurs?' The word "factor" here must not be assumed to stand for something simple.

We may, then, say '*X* causes *Y*' means 'Given that *X* happens, then *Y* happens'. We shall see later that this is not accurate, but it is sufficiently accurate to guide investigation in its earliest stage. 'Cause' and 'effect' are names used for the referent and the relatum, respectively, of the causal relation. This relation is asymmetrical; in certain usages of the word "causes" it is also a many-one relation.

§ 3. METHODS OF EXPERIMENTAL INQUIRY

J. S. Mill attempted to formulate with some precision various methodical procedures for the purpose of ascertaining the causes of specified phenomena (i.e. occurrences). He did not achieve all that he believed himself to have achieved but his 'methods', with certain qualifications, show the ways in which we must prepare the material in order to obtain an answer to the question, 'What is the cause of *Y*?' (where *Y* is an illustrative symbol). They have the merit of making clear the fundamental part played by elimination in causal inquiry. Our statements of Mill's methods must be very brief.*

The methods rest upon two principles fundamental to the concept of cause: (1) Nothing is the cause of an effect which is absent when the effect occurs; (2) Nothing is the cause of an effect which is present when the effect fails to occur. These are acceptable to common sense; indeed, Mill's methods do little more than organize the procedures of plain men when they seek to find the answers to such questions as: 'What makes the drawer stick?', 'Why won't the car start?', 'Why is honey so scarce in this district this year?'

In stating the methods we shall assume throughout that we are searching for the cause of an occurrence, *Y* (called by Mill a 'phenomenon'). In the next section we shall notice how large are the assumptions tacitly made as we proceed on our investigations. Plain men always make large, tacit assumptions.

We have to prepare our material in order to investigate the cause of *Y*; the two principles of causation given above show that we shall do well to: (i) compare different situations in which *Y* is present; (ii) compare situations in which *Y* occurs with other situations in which *Y* does not occur in spite of similarity in various respects.

(1) *The Method of Agreement. Rule:* If two or more instances of the occurrence of *Y* have only one factor in common, then this factor, in which alone all the instances agree, is the cause of *Y*.

For example, all the patients suffering from typhoid (in a given district) may be found all to have used the same water

* I shall not state the methods in Mill's own words, mainly in order to be briefer, but also to avoid certain mistakes in his formulation which he probably did not notice. The student must read Mill's own account (see *System of Logic*, Bk. III, Ch. VIII). It would also be advisable to read *M.I.L.*, Ch. XVII, especially § 2, where a *detailed* example of an experimental investigation is given. To read this section may suffice the lazy or over-worked student; others are advised to work out for themselves, *in detail*, some example of an experimental inquiry. The snippety examples often given in textbooks are of little value.

supply; hence, the water is causally connected with the patients having typhoid.

It will be noticed that the example does not fit the rule. Picture to yourself what happens when several people – in the *same* district – fall ill of typhoid (or any other disease). They all, *ex hypothesi*, live in the same neighbourhood; but certainly some will be men, some women, some fat, some thin, some fair-haired, some dark, some may be agricultural labourers, some plumbers, some university students, and so on. This 'and so on' is justified, for we can all quite easily fill up the details. We know that some of the patients will 'agree' in being males, others (or some of the former) 'agree' in being labourers, others 'agree' in being fair-skinned, etc. It is not possible to find instances in which all the circumstances *but one* differ. We cannot *begin* to use the rule until we have made an immense number of judgements of irrelevance. When we have done so then we may find that only one factor is always present in the set of instances in which *Y* is present; in that case we are justified in asserting that this factor is the cause of *Y*. But in most cases we cannot be sure that our judgements of irrelevance are correct; hence, we should at the level of practical common sense, begin to look for cases in which *Y* was absent even though these resembled the former to a considerable extent. Hence, we use the next method.*

(2) *The Joint Method of Agreement and Difference. Rule:* If a set of instances of the occurrence of *Y* have only one factor, *A*, in common while several instances in which *Y* does not occur have distributed among them the other factors that were present with *Y* except *A*, then *A* is probably causally connected with *Y*.

This method suggests that we must find a set of instances in which *Y* is present conjoined with a number of factors, but in *any two* instances only one factor *A* is present in both. These are called the *positive* instances. We then find a set of instances resembling the first as much as possible but all

* Mill gives next the Method of Difference. For reasons which, I hope, will be made clear in the text, I have put the Joint Method second. In formulating the Rule for the Joint Method I have departed widely from Mill's formulation. (For the reasons for this, see *M.I.L.*, pp. 336–7.)

agreeing in the absence of *Y*. These are the *negative* instances. Comparison between the two sets of instances shows that when *A* is present *Y* occurs, when *A* is absent *Y* does not occur. Hence, in accordance with the two fundamental principles we can conclude that *A* causes *Y* or is at least connected with its causation.

For example, in the typhoid investigation, it may be suspected that the *water* is the source of the typhoid infection. If all those who have typhoid have used the same water supply, it will be a help to consider people living in the district who have not got typhoid, and have water from another source, and to inquire whether some of these have meat from the same butcher as some of the typhoid patients, and if some of the former have milk from the same dairy as the latter. If so, then we can judge that the *meat* and the *milk* are irrelevant factors.

This method is well adapted to such inquiries as the following: Is the direct method of teaching Latin satisfactory? Are hasty marriages likely to end in divorce? Are limes as good as oranges as a protection against scurvy?

(3) *The Method of Difference. Rule:* If an instance in which *Y* occurs and an instance in which *Y* does not occur have in common all factors except *A*, and *A* occurs only in the instance when *Y* occurs, then *A* is the effect, or the cause, or an indispensable part of the cause of *Y*.

This method is clearly more cogent in its conclusion than either of the other two. The method of agreement might lead us to conclude that two concomitant occurrences, e.g. the sounding of a hooter in a factory and the ringing of a bell in a school, were cause or effect of each other. People have often assumed that a patent medicine is a cure for a disease because of the 'evidence' offered in 'unsolicited testimonials' printed in advertisements; they forget that those who were not cured did not write to the proprietors. If we can find a negative instance resembling the positive instance in all relevant factors but one, then that factor is undoubtedly causally connected with *Y*.

It is clear that it is difficult to secure these conditions, for it must be possible to introduce, or to withdraw, *A* without there being any other change than the non-recurrence of *Y*. If, however, we can be reasonably sure that the two instances differ in only *one relevant* respect, then the method is applicable under certain experimental conditions. For example, dropping a piece of blue litmus paper into an acid; it turns red; we conclude that the acid is the cause of the change in colour. We put sugar into a cup of tea, and it tastes different; the sugar is the cause of the different taste.

These examples are artificially adapted to illustrate the method; we know what examples to choose. But if we see, from the example, how the method is used, we may be able to put it into practice when we really *are investigating* an occurrence to discover its cause and not merely talking about someone else's investigation. Only we must be very careful to see that our judgements of irrelevance are justified. These remarks can be applied to all the methods, but are most obviously illustrated by the Method of Difference.

It should be noticed that we never use the Joint Method if we can secure the more stringent conditions required by the Method of Difference.

(4) *The Method of Concomitant Variations. Rule:* If, in a complex situation containing both *A* and *Y*, the factor *Y* varies in some manner whenever *A* varies, then *A* is causally connected with *Y*.

We reason in accordance with this method when we conclude that applying heat to a tube filled with mercury is the cause of the rise of mercury in the tube. This method is important in connexion with the investigation of quantitative variation; it requires data derived from measurement. If we seek to examine the effects of a rise in the price of tobacco upon the consumption of tobacco, we should be applying a principle of concomitant variation. But the variation would probably not be precise; there might be many disturbing factors (e.g. as the price rises, it so happens, that more people are at leisure, or there are air-raids and people smoke more during the night) which prevent us from being certain how much an increase in price would decrease consumption on occasions when those factors are absent.

(5) *The Method of Residues. Rule:* If in the case of a complex occurrence, certain factors, *W*, *V*, *Y*, are known, from previous investigations, to be the effects of *C*, *E*, *H*, then the residual effect *Z* is caused by the only other factor, *A*, which is jointly present with *W*, *V*, *Y*.

There is no good ground for considering this as an independent method. In so far as it is applicable it uses the method of difference theoretically to establish a conclusion that is dependent upon previous investigations.* The argument is in fact deductive.

In thus summarily stating Mill's methods we have incidentally suggested that they suffer from grave defects if they are to be regarded as complete methodical procedures for establishing causal connexinns. The following points should be noted: (1) Each method presupposes that judgements of irrelevance have been correctly made. (2) This means that the investigator is already in a position to formulate an hypothesis of the form: In *this* situation the possible cause of *Y* must be found among the factors *A*, *B*, *C*, *D*. But this step is one of the most difficult, and nothing in Mill's account of the methods shows that he recognized either its difficulty or its importance. (3) Each method, when it can be properly used, gives some grounds for the conclusion that is drawn, but these grounds are far from being conclusive.

The value of Mill's methods lies mainly in the fact that they lay down what may be described as minimal conditions for the investigation of causes of occurrences. By using them with due care we eliminate factors that might seem to be possible causes because these factors have been present when the investigated effect was at first observed. They show that *A* cannot be the cause of *Y* unless (i) *A* is regularly followed by *Y*, (ii) *A* is never present when *Y* is absent, (iii) *A* and *Y* vary together.

* The favourite example of this method is afforded by the discovery of the planet Neptune, as the result of calculating the orbit of Uranus from the known effects of the known planets, and finding a discrepancy between the calculated orbit and the observed orbit. It was suggested that another planet must be the cause of the residual effect. This reasoning is clearly deductive (see *M.I.L.*, pp. 346–7).

Mill himself recognized a *practical* difficulty in applying the Method of Agreement, namely, that on one occasion *A* may indeed cause *Y* but on another occasion *Y* may be caused by *B*. There can be no doubt that as 'cause' is used in ordinary discussion there can be such a *plurality of causes*. It is well known that men die from many different causes. That is to say the causal relation is assumed to be many-one. For practical purposes it is certainly convenient to know that there are many ways of encompassing the death of one's enemy or of giving enjoyment to one's friends. But is it in fact true that different causes result in *exactly the same effect*? The procedure of a coroner's court is based upon the denial that the causal relation is many-one; it is assumed that if the characteristics of the effect *Y* (viz. *this* person's death) be carefully analysed, then it will be seen that variation in the complex situation described by "*Y*" is in one-one correlation with variation in the complex situation described by "*A*". This assumption is plausible. At the same time it must be admitted that it accords ill with our common-sense use of the concept *cause*. If we admit that the plurality of causes is possible, then we cannot agree with Mill that it affects only his *Method of Agreement*. It is true that a rigorous use of the Method of Difference can assure us that *in the given case* no other cause was possible; but this does not suffice to show that in another situation the effect *Y* may not be the result of quite other factors.

As the admission that there may be a plurality of causes shows, Mill's methods are insufficiently analytic. He did not sufficiently recognize the truth of Francis Bacon's remark: 'the force of the negative instance is greater'. If we have reason to suppose that *A* is the cause of *Y*, it is vitally important that we should seek for instances of the occurrence of *Y* conjoined with *A* in which the factors other than *A* are varied as much as possible.* Repetition of instances of the conjunction of *A* with *Y* have little value unless these instances vary widely among themselves.

* J. M. Keynes has laid stress upon the importance of such variation: not resemblance but unlikeness is what we must look for. See *A Treatise on Probability*, Chs. XIX–XX, and cf. *M.I.L.*, Ch. XIV, § 3.

§4. THE NATURE AND IMPORTANCE OF HYPOTHESIS

If we are interested in the process whereby scientific discoveries are made, we can hardly over-emphasize the part played by the formulation and development of hypotheses. An hypothesis is a proposition *suggested* by the evidence available to establish the conclusion but insufficient to *demonstrate* the conclusion. Hypotheses are formed when we seek to ask *why* something has happened. Why, for instance, are booms followed by slumps? (If booms are *not* followed by slumps, *cadit quaestio.*) Why does water not run uphill and yet it rises in a pump? Why does water not rise in a pump to a height greater than thirty-three feet at sea-level? Why are some people so much afflicted by nightmares?

The question asked by "Why" may require an answer in terms of human, or divine, purpose, or it may require an answer in terms of what previously happened on account of which this (which initiated the question) happened. The first is a demand for a teleological explanation, the second demands *how* things are connected independently of anyone's purposes and desires. This is often called scientific explanation; it would be a mistake, however, to suppose that scientific explanations cannot involve reference to purposes; they must involve such reference when actions, as distinct from natural occurrences, are involved.

It must be noticed that an intelligent question beginning with 'Why' or with 'How' cannot be asked except on the basis of some knowledge about the situation which prompted the question. It cannot be answered without considerably more knowledge than the questioner possessed. The question and answer may be formulated by the *same* person; in that case, he is first *seeking* for knowledge, later he is in possession of the knowledge sought – assuming that he has answered the question correctly. Even a cursory acquaintance with the history of a scientific discovery suffices to show how indispensable is a background of relevant knowledge.* In this short sketch we take the possession of relevant knowledge for

* See *M.I.L.*, Ch. XIII, §§ 3–4; XVI, §§ 1, 2.

granted, but it must not be forgotten that we have done so.

The method of using an hypothesis to answer a question is commonly regarded as consisting of four steps: (1) Awareness of a complex familiar situation in which something is felt to call for explanation. (2) Formulation of an hypothesis; i.e. the statement of a proposition which connects the unexplained occurrence with data derived from previous observations, the proposition being such that, if it is true, then the given occurrence, together with other occurrences not yet observed, could be deduced. (3) Deduction from the hypothesis of its consequences; these consequences must include both the given occurrence and other *supposed* occurrences which will happen provided the proposition is true. (4) Testing the hypothesis by appeal to observable occurrences. This last stage is usually called the 'verification' of the hypothesis. The name is not very fortunate, since what is verified is *that the consequences take place*, rather than that the original proposition – the hypothesis – is true. Various hypotheses may be consistent with the happening of the occurrence which is being investigated.

To state a simple example, we will suppose that someone asks: Why is there no meat in the meat-safe, for I put the week's ration there this morning? First hypothesis (h_1): Perhaps someone got in and has stolen it. If so, then you must have seen someone pass the window for [the meat-safe is in the back garden and no one could get over the back-garden wall; the only approach is by a path down the side of the house; anyone who goes there passes the window of the front sitting-room]. But you did not see anyone pass the window; we shall conclude that no one did, as you always notice a shadow – at this time of day – falling across the window. Perhaps the maid has put the meat in the scullery (h_2). If so, then it will be there still; but it is not there. Perhaps a dog jumped the wall and stole the joint (h_3). If so, there will be scrabbles on the wood of the safe; there are marks of scrabbling; therefore, a dog got in and stole the joint.*

* This records an instance which actually happened. The remarks in brackets give information to the reader that was taken for granted by the occupiers of the house.

The form of this reasoning is as follows: If h_1 then $p(A)$ (where "A" is shorthand for the alleged occurrence deduced from h_1, and "$p(A)$" is shorthand for *the proposition that* the occurrence took place. Analogous shorthand symbols are used throughout). But not-$p(A)$. If h_2, then $p(B)$; but not-$p(B)$. If h_3, then $p(C)$; but $p(C)$. The rules of formal deduction show that if h_1 *implies* $p(A)$, then *not*-$p(A)$ *implies* h_1. Hence, the truth of *not* $p(A)$ (i.e. the *falsity of* $p(A)$) justifies us in asserting that h_1 is false. The formal procedure is the same with regard to h_2. But in the case of h_3 the position is different; here we have: If h_3, then $p(C)$; but $p(C)$; therefore h_3. This commits the fallacy of the consequent. We can, therefore, accept h_3 only on condition that h_1, h_2, h_3 together exhaust the possible hypotheses; we should then have the following valid argument: (where "$p(O)$" is shorthand for the proposition *The meat has disappeared*).

(i) If $p(O)$, then either h_1 or h_2 or h_3;
h_1 *or* h_2 *or* h_3 $\equiv$ h_1 *and* h_2 *and* h_3 *is false*.
(ii) If h_1, then $p(A)$; but $p(A)$ is false; $\therefore$ h_1 is false.
(iii) If h_2, then $p(B)$; but $p(B)$ is false; $\therefore$ h_2 is false.
(iv) If $p(O)$, then either h_1 or h_2 or h_3; but not h_1 or h_2;
$\therefore$ If $p(O)$, then h_3; but $p(O)$; $\therefore$ h_3.

It may be said that in the investigation of matters of fact it is never possible to assert a proposition of the form (i) above; we cannot be sure that we have exhausted all possible hypotheses. Thus the assertion that our hypothesis is 'verified' by the consequences does not amount to the assertion that *the hypothesis is certainly true*; rather we should say that the *deduced* consequences are verified and the hypothesis is confirmed.

When the deduced consequences are not verified (i.e. the proposition stating that *such and such an occurrence has happened* is false), it is by no means always the case that the original hypothesis is totally discredited; it may be that it can be emended in such a way that the original deduced consequence is no longer implied.

A successful prediction is often regarded as of very great importance in establishing an hypothesis. It is, however, easy to overestimate its significance, as we shall see if we remember that more than one hypothesis may be consistent with the facts. Those who rely on the predictions of newspaper astrologists forget this; they seem to think that the only hypothesis consistent with the successful prediction is that the astrologer obtained his information from the stars.

§ 5. SYSTEMATIZATION IN SCIENCE

Although a science begins with such piecemeal discoveries as, e.g. *Water rises in a pump*, *It becomes more difficult to breathe as one ascends higher and higher up a mountain*, it does not advance very far until sets of discoveries (established by means of the method discussed in the last section) can be connected together. The discovery that air has weight connected the rise of mercury in a barometer, the rise of water in a pump, the difference in the boiling-point of water at sea-level and on the top of Snowdon, etc. To be brief, Newton's great physical synthesis connected together the fall of unsupported bodies, the phenomena of high and low tides and of neap and spring tides, the movements of the moon, the revolution of the planets round the sun and . . ., for the list could be much extended. Discoveries made in one small department of one branch of science are relevantly connected with those made in another department of the same branch; discoveries in one branch of science (say, chemistry) are connected with discoveries in another branch of science (say, physiology); the outcome may be a body of specialized knowledge reaching the dignity of a *new* branch of science (say, biochemistry). The metaphor of "branches" – if not pressed – is significant, for it suggests that the various sciences tend to develop and grow together, so that discoveries in one reinforce discoveries in another. This is all too brief, and, if it be forgotten that we are here engaged merely in making comments on a vast subject, what has just been said may be downright misleading. The point to be insisted upon is that, with many qualifications, we can assert that natural occurrences are interconnected in such a way that, for example, a thorough understanding of how it is that sap rises in trees would involve taking note of the law of gravitation and the behaviour of living matter.

We might put the point in this way: On what grounds are we *justified* in believing that *water runs downhill*? That we do believe it is not questioned. The child's answer is: 'Because water always does run downhill'; a more advanced answer is, 'Because water seeks its own level'; another answer is, 'Because water is a very good example of a fluid.' Each of these answers does something to connect the behaviour of water with something else; even the child's answer asserts that *this* water running down *this* hill is not to be regarded as an isolated phenomenon. Perhaps the answer we should give today is: That water runs downhill *follows from* the principles of mechanics. Accordingly, either there is something wrong with the principles of mechanics *or* water runs downhill. To dispute the principles of mechanics is to upset a whole domain of ordered knowledge. This may have to be done; to some extent it has been done as the result of the work of Einstein, but this work would not have been acceptable unless it had fulfilled two conditions: (1) the new hypothesis is in accordance with all the observed occurrences including those hitherto accounted for satisfactorily by the Newtonian scheme and those discrepant with it; (2) the new hypothesis does itself offer fruitful deductions guiding subsequent experimental inquiry. It is well known that Einstein's theory satisfies these conditions.

The method of science is sometimes called *hypothetico-deductive*. There is some merit in this appellation. Einstein has said: 'Theory is compelled to pass more and more from the inductive to the deductive method, even though the most important demand to be made of every scientific theory will always remain that it must fit the facts.' The more advanced a theory is the more its exposition assumes deductive form; in consequence, an advanced science is an immense system of interconnected facts; new discoveries are fitted in to the system, even if at times the system must be modified to accommodate them. Our trust in any one generalization (which may have begun with the 'precarious and childish' method of simple enumeration) is in no small part dependent upon our trust in the system as a whole. We have trust in the fidelity of the system to the observable occurrences because we find that *it works* – it guides us to further experimental observations; it connects what had hitherto been isolated and thus unexplained; finally, it shows us what are the right questions to ask if we seek to understand the world in which we live. To understand a statement is to know what implied it and what it implies. Little though the activities of men can be thought to be in harmony with Aristotle's belief in *homo sapiens*, we understand how he could have entertained it when we reflect upon the fact that man alone (so far as we know) asks questions – occasionally – solely in order that he may know the intellectual satisfaction of having his questions answered.

APPENDIX

Containing References for Further Reading, Exercises, and a Key

REFERENCES FOR FURTHER READING, AND EXERCISES

Abbreviations used in citing the titles of books to which frequent reference is made will be given in square brackets after the first citation of the book in question. The references have been kept to a minimum; the student who consults any of these books will find further guidance in them for his future reading. Those references marked with an asterisk may be regarded as alternative readings on the same topic; those marked with a dagger are intended for more advanced students.

CHAPTER I

REFERENCES

Stebbing, L. Susan. *A Modern Introduction to Logic* (Methuen: 2nd or 3rd edition only). Chs. I, II, XXIV, § 1. [*M.I.L.*]

* Cohen, M. R. and Nagel, Ernest. *An Introduction to Logic and Scientific Method* (Geo. Routledge & Sons Ltd, 1934). Ch. I. [*C. and N.*]

* Eaton, R. M. *General Logic* (New York: Charles Scribner's Sons, 1931). Pt. I, §§ 1, 2, 8. [*Eaton.*]

Keynes, John Neville. *Studies and Exercises in Formal Logic* (Macmillan: 4th ed., 1906). Introduction. [*F.L.*]

Chapman, F. M. and Henle, P. *The Fundamentals of Logic* (Charles Scribner's Sons, 1933). Pt. I, Ch. I.

† Joseph, H. W. B. *An Introduction to Logic* (Oxford University Press: 2nd ed., 1916). Ch. I.

EXERCISES

1. In the case of each of the following statements, find *two* statements from which the given statement would follow: (*a*) Some taxes are uneconomic. (*b*) Mr Crab is a bore. (*c*) Corn ripens in the sun. (*d*) Some monkeys can be taught tricks.
2. Find an example of argumentative discussion (taken from any book or newspaper); set out the conclusion the writer seeks to establish, and specify the premisses given in support of it.
3. Distinguish between validity and truth.

CHAPTER II

REFERENCES

* *M.I.L.* Chs. IV, V.
* *C. and N.* Chs. II, III.
Eaton. Pt. I, Ch. V, § 1.
† *F.L.* Pt. II, Chs. III, IV.

EXERCISES

4. What is the purpose of restating categorical propositions in regular *A, E, I, O* forms? Try to restate each of the following statements in one (or more) of these forms; indicate whether anything has been lost in the restatement:

(1) Only metals are good conductors of heat.
(2) 'He that fights and runs away may live to fight another day.
(3) Sometimes all our efforts fail.
(4) 'Who drives fat oxen should himself be fat.'
(5) No admittance except on business.
(6) Man alone repines.
(7) 'A man may smile and smile and be a villain.'
(8) 'To be great is to be misunderstood.'
(9) 'Nothing ever becomes real till it is experienced.'
(10) 'He who praises everybody praises nobody.'
(11) 'Where you see a Whig you see a rascal.'
(12) 'Popular preachers are not always sound reasoners.'
(13) 'All that glisters is not gold.'
(14) 'To the pure all things are pure.'
(15) Humour is not given to all great teachers.

5. Construct a set of propositions to illustrate the square of opposition. Which terms in these propositions are distributed, and which are undistributed?

6. Determine the logical relation holding between each pair of the following propositions:*

(1) All cruel actions are unjustifiable.
(2) All unjustifiable actions are cruel.
(3) Some justifiable actions are not cruel.
(4) No justifiable actions are cruel.
(5) Some justifiable actions are cruel.
(6) Some cruel actions are not unjustifiable.
(7) Some actions that are not cruel are not unjustifiable.

7. Give the obverse and the contrapositive (where possible) of the following: (i) All are not saints that go to Church. (ii) Only small children love tin soldiers. (iii) No shrimps are obtainable today.

8. Restate the following propositions in such a way that without being weakened they may all have the same subject-term and the same

* In answering questions of this kind the student will probably find it helpful to formulate the propositions in various ways (e.g. obverse, etc.) so that equivalent and non-equivalent propositions can be easily recognized by means of immediate inference.

predicate-term: (i) *All F is not-C*; (ii) *Some not-F is C*; (iii) *No not-F is C*; (iv) *Some F is C*.

9. Granted that *Some sailors are patriotic* is true, show which of the following statements may be inferred to be true, which false, and which doubtful:

(1) Some who are not sailors are unpatriotic.
(2) No patriotic people are sailors.
(3) Some patriotic people are not other than sailors.
(4) No unpatriotic people are sailors.
(5) Some sailors are not unpatriotic.

10. Give the contradictory and a contrary of: '*No man can be a politician except he be first a historian or a traveller.*'

11. Show that *Some aeroplanes are bi-planes* is the subimplicant of the contradictory of the subimplicant of the contrary of the contradictory of the subcontrary of itself.

12. Consider whether there are any ambiguities in the following statements: (i) All are not just that seem so. (ii) Some of the soldiers were not afraid. (iii) All the fish weighed 4 lb. Assign the contradictory of each of the interpretations you give.

CHAPTER III

REFERENCES

M.I.L. Chs. V, VII.
C. and N. Ch. II, § 3. Ch. III, §§ 3, 5.
† *F.L.* Pt. II, Chs. IX, X.
† Johnson, W. E. *Logic.* Pt. I, Ch. II.
Joseph, H. W. B. *An Introduction to Logic.* Ch. IX.

EXERCISES

13. Give the contradictory of: 'Man is born free; and everywhere he is in chains.'

14. In the case of each of the following propositions give three other composite propositions equivalent to the original:

(i) If wages are increased, prices will rise.
(ii) Either the child was badly taught or he is exceptionally stupid.
(iii) You cannot both eat your cake and have it.
(iv) If a man will begin with certainties, he shall end in doubts.
(v) Either we are not responsible for our actions or our actions are within our own power.
(vi) If *C* is *D*, then *Q* is not *R*.

15. Suppose you wish to choose a tutor who will teach you enough logic to pass your examination. You have the following evidence with regard to four tutors, *A*, *B*, *C*, *D*:

(*a*) Either a student is not taught by *A* or he fails to pass.
(*b*) Unless a student is not taught by *B*, he fails to pass.
(*c*) Only if a student is not taught by *C* does he not pass.
(*d*) Only if a student is not taught by *D* does he pass.

How can you decide which tutor to select?

16. Construct an argument in the *Modus tollendo tollens*; obtain the same conclusion from equivalent premisses but stated in (i) *modus tollendo ponens*, (ii) *modus ponendo tollens*, (iii) *modus ponendo ponens*.

17. Exhibit the logical structure of the following arguments, adding any premisses that may be required; determine in each case whether the argument is valid:

(i) 'If Abraham Lincoln were alive today, a just and reasonable peace would be made. But, since he is dead, a just and reasonable peace will not be made.'

(ii) ' "If the law supposes that", said Mr Bumble, "the law is an ass – a idiot".'

(iii) 'Either the Pythagorean theorem in geometry is true or it is not worth the labour of studying it; but it is true; therefore, it is not worth while to study it.'

(iv) 'Prices only fall if there is over-production. But if there is not over-production, factories close; if factories close, the number of the unemployed increases. If more people are unemployed, there is dissatisfaction and social unrest. Consequently, if prices fall, there is dissatisfaction and social unrest.'

(v) 'This author is certainly muddle-headed; for, if I follow his argument, he is certainly muddled, and if I do not follow it, he is obscure in his statement of the argument.'

(vi) 'If your uncle is rich, you will not be afraid of asking him for a loan. But you are not afraid. Consequently, I conclude that your uncle is rich.'

(vii) 'It is an undertaking of some degree of delicacy to examine into the cause of public disorders. If a man happens not to succeed in such an inquiry, he will be thought weak and visionary; if he touches the true grievance, there is a danger that he may come near to persons of weight and consequence, who will rather be exasperated at the discovery of their errors, than thankful for the occasion of correcting them. If he should be obliged to blame the favourites of the people, he will be considered as the tool of power; if he censures those in power, he will be looked on as an instrument of faction. But in all exertions of duty something has to be hazarded' (*Burke*).

18. Select from the following, those statements which are equivalent:

(1) Where you see a Whig you see a rascal.
(2) If you see a Whig you don't see a rascal.
(3) If you see a Whig you see a rascal.
(4) Either you see a rascal or you don't see a Whig.
(5) Only if you see a rascal do you see a Whig.
(6) Only if you do not see a rascal do you not see a Whig.
(7) Unless you see a rascal you do not see a Whig.

19. Give the contradictory and a contrary of each of the following:

(1) 'If poetry comes not as naturally as leaves to a tree, it had better not come at all.'
(2) I am certain that you are wrong.
(3) All endogens are all parallel-leaved plants.

CHAPTER IV

REFERENCES

M.I.L. Chs. VI, VII.
C. and N. Ch. IV.
† *F.L.* Pt. III, Chs. I–VIII.
† H. W. B. Joseph. *An Introduction to Logic.* Chs. XII–XVI.

EXERCISES

20. State the rules that are necessary and sufficient to ensure the validity of a categorical syllogism. *Prove directly from these rules:**

(1) That the mood *EIO* is valid, and the mood *IEO* invalid, in every figure.
(2) That *O* cannot be a premiss in figure I, a major premiss in figure II, a minor premiss in figure III, nor a premiss in figure IV.
(3) That, if the major term is predicate in its own premiss, the minor premiss cannot be negative.
(4) That an *A* proposition can be proved only in figure 1.
(5) That if the middle term is distributed in both premisses, the conclusion must be particular.

21. Show, by means of the general rules of the syllogism, in how many ways it is possible to prove a proposition of the form *SeP*.

22. (i) All intelligent people are competent.
(ii) No unintelligent people are reliable.
(iii) Not all competent people are unreliable.
(iv) Some unreliable people are not competent.

Determine whether (iii) and (iv) are implied by (i) and (ii) jointly.

23. Determine the mood and figure of a valid syllogism which conforms to the conditions: (i) the major premiss is affirmative; (ii) the major term is distributed both in the conclusion and in its own premiss; (iii) the minor term is undistributed in both premiss and conclusion.

24. Construct a significant syllogism in *Bocardo*; restate the argument so as to obtain an equivalent conclusion from equivalent premisses in the mood *Darii*.

25. Given the special rules of figure I, show by *reductio per impossibile* that, in figure II the conclusion must be negative, and in figure III the conclusion must be particular.

26. Construct a valid Sorites consisting of five propositions and having *Some young men are not shy in advising their elders* for its conclusion. Name the form of the *Sorites* you give.

27. If *C* is a sign of the presence of *A*, and *B* is likewise a sign of *D*, and if *B* and *C* never co-exist, can it be validly inferred that *A* and *D* may sometimes not be found together?

* It should be carefully noted that the proof asked for is to be a deduction from the *general* rules of the syllogism, not from the *special* rules for each figure; thus (1) cannot be proved by examining each of the four figures in turn; it is necessary to show that the validity of *EIO* and the invalidity of *IEO* follows *directly* from the general rules irrespective of the position of the terms, i.e. without reference to the special rules.

28. Examine the validity of the following arguments, supplying any premiss that is implicit:

(1) 'His generosity might have been inferred from his humanity, for all generous people are humane.'
(2) 'Of course the U.S.A. is an Anglo-Saxon nation, in spite of its mixture of races; for all Anglo-Saxon nations are devoted to freedom, and devotion to freedom is nowhere more evident than in America.'
(3) 'I cannot help you to do this because I am not able to do it myself.'
(4) 'Only sensitive people resent criticism and, since only sensitive people are musical, it follows that all musical people resent criticism.'
(5) 'Two bodies must touch each other when there is nothing between them; consequently a vacuum is impossible.'
(6) 'You cannot consistently maintain that no one who does not work ought to have money that he has not earned, for you hold that a man should be permitted to leave his sons and daughters his whole fortune, and in many cases this suffices to maintain them in idleness for the rest of their lives.'
(7) 'He cannot maintain that all wars are unjustifiable, since he denies that persecution is justifiable, and it is sometimes not possible to prevent persecution except by making war upon the persecutors.'
(8) 'Only pacifists are Quakers, but not all pacifists are Quakers; only Socialists – and not all of them – are Marxists; among both pacifists and Socialists you will find those who support the raising of the school-leaving age. Hence we can conclude that no Quakers are Marxists, but not all non-Marxists are Quakers; further, some of those who are not Quakers and also some who are not Marxists support the raising of the school-leaving age.'
(9) 'If you deny that industry and intelligence are incompatible, and I deny that they are inseparable, we can nevertheless agree that some industrious people are intelligent.'
(10) 'The country needs clever politicians; a clever politician is one who knows how to control his party-machine; anyone who knows how to control his party-machine is apt to engage in shady practices. Hence, we conclude that the country needs those who are apt to engage in shady practices.'
(11) Whatever is desired by all is desirable; all men desire their own happiness; therefore every man desires the happiness of all men, so universal happiness is desirable.
(12) 'Some fashionable views are not true, for no fashionable views are subtle and some true views are subtle.'
(13) To be wealthy is not to be healthy; not to be healthy is to be miserable; therefore, to be wealthy is to be miserable.
(14) It is impossible to prove that industry can flourish without competition unless you can also prove that the lack of any competition does not lead to decreased effort on the part of the workers; for it is certainly the case that when the efforts of the workers decrease, industry does not flourish.
(15) Most of those present at the meeting were in favour of opening a 'second front' now, and most of those present were Conservatives; hence, some Conservatives are in favour of opening a 'second front' now.

CHAPTER V

REFERENCES

M.I.L. Ch. I, § 1. Ch. IV, §§ 5, 6. Ch. VII, § 5. Ch. IX, § 1. Ch. X, §§ 1, 2, 3.

* *C. and N.* Ch. VI, §§ 1, 2, 3.

* Eaton. Pt. I, Ch. VIII.

Chapman, F. M. and Henle, P. *The Fundamentals of Logic.* Chs. III, VII.

Johnson, W. E. *Logic.* Pt. I, Chs. VIII, X, XIII.

Langer, S. K. *An Introduction to Symbolic Logic* (Geo. Allen & Unwin, 1937). Chs. I, II.

† Russell, Bertrand. *An Introduction to Mathematical Philosophy* (Geo. Allen & Unwin, 1920). Ch. V.

EXERCISES

29. Construct a significant example of each of the relations listed below, and assign the logical properties of the relation in each case: greater than, twin of, ancestor of, married to, factor of, exactly matches in colour, aunt of, in debt to, imply, lover of.

30. Give examples of: (i) many-one relation; (ii) one-one relation; (iii) relative product. Construct three propositions each of which contains the converse of *one* of your examples.

31. What is a class? How can there be (i) empty classes, (ii) single-membered classes?

32. Formulate the following propositions existentially:

(1) Some Italians are not Fascists.
(2) None but the brave deserve the fair.
(3) No butterflies live long.
(4) Only legal experts can draft an act of parliament.

33. 'All deductive inference depends on the logical properties of relations.' Discuss.

34. Discuss the validity of the inference of *Some not-S is not-P* from the premiss *All S is P.* Illustrate your answer by using the proposition *All far-sighted statesmen have failed to find a means of abolishing war.*

35. Given that universal propositions are existentially negative and particular propositions are existentially affirmative, determine the validity of the following inferences: (i) $SaP \therefore Po\bar{S}$; (ii) MaP and SaM, $\therefore SiP$; (iii) $PeS \therefore \bar{S}i\bar{P}$.

CHAPTER VI

REFERENCES

M.I.L. Chs. III, XXII.

C. and N. Ch. XII.

Eaton. Pt. II, Chs. VI, VII.

Joseph, H. W. B. *An Introduction to Logic.* Chs. IV, V, VI.

† Russell, Bertrand. *An Introduction to Mathematical Philosophy.* Ch. XVI.

Mill, John Stuart. *A System of Logic.* Chs. II, VIII.

EXERCISES

36. Distinguish between extension and denotation, giving examples.

37. With regard to each of the following terms cite not less than six and not more than ten subclasses: *plane figure*, *symbol*, *vehicle*, *university student*, *metal*.

38. What do you understand by "connotation"? How would you answer the question asked by a schoolboy: 'What is "rationalize"?'

39. Assign the various predicables for (i) aviator, (ii) sonnet, (iii) schooner, (iv) paviour, (v) communiqué.

40. Which of the following definitions seem to you to be faulty? For what reason? Suggest an emended definition in any *two* of the examples:

(1) A square is a rectangle; (2) spinster means one who spins cotton; (3) negligence is want of proper care; (4) twinkle means scintillate; (5) a soldier is a man of military skill serving in the army.

41. Illustrate, by reference to the term *ship*, what is meant by the inverse variation of extension and connotation.

42. Arrange the following in an orderly manner: lyric, novel, literary work of art, sonnet, epic poem, comedy, narrative prose work, historical work, scientific treatise, ode, *Origin of Species*, Lyell's *Principles of Geology*, fiction, triolet, *Moll Flanders*, drama, *Alice in Wonderland*.

43. How do you account for the omission of ordinary proper names from a dictionary? Discuss the logical characteristics of such names.

CHAPTER VII

REFERENCES

M.I.L. Chs. II, VIII, IX, §§ 1, 2. Ch. X, § 5.
C. and N. Ch. VI, § 4.
† Johnson, W. E. *Logic*. Pt. II, Ch. III.
Langer, S. K. *An Introduction to Symbolic Logic*. Ch. II, §§ 3–6.
† Russell, Bertrand. *An Introduction to Mathematical Philosophy*. Ch. XV.

EXERCISES

44. Explain the use of illustrative symbols, giving examples. Distinguish illustrative symbols from variables.

45. Explain and illustrate: propositional form, variable proposition, values of a function, range of significance of a propositional form.

46. Define " $\supset$ ", and give examples.

47. What is an 'extensional interpretation' of logical relations?

CHAPTER VIII

REFERENCES

M.I.L. Ch. XXIV. Ch. IX, § 4. Chs. X, XI, XII.
C. and N. Chs. VII, IX.
Eaton. Pt. II, Ch. V, §§ 5, 6.
Johnson, W. E. *Logic*. Pt. I, Chs. III, IV.

EXERCISES

48. What is meant by "the laws of thought"? Comment upon the statement, 'Logic is the *science* which investigates the general *principles* of *valid thought*', with special reference to the words italicized.

49. Indicate the kind of evidence required to establish *each* of the following statements:

(1) There is a cathedral in Salisbury.
(2) A square has four right angles.
(3) Iron expands when heated.
(4) Jack is taller than Tim *implies* Tim is shorter than Jack.
(5) Red roses are red.
(6) There are mountains on the other side of the moon.
(7) Light waves are electromagnetic.
(8) There are three feet in a yard.
(9) A married man has a wife.
(10) No two people have the same finger-prints.

50. What is a circular proof?

51. Distinguish between persuasion and proof.

52. Give examples of (i) contingent, (ii) tautological, (iii) self-contradictory statements.

53. How would you define "logic"?

CHAPTER IX

REFERENCES

M.I.L. Pt. II.
C. and N. Chs. X–XIV.
Joseph, H. W. B. *Introduction to Logic*. Chs. XVIII–XXIV.
Mill, J. S. *A System of Logic*. Introd. Bk. II, Ch. I, Bk. III, Chs. I–XIV, XXI.

KEY TO THE EXERCISES

Full answers are given only to those questions which admit of a definitive solution.

1. (*a*) All taxes which are costly to collect are uneconomic; Some taxes are costly to collect. (*b*) All people whose conversation is mainly about their own exploits are bores; Mr Crab's conversation is mainly about his own exploits. (*c*) All cereals ripen in the sun; Corn is a cereal. (*d*) Any animal that is attentive and imitative can be taught tricks; Some monkeys are attentive and imitative.

Note. – These are examples of premisses fulfilling the condition specified in the question. It should be noticed that, in every case, the terms in the conclusion each appear in one premiss.

2. See Ch. I, § 2.

3. See Ch. I, § 3.

4. See Ch. II, § 3. The purpose of restating any proposition is to exhibit clearly the way in which its constituent elements are put together; if we can find certain formulations that can be taken as standard forms, we can more easily see how different statements are related logically to one another. So-called 'reduction to logical form' is a matter of convenience, but convenience is important; we need aid in deciding what inferences are permissible. Thus, for example, $8x^2 = 3x - 8$ is usually rewritten $8x^2 - 3x + 8 = 0$ in order to bring out its resemblance to $ax^2 + bx + c = 0$, which is the standard form.

(1) All good conductors of heat are metals. (This statement can also be restated *No non-metals are good conductors of heat.*)

(2) All who fight and run away are among those who may live to fight another day. (This restatement has less force, since the significance of the verb *may* is weakened when it is used in an adjectival sentence.)

(3) Some failures are failures of all our efforts.

(4) All who drive fat oxen are properly themselves fat. (In replacing *should be* by *are properly* the significance is weakened.)

(5) All who are allowed to be admitted are those on business.

(6) No non-human creature is one who repines. (Alternatively, *All who repine are human and none who are non-human are those who repine.*)

(7) Some who smile and smile are villains. (This restatement loses the implication that *smiling and villainy* seem to be incompatible but are not so in fact.)

(8) All who are great are misunderstood. (This restatement fails to bring out the implication that *being misunderstood* is a consequence of *being great*. In the traditional reformulation of propositions the *A, E, I, O* forms are interpreted as existentially affirmative, i.e. it is assumed that classes determined by the subject- and predicate-terms have members. The statement *All S's are P's* may be asserted as the result of an examination of the members of the class *S*; this leaves open the possibility that every member of *S* happens to be also a member of *P* even though there is no essential connexion between *S* and *P*. See page 25 above.)

(9) Nothing not-experienced is real. (Alternatively, *All that is real is experienced.*)

(10) All who praise everybody are praisers of nobody. (See comment on (8).)

(11) All Whigs are rascals. (This is much less emphatic than the original. See further, exercise 18.)

(12) Some popular preachers are not sound reasoners.

(13) Some glistering things are not gold. (Note that 'All . . . not . . .', in the example, is used so as to distribute *gold things* but to leave *glistering things* undistributed.)

(14) All who are pure are those who find all things pure. (Alternatively, *All things are pure to those who are pure.*)

(15) Some great teachers are not endowed with humour.

5. (i) All sea-gulls are greedy; (ii) No sea-gulls are greedy; (iii) Some sea-gulls are greedy; (iv) Some sea-gulls are not greedy.

(i) and (iv) are contradictories; (ii) and (iii) are contradictories; (i) and (ii) are contraries; (iii) and (iv) are subcontraries; (i) is superimplicant to (iii), (ii) is superimplicant to (iv), whilst (iii) is subimplicant to (i) and (iv) subimplicant to (ii); (iii) and (iv) are subcontraries. Hence the four given propositions illustrate the square (or figure) of opposition.

6. (*Note.* – The answer given here provides an example of the procedure recommended in the note added to the question. It should, however, be observed that the question is fully answered once the name of the logical relation in each case has been assigned.)

Let C, U, $\bar{C}$, $\bar{U}$ represent *cruel actions*, *unjustifiable actions*, and their contradictories, in accordance with the usual convention. We shall first write down each proposition with, on the same line, some immediate inferences from it; we then set out the full answer to the question as stated:

(1) $CaU \equiv Ce\bar{U}$ (*obv.*) $\equiv \bar{U}eC$ (*conv. of obv.*).

(2) $UaC \equiv Ue\bar{C}$ (*obv.*) $\equiv \bar{C}eU$ (*conv. of obv.*) $\equiv \bar{C}a\bar{U}$ (*obv. of conv. of obv.*).

(3) $\bar{U}oC \equiv \bar{U}i\bar{C}$ (*obv.*) $\equiv \bar{C}i\bar{U}$ (*conv. of obv.*) $\equiv \bar{C}oU$ (*obv. of conv. of obv.*).

(4) $\bar{U}eC \equiv \bar{U}a\bar{C}$ (*obv.*) $\rightarrow \bar{C}i\bar{U}$ (*conv. of obv.*).

(5) $\bar{U}iC \equiv Ci\bar{U}$ (*conv.*) $\equiv CoU$ (*obv. of conv.*).

(6) $CoU \equiv Ci\bar{U}$ (*obv.*) $\equiv \bar{U}iC$ (*conv. of obv.*) $\equiv \bar{U}o\bar{C}$ (*obv. of conv. of obv.*).

(7) $\bar{C}oU \equiv \bar{C}i\bar{U}$ (*obv.*) $\equiv \bar{U}i\bar{C}$ (*conv. of obv.*) $\equiv \bar{U}oC$ (*obv. of conv. of obv.*).

1 and 2 independent (complementary); 3 subimplicant to 1; 1 and 4 equivalent; 1 and 5 contradictories; 1 and 6 contradictories; 1 superimplicant to 7 (inverse); 2 superimplicant to 3 (inverse); 2 and 4 independent; 2 and 5 independent; 2 and 6 independent (contracomplementary); 2 superimplicant to 7 (inverse); 3 subimplicant to 4; 3 and 5 subcontraries; 3 and 6 subcontraries; 3 and 7 equivalent; 4 and 5 contradictories; 4 and 6 contradictories; 4 superimplicant to 7; 5 and 6 equivalent; 5 and 7 subcontraries; 6 and 7 independent.

7. (i) $\equiv$ Some who go to church are not saints. *Obverse:* Some who go to church are other than saints; *Contrapositive:* Some who are other than

saints go to church. (ii) ≡ All who love tin soldiers are small children. *Obverse:* None who love tin soldiers are other than small children; *Contrapositive:* None other than small children love tin soldiers. (iii) *Obverse:* All shrimps are unobtainable today; *Contrapositive:* Some things unobtainable today are shrimps.

8. (i) $Fa\bar{C} \equiv FeC \equiv CeF$.
(ii) $\bar{F}iC \equiv Ci\bar{F} \equiv CoF$.
(iii) $\bar{F}eC \equiv Ce\bar{F} \equiv CaF$.
(iv) $FiC \equiv CiF$.

The required forms are *CeF*, *CoF*, *CaF*, *CiF*.

9. By reformulating these five propositions as immediate inferences, we can exhibit their relation to one another:

(1) $\bar{S}i\bar{P}$ (using S for *sailors*, $\bar{S}$ for its contradictory, P for *patriotic people*, $\bar{P}$ for its contradictory).
(2) $PeS \equiv SeP$.
(3) $Po\bar{S} \equiv PiS$ (*obv.*) $\equiv SiP$ (*conv.*).
(4) $\bar{P}eS \equiv Se\bar{P} \equiv SaP$.
(5) $So\bar{P} \equiv SiP$.

Thus (2) to (5) form the square of opposition (omitting the *o* proposition), whilst (1) is an inverse of (4); hence, given *SiP* is true, then (1) and (4) are doubtful; (2) is false; (3) and (5) are true.

10. *Contradictory.* Some man can be a politician without being either a historian or a traveller.

Contrary. All men can be politicians without being either historians or travellers.

11. Let *A* stand for *aeroplanes*, *B* for *bi-planes*, then the given proposition is *AiB*. The following diagram *shows* what is required:

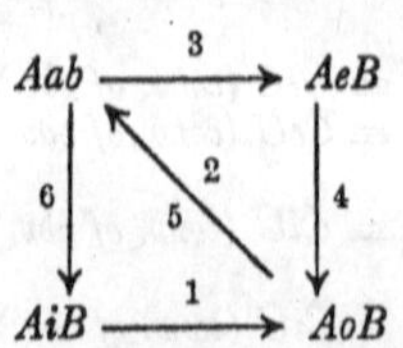

The four propositions are assumed to stand at the corners of the figure of opposition. The arrows show the passage from *AiB* to its subcontrary *AoB*, to *AaB*, contradictory of *AoB*, and so on, in accordance with the numbered steps.

12. (i) This statement might mean that no one who seems just is just (an *E* proposition), or it might mean *some are not* (an *O* proposition).
(ii) This statement may mean that some of the soldiers *were* and some *were not* afraid, i.e. "some" may be used for "some only"; it might also be used to assert that *at least some and perhaps all* were afraid.
(iii) This statement may mean either that the *fish together* weighed 4 lb. or that *each fish* weighed 4 lb. The contradictories (given in the order of interpretation) are:
(*i*) Some who seem just are just. All who seem just are just.

(*ii*) Either no soldiers were afraid or all soldiers were afraid. No soldiers were afraid.

(*iii*) The total weight of the fish was less than, or more than, 4 lb. Some of the fish weighed less, or more, than 4 lb.

13. Either man is not born free or he is not everywhere in chains.

14. (i) If prices do not rise, wages are not increased.
Either prices will rise or wages will not increase.
It is not the case both that prices will not rise and wages will increase.

(ii) If the child is not badly taught, then he is exceptionally stupid.
If the child is not exceptionally stupid, then he is badly taught.
It is not the case both that the child was not badly taught and also that he is not exceptionally stupid.

(iii) Either you do not eat your cake or you do not have it.
If you eat your cake, you do not have it.
If you have your cake, you do not eat it.

(iv) Either a man will not begin with certainties or he will end in doubts.
If a man shall not end in doubts, he will not begin with certainties.
It is not the case both that a man will begin with certainties and also not end in doubts.

(v) If we are responsible for our actions, then our actions are within our own power.
If our actions are not within our own power, then we are not responsible for our actions.
It is not the case both that we are responsible for our actions and that our actions are not within our own power.

(vi) Either *C* is not *D* or *Q* is not *R*.
If *Q* is *R*, then *C* is not *D*.
It is not the case both that *C* is *D* and *Q* is *R*.

15. The four given statements can be reformulated as hypothetical propositions as follows:

(*a*) If a student is taught by *A*, he fails.
(*b*) If a student is taught by *B*, he fails.
(*c*) If a student is taught by *C*, he passes.
(*d*) If a student is taught by *D*, he fails.

By successively affirming the antecedents of (*a*), (*b*) and (*d*), we affirm in turn their consequents; hence, the tutors *A*, *B*, *D* are each excluded; the antecedent of (*c*) being affirmed, we can affirm its consequent, viz. *he passes*. Thus we decide that *C* is the tutor who will ensure that the student passes the examination.

Note. – The student will find it useful to study the following equivalences, assuring himself (by means of the intuitive apprehension of a significant example) that these equivalences hold:

If p, *then* $q \equiv$ *If* $\bar{q}$, *then* $\bar{p} \equiv$ *Either* $\bar{p}$ *or* $q \equiv$ *Only if* $\bar{p}$, $\bar{q} \equiv$ *Only if* q, p $\equiv$ *Unless* $\bar{p}$, $q \equiv$ *Unless* q, $\bar{p}$.

16. *Modus tollendo tollens:* If civilians are cowardly, then factories stop work in an air-raid; but factories do not stop in an air-raid; ∴ civilians are not cowardly.

Equivalences:

(i) Either civilians are not cowardly or factories stop work in an air-raid.
But, Factories do not stop work in an air-raid;
∴ Civilians are not cowardly.

(ii) It is not the case both that civilians are cowardly and that factories do not stop in an air-raid.
But, Factories do not stop work in an air-raid.
∴ Civilians are not cowardly.

(iii) If factories do not stop work in an air-raid, then civilians are not cowardly.
But, Factories do not stop work in an air-raid.
∴ Civilians are not cowardly.

Note. – In the example given above the antecedent and the consequent of the original argument are both affirmative statements; this is by no means necessary.

17. (i) If Abraham Lincoln were alive today, then a just and reasonable peace would be made. Abraham Lincoln is not alive today;
∴ A just and reasonable peace will not be made.
Invalid: fallacy of denying the antecedent.

(ii) If the law supposes that, the law is an ass, a idiot.
(But the law supposes that);
∴ The law is an ass, a idiot.
Valid (provided the premiss in parentheses is granted).

(iii) Either the Pythagorean theorem . . . of studying it.
But the Pythagorean theorem . . . is true;
∴ It is not worth while to study it.
Invalid: fallacy of affirming an alternant.

(iv) (*a*) If prices fall, then there is over-production; and if there is not over-production, then factories close;
(But either there is over-production or there is not over-production);
∴ Either prices fall or the factories close.
Invalid: The omitted premiss is almost certainly the premiss given in parentheses. But this premiss affirms the consequent of the first proposition and the antecedent of the second, whereas, what is required for establishing the conclusion is the alternative affirmation of both antecedents.

(*b*) If factories close, the number of unemployed increases;
If the number of unemployed increases, there is dissatisfaction and social unrest;
(∴ If factories close, there is dissatisfaction and social unrest).
Valid.

Although these two arguments are valid, the conclusion given in the original argument, viz. – *If prices fall, there is dissatisfaction and unrest* – does not follow. The conclusions of (*a*) and (*b*) taken together warrant only the conclusion: *Either prices fall or there is dissatisfaction and social unrest.*

(v) If I follow his argument he is muddled; if I do not follow his argument, he is obscure in his statement.
(But either I follow his argument or I do not);
∴ Either he is muddled or obscure in his statement.
Valid. Note, however, that the speaker has made the doubtful assumption that his inability to follow the argument could not be due to any other cause than the author's obscurity in statement.

(vi) If your uncle is rich, you will not be afraid . . . a loan.
But you are not afraid;
∴ Your uncle is rich.
Invalid: fallacy of affirming the consequent. (Probably the speaker has in mind the premiss, *Only if your uncle is rich . . .*, and this is equivalent to *If you are not afraid, then your uncle is . . .*) The argument would then be a valid *modus ponendo ponens.*

(vii) (*a*) If a man happens not to succeed . . ., he will be thought weak and visionary; and if he succeeds (touches the true grievance), he may come near . . . correcting them.
(But he will succeed or not succeed);
∴ Either he will be thought weak . . . or come near . . . correcting them.

(*b*) If he should be obliged . . . people, he will be considered . . . power, and if he censures those in power, he will be looked on . . . faction.
(But either he will be obliged to blame the favourites or will censure those in power);
∴ Either he will be considered the tool of power or he will be looked on as an instrument of faction.

(*c*) If anyone is thought weak . . . or comes near . . . be exasperated, or is considered the tool of power or as . . . faction, then he is engaged in an undertaking of some degree of delicacy.
(But anyone who examines the cause of public disorders is thought weak . . . or comes near . . . or is considered the tool of power or as . . . faction);
∴ Anyone who examines the causes of public disorders is engaged in an undertaking of some degree of delicacy.

(*d*) If anyone is engaged in an undertaking of some degree of delicacy, he has to hazard something;
(If anyone is exerting himself in duty, he has to engage in an undertaking of some degree of delicacy);
∴ If anyone is exerting himself in duty, he has to hazard something.
These four arguments are valid, provided that the implicit premisses – enclosed in parentheses – are granted.

18. Statements (1), (3), (4), (5), (7) are all equivalent; each is equivalent to the categorical statement, *All Whigs are rascals.* Statement (2) is equivalent to the categorical statement, *No Whigs are rascals.* (6) is independent and equivalent to *All rascals are Whigs.*

19. (1) *Contradictory:* It is the case both that poetry does not come as naturally as leaves to a tree and that it had better come than not come. *Contrary:* If poetry comes as naturally as leaves to a tree, it had better come.

(2) *Contradictory:* I am not certain that you are wrong. *Contrary:* I am certain you are right.

(3) *Contradictory:* Either some endogens are not parallel-leaved or some parallel-leaved plants are not endogens. *Contrary:* No endogens are parallel-leaved plants.

20. For the rules, see p. 57.

(1) *To prove that EIO is valid in every figure:*

Since the major premiss is universal its subject is distributed, and since it is also negative, its predicate is distributed; ∴ both major and middle terms are distributed in this premiss whether it is of the form *P-M* or *M-P*. Since the conclusion is particular the minor term is not distributed; accordingly the minor premiss *SiM*, or *MiS*, can be combined alternatively with *PeM*, or *MeP*. The mood *EIO is thus valid in every figure.*

To prove that IEO is invalid in every figure:

Since the major premiss is particular affirmative, the major term will be undistributed whether it is subject or predicate; but, since the minor premiss is negative, the conclusion must be negative; hence, *P*, the major term, will be distributed in the conclusion. Thus the mood *IEO* involves illicit major, no matter what the position of the major term may be in its own premiss; accordingly, *IEO is invalid in every figure.*

(2) * (*a*) *O* cannot be major premiss in figure I, for, if it were the minor premiss must be affirmative; in that case, *M* will be undistributed in the minor premiss, so *M* must be distributed in the major premiss of which it is subject. But *O* is particular; hence its subject is undistributed; ∴ *O cannot be the major premiss in figure I.*

(*b*) *O* cannot be minor premiss in figure I, for, if it were, the major premiss must be affirmative and the conclusion must be negative. But *P* is predicate in the major premiss, and would be undistributed if this premiss were affirmative; thus, there would be a fallacy of illicit major; ∴ *O cannot be the minor premiss in figure I.*

(*c*) *O* cannot be major premiss in figure II, since one premiss must be negative (in order to distribute *M*, which is predicate in both premisses), and, in consequence, the conclusion will be negative with a distributed predicate, viz. *P*. But *P* is subject in the major premiss which must, then, be universal to secure the distribution of *P*; ∴ *O cannot be the major premiss in figure II.*

(*d*) *O* cannot be a minor premiss in figure III, for the same reason as in figure I (see *b* above).

* The student should notice that there are a variety of slightly different ways in which such proofs as these can be given. The exact wording is not important; consequently, in the following answers variations are deliberately introduced in order to show that the relevant points can be differently stated. Henceforth, *S*, *M*, *P* will be used to stand respectively for *minor*, *middle*, and *major* terms. Proofs will be less and less fully stated, since, once a student has grasped the procedure, he should have no difficulty in fitting in the indications provided in the answers.

(*e*) *O* cannot be a major premiss in figure IV, for the same reason as in figure II (see *c* above).

(*f*) *O* cannot be a minor premiss in figure IV, for the same reason as in figure I, except that, *in this case*, the illicitly undistributed term would be *M*, which would be subject of a particular minor premiss, and predicate of an affirmative major premiss, and thus would not be distributed in either premiss.

(3) This theorem can be proved from the considerations already adduced in the answer to (2). (*Note* that, if *P* is predicate (i.e. the major premiss is *M-P*), it can be distributed only if the major premiss be negative; but, if *either* premiss is negative, *P* will be distributed in the conclusion.)

(4) To prove an *A* proposition both premisses must be affirmative, and the minor must be universal to distribute *S*; hence the minor premiss must be *SaM*. In this premiss *M* is undistributed; it must, therefore, be distributed in the major, which is affirmative; hence, the major premiss must be universal affirmative with *M* as subject. The syllogism is, therefore, *MaP*, *SaM*, ∴ *SaP*, and no other combination of premisses will yield *SaP*.

(5) There are three cases: (*a*) *Both affirmative:* Since *M* is to be distributed in both, it must be subject of both, and the premisses must be universal; *S* will be predicate of an affirmative premiss, and will thus be undistributed; hence, the conclusion must be *SiP*.

(*b*) *One affirmative and one negative premiss:* Together these can distribute three terms; of these terms two must be *M*, and the remaining term *P* (since the conclusion must be negative). Thus *S* cannot be distributed, i.e. the conclusion must be *SoP*.

(*c*) *Both premisses negative:* excluded by general rules of quality.

21. To prove *SeP*.

Both premisses must be universal, with one affirmative, and one negative; i.e. the premisses must be *A* and *E* in either order.

(i) Let the major be *E*, i.e. either *MeP* or *PeM*. The minor must then be affirmative, with *S* distributed; ∴ it must be *SaM*.

(ii) Let the minor be *E*, i.e. either *SeM* or *MeS*. The major must then be affirmative, with *P* distributed; ∴ it must be *PaM*.

Accordingly, *SeP* can be proved in four different moods, viz.:

(1) *MeP*	(2) *PeM*	(3) *PaM*	(4) *PaM*
SaM	*SaM*	*SeM*	*MeS*
∴ *SeP*	∴ *SeP*	∴ *SeP*	∴ *SeP*

(*Note.* – In (1) and (2) the major, and in (3) and (4) the minor, premisses are simple converses of each other.)

22. Let *I* stand for intelligent, $\bar{I}$ for unintelligent, people; and let *R* stand for reliable, $\bar{R}$ for unreliable, people. Then the four given propositions can be represented as follows:

(i) *IaC*, (ii) $\bar{I}eR$, (iii) $Co\bar{R}$, (iv) $\bar{R}oC$.

Now (ii) $\bar{I}eR \equiv Re\bar{I}$ (*conv.*) $\equiv$ *RaI* (*obv.*). Combine *RaI* with (i) *IaC*, and thus obtain the *Barbara* syllogism: *IaC*, *RaI*, ∴ *RaC*.

Now (iii) $Co\bar{R} \equiv$ *CiR* (*obv.*), which is the *converse per accidens of RaC*; hence (i) and (ii) jointly imply (iii).

Now (iv) $\bar{R}oC \equiv \bar{R}i\bar{C}$ (*obv.*), and $\bar{R}i\bar{C}$ is the inverse of *RaC*; hence (i) and (ii) jointly imply (iv), provided that $\bar{R}$ and $\bar{C}$ exist.

23. By (i) the major premiss is affirmative, and by (ii) the major term is distributed in this premiss, of which it must, therefore, be the subject and the premiss must be universal; hence the required premiss is *PaM*. By (ii) the major term is given as distributed in the conclusion, which must, therefore, be negative, and, since by (iii), the minor term is undistributed in the conclusion, the conclusion must be *SoP*. Since *M* is undistributed in *PaM*, it must be distributed in the minor premiss, which must be negative, with *S* undistributed (by iii); hence, the minor premiss is *SoM*. The required syllogism is thus *PaM*, *SoM*, ∴ *SoP* (i.e. *AOO* in figure II).

24. *Bocardo: Some archers are not graceful, All archers are athletes,* ∴ *Some athletes are not graceful*. In order to obtain an equivalent conclusion from equivalent premisses in the mood *Darii*, we require the *A* proposition as major premiss with the subject and predicate reversed. This cannot, however, be done, since *A* converts to *I*, which is non-equivalent, and would not, with another particular premiss, yield any conclusion at all. There is the further difficulty that an *O* proposition has no convert. Hence, to obtain equivalent premisses we must use obversion as well as conversion. The required steps are as follows: (1) obvert the original major; (2) convert this obvert; (3) transpose the premisses; (4) draw a conclusion from the premisses thus obtained. This syllogism will be in *Darii*; (5) convert the new conclusion; (6) obvert the convert; this yields the original conclusion.

(1) Some archers are not graceful ≡ Some archers are ungraceful.
(2) Some ungraceful people are archers.
(3) (Major) All archers are athletes.
    (Minor) Some ungraceful people are archers;
(4) ∴ Some ungraceful people are athletes,
(5) ≡ Some athletes are ungraceful,
(6) ≡ Some athletes are not graceful.

25. See pp. 62–4, above. Since we are given that the major premiss is universal and the minor is affirmative, we find that the moods in figure I must fit into the scheme:

If every (or some) *X* is *Y* (or not),
And every (or some) *Z* is *X*;
Then, every (or some) *Z* is *Y* (or not).

In *reductio per impossibile* we deny the conclusion; we thus obtain the schema, Every (or some) *Z* is not *Y* (or is). Combining this successively with the schemas for the two premisses, we obtain:

(i)	If every (or some) *Z* is not *Y* (or is)	minor premiss,
	and every *X* is *Y* (or not)	major premiss,
	then, every (or some) *Z* is not *X*	conclusion.
(ii)	If every (or some) *Z* is not *Y* (or is)	major premiss,
	and every (or some) *Z* is *X*	minor premiss,
	then, some *X* is not *Y* (or is)	conclusion.

(i) yields the moods of figure II, in each of which the conclusion must be negative; (ii) yields the moods of figure III, in each of which the conclusion must be particular.

26. No self-confident people are shy in advising their elders.
All good administrators are self-confident.
All Civil Service officials are good administrators.
Some young men are Civil Service officials,
∴ Some young men are not shy in advising their elders.

This is a Goclenian Sorites.

27. The information provided can be stated in the premisses:

CaA
BaD
BeC.

To establish the desired conclusion, we must be able to deduce from these premisses at least one of the propositions *AoD* or *DoA*. But neither *D* nor *A* is distributed in the original premisses, whilst *D* is distributed in *AoD*, and *A* in *DoA*; therefore, neither of these conclusions can be obtained. Accordingly, the answer to the question is in the negative.

28. (*Note.* – In answering this question only brief indications of the premisses will be given.)

(1) All generous people are humane. (*Invalid,* ∵ *undistributed middle.*)
He is humane;
∴ He is generous.

(2) All A.–S. nations are . . . to freedom. (*Invalid,* ∵ *undistributed middle.*)
The U.S.A. is . . . to freedom.
∴ The U.S.A. is an A.–S. nation.

(3) This argument is invalid because it assumes that what I cannot do alone, I cannot do with others. The fallacy is analogous to the fallacy of *composition.*

(4) All who resent criticism are sensitive. (*Invalid,* ∵ *undistributed middle.*)
All musical people are sensitive,
∴ All musical people resent criticism.

(5) Invalid, for the conclusion, *Two bodies with nothing between must touch,* assumes the point to be proved, viz. *There cannot be nothing between bodies,* i.e. *a vacuum is impossible.* Thus the argument commits the fallacy of begging the question.

(6) *You admit:* A fortune can be left to a man's children which is sufficient to keep them in idleness, i.e. it is permissible for heirs to a fortune to have unearned money without working.

You maintain: No one ought to have unearned money without working.

These two statements are contradictory.

The argument is valid.

(7) Persecution is not justifiable.

∴ Whatever is needed to prevent persecution is justifiable.

The conclusion does not follow; accordingly, the remainder of the argument is irrelevant.

(8) Using *P, Q, S, M, R,* for *pacifists, Quakers, Socialists, Marxists,* and *those who support the raising of the school-leaving age*, respectively, the information given can be summed up in the premisses:

QaP, PoQ, MaS, SoM, PiR, SiR.

The conclusion is said to be: *QeM* and $\bar{M}oQ$; $\bar{Q}iR$ and $\bar{M}iR$.

On examination it will be found that the conclusion does not follow, although none of the four constituent propositions is inconsistent with the premisses $\bar{Q}iR \equiv RoQ$, and $\bar{M}iR \equiv RoM$, but any attempt to connect Q and M, or Q and R, or M and R, or their contradictories, by combining the premisses in any order would involve illicit distribution.

(9) Let S represent *those who are industrious* and P represent *those who are intelligent*. Then, you deny SeP, I deny SaP *and* PaS.

Now, *denying* $SeP \equiv$ *affirming* SiP;

and *denying* SaP *and* $PaS \equiv$ *affirming either* SoP *or* PoS.

Question is whether these two denials can be said to 'agree that some industrious people are intelligent', i.e. whether SiP is true. *Either* SoP *or* PoS neither implies nor is implied by SiP, but these are consistent. Hence, if 'agree that SiP is true' means 'do not assert SeP', then you and I agree; if, however, 'agree, etc.' means 'assert that SeP is false', we do not agree.

(10) This argument is valid only on the assumption that to need X, when X is inseparable from Y, implies needing Y also. This assumption is manifestly untrue.

(11) *All men desire their own happiness* does not imply that *each man desires the happiness of all*. Hence, even if it be granted that *whatever is desired by all is desirable*, it does not follow that *the happiness of all* (i.e. universal happiness) *is desirable*. The conclusion is consistent with the premisses (provided it is assumed that it is possible *both* to desire one's own happiness *and* the happiness of all other people); but to assert that the premisses *imply* the conclusion is to commit the fallacy of composition.

(12) No fashionable views are subtle.
Some true views are subtle;
∴ Some fashionable views are not true.

This argument is *invalid:* it commits the fallacy of the illicit major.

(13) Using initial letters for class-names, these propositions may be symbolized as follows: WoH and $\bar{H}aM$, ∴ WaM.

Now $WoH \equiv Wi\bar{H}$; then we have the syllogism, $\bar{H}aM$, $Wi\bar{H}$, ∴ WaM, which involves the fallacy of illicit minor. But 'to be wealthy is not to be healthy' is ambiguous; it may be used to assert WeH which obverts to $Wa\bar{H}$, and $Wa\bar{H}$ *and* $\bar{H}aM$ implies WaM.

(14) This argument may be briefly formulated as follows:
If decreased effort, then industry does not flourish.
If no competition, then decreased effort;
∴ If no competition, then industry does not flourish.

It is valid. It should be noted that the validity depends upon the assumption that "competition" has exactly the same force in both statements. It may well be relevant to stress the difference between *competition between different firms* and *competition between different workers in the same firm* (as in piece-work).

(15) This argument is of the form: *Most M is C, Most M is S;* ∴ *Some S is C.* This is valid, since "most" means "more than half", so that, taking the two premisses together, the middle term, M, is referred to in its whole extent, i.e. is distributed.

29. His income is *greater than* yours: *asymmetrical, transitive.*
Castor is *twin of* Pollux: *symmetrical, intransitive.*
Henry VII is *ancestor of* Elizabeth: *asymmetrical, transitive.*

Othello is *married to* Desdemona: *symmetrical, non-transitive.*
7 is *a factor of* 42: *asymmetrical, non-transitive.*
This ribbon *exactly matches in colour* that dress: *symmetrical, transitive.*
Jane is *aunt of* Thomas: *asymmetrical, intransitive.*
Tom is *in debt to* Dick: *asymmetrical, non-transitive.*
The falsity of the conclusion *implies* the falsity of at least one premiss in a valid syllogism: *non-symmetrical, transitive.*
John is a *lover of* Mary: *non-symmetrical, non-transitive.*

30. (i) servant of; child of; (ii) eldest son of a father; double of; (iii) cousin of; step-father of.

(i) Edward is Jacob's master; (ii) 10 is the half of 20; (iii) Marina is the cousin of George.

31. See pp. 78–81; 87–9.

32. (1) Non-Fascist Italians $\neq O$.
(2) Non-brave people deserving the fair $= O$.
(3) Long-lived butterflies $= O$.
(4) Non-legal experts able to draft an act of parliament $= O$.

33. See pp. 81–4; 93–9.

34. See pp. 88–93.

35. (i) *SaP*, on the given assumption, states that $S\bar{P} = O$, whilst $Po\bar{S}$ states $\bar{S}P \neq O$. But *SaP* does not imply the existence of *P* or of $\bar{S}$; hence, the inference is invalid.
(ii) *MaP* states $M\bar{P} = O$ and *SaM* states $S\bar{M} = O$, whereas the conclusion *SiP* states $SP \neq O$. But the premisses do not suffice to establish the existence of *S* (i.e. the minor term); hence the inference is valid.
(iii) *PeS* states $PS = O$, whereas $\bar{S}i\bar{P}$ states $\bar{S}\bar{P} \neq O$; but if nothing is both *P* and *S*, either $P = O$ or $\bar{S} \neq O$; consequently *PeS* implies $\bar{S} \neq O$ unless nothing is *P*. But, if $P = O$, then $P \neq O$. It follows that $\bar{S}i\bar{P}$, and thus the inference is valid.

36. See pp. 102–7.

37. See pp. 107–12.

38. See p. 102. In answering a schoolboy's question: 'What is "rationalize"?', it would be necessary to ascertain the context, since the verbal form *rationalize* has three wholly distinct meanings in common use, and a fourth meaning from which, in devious ways, the other three meanings have been derived. Context alone can settle which meaning is relevant. (See any *Dictionary* for these meanings, viz. original, used in mathematics, in economics, in psychoanalysis. To explain properly the meaning of a word it is essential to give examples illustrating its use, for we do not *understand* a word until we know how to use it in different sentences.)

39. It should be remembered that various definitions of a word can be given, and that there are various *propria* and *accidens*. The following are illustrative examples:

Genus	*Differentia*	*Propria*	*Accidens*
(i) (*Aviator*), man.	Able to pilot an aeroplane.	Having knowledge of altimeters.	Member of R.A.F.

	Genus	Differentia	Propria	Accidens
(ii)	(*Sonnet*), poem.	Having 14 deca-syllabic lines, expressing one idea.	Having a rhyme scheme.	Having the rhyme scheme *abba cdcdcd.*
(iii)	(*Schooner*), sailing-ship.	Fore-and-aft rigged.	Having masts.	Having a Scots skipper.
(iv)	(*Paviour*), workman.	Employed to lay pavements.	Having arms.	Being English.
(v)	(*Communiqué*), announce-ment.	Official.	Concerning matters of national importance.	Depressing in content.

40. (1) Too wide; it requires the differentia – *having four equal sides.* (2) Too narrow, since the spinning need not be confined to cotton. There is an additional (and now distinct) meaning, viz. "unmarried woman". (3) Satisfactory. (4) Errs by defining the unknown by what is likely to be more unknown. *Def.*: "Shine with quivering or intermittent light". (5) Too narrow, since military *skill* may be lacking. *Def.*: "A person serving in an army".

41. *Ship* is a class-name used for a variety of sea-going vessels; hence there are numerous subclasses constituting the *extension* of *ship*, the connotation of which is "large sea-going vessel". If we arrange the subclasses in an orderly classification, then any *subclass* has smaller extension than its *superclass*, but has increased *connotation*, since its connotation will contain the property (or properties) differentiating one subclass from a co-ordinate class and from the superclasses. For example, *sailing ship* excludes *steam-ship*, etc., and adds differentiating property *sailing.* Again, the subclass *brigantine* excludes *schooners* and *brigs*, etc., and adds to *sailing ship*, the differentia *having two masts – a brig's foremast, square-rigged, a schooner's main-mast, fore-and-aft rigged* (see pp. 107–12, above).

42. We clearly need a class not included in the list, under which *literary work of art* and *scientific treatise* may find an appropriate place. The following is a possible arrangement:

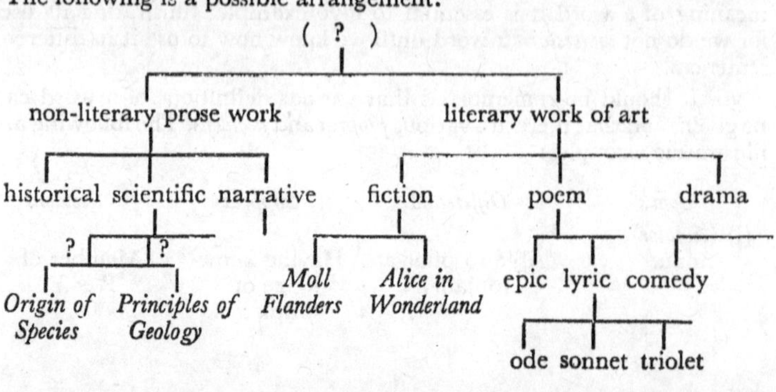

This is a logically unsatisfactory arrangement, but it is difficult to see what good purpose could be served by classifying the various classes given in a single classificatory table. To mark the criticism, queries have been put to indicate omission of essential superclasses. To include in the table *individuals*, e.g. *Origin of Species*, is to make a muddle of any classificatory scheme (see p. 105 above).

It must be noticed that familiarity with the nature of the subclass is essential for the purpose of classifying.

43. See pp. 103–5, above. Main points to be noted: (i) the sen in which ordinary proper names lack connotation, whereas dictionary meaning is usually the connotation; (ii) the significant use of ordinary proper names depends upon the speaker's knowledge that many *descriptions* do in fact *describe* the individual so named (cf. *M.I.L.*, Ch. III, § 2).

44. See above, pp. 14–15 and pp. 126–9.

45. See above, pp. 130–5.

46. See above, pp. 135–41.

47. See above, pp. 141–4.

48. See pp. 146–52.

49. (1) *Empirical proposition:* Granted that there is agreement with regard to the meaning of "cathedral", the evidence required is observational. Testimony may be used to establish it, but those who testify to its truth must have relied upon observation at some stage.

(2) This statement is true by definition; hence, the evidence required is given provided "square" has been defined.

(3) *Causal law:* Observation and assumptions with regard to natural happenings provide the evidence.

(4) The second of these two propositions follows from the first, since the *meaning* of "taller than" necessitates the second.

(5) Tautology.

(6) Observation would suffice to establish this proposition, in the same way as in example (1). It might also be established by indirect observational methods, depending upon measurement of shadows. It is not *in fact* possible for anyone dwelling on the earth to test its truth or falsity, since there is no practicable way of observing the other side of the moon. This fact does not in the least affect the logical status of the evidence required.

(7) Observation and experiment, together with mathematical deduction.

(8) This is a tautology, true by definition.

(9) Similar to (8).

(10) This can be established only by induction by simple enumeration (see Ch. IX, § 1). It is not logically impossible that two people should have the same finger-prints, but the amount of evidence suffices to make the acceptance of the proposition reasonable.

50. See p. 163.

51. See p. 160, and cf. *M.I.L.*, Ch. XXIV, § 1.

52. (i) It will rain tomorrow. Examples are provided by nos. (1), (3), (6), (10), and (7), in question 49.
(ii) A right-angled triangle is right-angled. Examples given in nos. (2), (4), (5), (8), (9), in question 49.

(iii) Red roses are not red. The widower's wife has called. Five times six is forty.

53. *Note.* – Your definition must cover all the topics which you consider should be dealt with by logicians, and exclude any topic lying outside their scope.

Index

The paragraph-headings given in the Table of Contents should also be consulted. No references are given to the names of authors or titles of books cited in the Appendix